# FRENCH
*Phrase book*

Carol Stanley and Philippa Goodrich

**BBC Books**

Consultant: Jacqueline Chnéour

Published by BBC Books
A division of BBC Enterprises Ltd
Woodlands, 80 Wood Lane, London W12 0TT

ISBN 0 563 21518 6
First published 1991
© Carol Stanley and Philippa Goodrich 1990
Set in 8 on 9 point Times Roman by
Ace Filmsetting Ltd, Frome, Somerset
Printed and bound in England by
Richard Clay Ltd, Bungay
Cover printed by Richard Clay Ltd, Norwich

Published in consultation with the
BBC Continuing Education Advisory Council

# Contents

# HOW TO USE THIS BOOK

Communicating in a foreign language doesn't have to be difficult – you can convey a lot with just a few words (plus a few gestures and a bit of mime). Just remember: keep it simple. Don't try to come out with long, grammatically perfect sentences when one or two words will get your meaning across.

Inside the front and back cover of this book is a list of All-purpose phrases. Some will help you to make contact – greetings, 'please' and 'thank you', 'yes' and 'no'. Some are to help you to understand what people are saying to you. And some are questions like 'do you have . . . ?' and 'where is . . . ?', to which you can add words from the Dictionary in the book.

The book is divided into sections for different situations, such as Road travel, Shopping, Health and so on. In each section you'll find
● Useful tips and information
● Words and phrases that you'll see on signs or in print
● Phrases you are likely to want to say
● Things that people may say to you

Many of the phrases can be adapted simply by using another word from the Dictionary. For instance, take the question **Est-ce que l'aéroport est loin?** (Is the airport far away?). If you want to know if the *station* is far away, just substitute **la gare** (the station) for **l'aéroport** to give **Est-ce que la gare est loin?**

All the phrases have a simple pronunciation guide underneath based on English sounds. This is explained in Pronunciation (page 5).

If you want some guidance on how the French language works, see Basic grammar (page 187).

There's a handy reference section (starts on page 198) which contains lists of days and months, countries and nationalities, general signs and notices that you'll see, conversion tables, national holidays, useful addresses and numbers.

The 5000-word Dictionary (page 220) comes in two sections – French–English and English–French.

Towards the end of the book is an Emergencies section (which we hope you *won't* have to use).

Wherever possible, work out in advance what you want to say. If you're going shopping, for instance, write out a shopping list in French. If you're buying travel tickets, work out how to say where you want to go, how many tickets you want, single or return, etc.

Practise saying things out loud – the cassette that goes with this book will help you get used to the sounds of French.

Above all – don't be shy! It will be appreciated if you try to say a few words, even if it's only 'good morning' and 'goodbye' – and in fact those are the very sorts of phrases that are worth learning, as you'll hear them and need to use them all the time.

If you would like to learn more French, BBC Books also publish *Get by in French, When in France* and *A vous la France!* BBC phrase books are also available for the following languages: German, Italian and Spanish. Future titles will include Arabic, Greek, Portuguese and Turkish.

The authors would welcome any suggestions or comments about this book, but in the meantime, have a good trip! – **bon voyage!**

# PRONUNCIATION

You don't need perfect pronunciation to be able to communicate – it's enough to get the sounds approximately right. If you want to hear real French voices and practise trying to sound like them, then listen to the cassette.

A pronunciation guide is given with the phrases in this book – the system is based on English sounds, as described below.

## Consonants

Many French consonants are pronounced in a similar way to English. The main differences are with **c, g, h, j, ll, q, r, w**.

Consonants at the ends of words are not normally pronounced, except when followed by another word beginning with a vowel, e.g.:

**vous** (*voo*)      **vous avez** (*vooz avay*)

## Vowels

French vowels don't vary so much as English ones, but the way they're pronounced is affected if: (1) there's a written accent; (2) they're followed by an **n** or **m**; (3) they're in a combination of vowels.

Vowels followed by **n** or **m** have a nasal sound – say them through your nose and mouth at the same time. The **n** or **m** itself is not pronounced. In the pronunciation guide the nasal sound is shown by the symbol **ñ**.

## Stress

French words are pronounced with almost equal stress on every syllable, so no stresses are shown in this book.

For the French alphabet, see page 9.

## Consonants

|  | Approx. English equivalent | Shown in book as | Example | |
|---|---|---|---|---|
| b | b in 'but' | b | **bain** | *bañ* |
| c followed by e or i, and ç | s in 'sat' | s | **citron** | *seetrawñ* |
|  |  |  | **ça** | *sa* |
| ch | sh in 'shut' | sh | **chambre** | *shombr* |
| c otherwise | c in 'can' | k | **comme** | *kom* |
| d | d in 'dog' | d | **douane** | *doo-an* |
| f | f in 'feet' | f | **français** | *froñsay* |
| g followed by e or i | s in 'measure' | j | **gentil** | *joñteey* |
| gn | ni in 'onion' | ny | **oignon** | *unyawñ* |
| g otherwise | g in 'got' | g | **grand** | *groñ* |
| h | always silent | – | **herbe** | *erb* |
| j | s in 'measure' | j | **je** | *juh* |
| k | k in 'kit' | k | **kilo** | *keelo* |
| l | l in 'look' | l | **livre** | *leevr* |
| ll | y in 'yet' | y | **fille** | *feey* |
| m | m in 'mat' | m | **main** | *mañ* |
| n | n in 'not' | n | **nous** | *noo* |
| (but see **Vowels** below) |  |  |  |  |
| p | p in 'pack' | p | **pêche** | *pesh* |
| qu | k in 'kit' | k | **que** | *kuh* |
| r | rolled in the back of the throat | r | **rouge** | *rooj* |
| s between vowels | z in 'zoo' | z | **chose** | *shohz* |
| s otherwise | s in 'set' | s | **sortie** | *sortee* |
| t | t in 'tin' | t | **table** | *tabl* |
| v | v in 'vet' | v | **vin** | *vañ* |

| | | | | |
|---|---|---|---|---|
| **w** | v in 'vet' | **v** | **wagon** | *vagawñ* |
| | except in English words like **weekend** | **w** | | |
| **x** at end of words | s in 'six' | **s** | **six** | *sees* |
| **x** otherwise | x in 'six' | **x** | **taxi** | *taxee* |
| **y** | y in 'yet' | **y** | **payer** | *payay* |
| **z** | z in 'zoo' | **z** | **douze** | *dooz* |

## Vowels

| | | | | |
|---|---|---|---|---|
| **a, à, â** | between a in 'cat' and 'cart' | **a** | **ami** | *amee* |
| **é; er, ez** at end of word | a in 'gate', but a bit shorter | **ay** | **café** **avez** | *kafay* *avay* |
| **e, è, ê** | e in 'get' | **e** | **cette** **chèque** | *set* *shek* |
| **e** at end of word | not pronounced | **–** | **carte** | *kart* |
| **e** at end of syllable or in one-syllable word | often pronounced weakly, like er in 'other' | **uh** | **petit** **je, de** | *puhtee* *juh, duh* |
| **i** | ee in 'meet' | **ee** | **ami** | *amee* |
| 'weak' **i** | y in 'yet' | **y** | **mieux** | *myuh* |
| **o** | o in 'lot' | **o** | **opéra** | *opayra* |
| **ô** | o in 'note' | **oh** | **hôtel** | *ohtel* |
| **u** | to make this sound, shape your lips to say **oo**, but say **ee** | **ew** | **une** | *ewn* |

7

## Vowel combinations

| | | | | |
|---|---|---|---|---|
| ai | a in 'gate' | ay | **français** | *fronsay* |
| aî | e in 'get' | e | **fraîche** | *fresh* |
| ail | i in 'bite' | iy | **travail** | *traviy* |
| au, eau | o in 'note' | oh | **cadeau** | *kadoh* |
| ei | e in 'get' | e | **Seine** | *sen* |
| eu, œu | er in 'other' | uh | **peu** | *puh* |
| oi | wa in 'swam' | wa | **moi** | *mwa* |
| oy | 'why' | wiy | **voyage** | *vwiyaj* |
| ui | wee in 'between' | wee | **huit** | *weet* |

## Nasal vowels

| | | | | |
|---|---|---|---|---|
| an, en | o in 'hot' + nasal sound | oñ | **banc** | *boñ* |
| ain, ein, in | a in 'cat' + nasal sound | añ | **bain** | *bañ* |
| on | aw in 'saw' + nasal sound | awñ | **bon** | *bawñ* |
| un | u in 'cut' + nasal sound | uñ | **chacun** | *shacuñ* |

# THE FRENCH ALPHABET

## Spelling

How is it spelt?
**Comment ça s'écrit?**
*komoñ sa saykree*

| Letter | Pronounced |
|--------|-----------|
| A | *a* |
| B | *bay* |
| C | *say* |
| D | *day* |
| E | *uh* |
| F | *ef* |
| G | *jay* |
| H | *ash* |
| I | *ee* |
| J | *jee* |
| K | *ka* |
| L | *el* |
| M | *em* |
| N | *en* |
| O | *oh* |
| P | *pay* |
| Q | *kew* |
| R | *er* |
| S | *es* |
| T | *tay* |
| U | *ew* |
| V | *vay* |
| **W (double V)** | *doobluh vay* |
| X | *eex* |
| **Y (I grec)** | *ee grek* |
| Z | *zed* |

# GENERAL CONVERSATION

● The word **bonjour** literally means 'good day' and is used at any time during the day (there's no distinction between 'good morning' and 'good afternoon'). In the evening you use **bonsoir** for 'good evening' and **bonne nuit** for 'goodnight'. **Salut** (hello) is a far more casual greeting.

**Au revoir** is 'goodbye', but you'll also hear **à tout à l'heure** and **à bientôt** (see you later).

● The French generally shake hands when they meet and when they say goodbye. Women, and men and women (though not two men) often exchange kisses on both cheeks.

● The words **monsieur**, **madame** and **mademoiselle** are used far more often than the English 'sir', 'madam' or 'miss' – it isn't as formal-sounding in French.

● When you're talking to someone in English you vary your tone of voice and your way of saying things depending on whether you're addressing them formally, showing respect, or more casually, as with a friend or member of the family.

In French, there's an extra way of making this distinction – by using different words to say 'you' and different parts of verbs. One way is more formal, the other more casual. There's more about this on page 192, but in this book we have used the more formal way, on the assumption that you will mostly be talking to people you don't know. The formal word for 'you' is **vous** (*voo*).

People may address *you* in the informal way (this is quite general among younger people). The informal word for 'you' is **tu** (*tew*). The verb forms are different as well, e.g. you'll hear **est-ce que tu veux?** instead of **est-ce que vous voulez?** (do you want?), **tu as** instead of **vous avez**. The **tu** form is always used when talking to a child.

## Greetings

| | |
|---|---|
| Hello<br>**Salut**<br>*salew* | See you later<br>**À tout à l'heure/À bientôt**<br>*a toot a luhr/a byañtoh* |
| Good morning/afternoon<br>**Bonjour**<br>*bawñjoor* | How are things?<br>**Comment ça va?**<br>*komoñ sa va* |
| Good evening<br>**Bonsoir**<br>*bawñswar* | How are you?<br>**Comment allez-vous?**<br>*komoñt alay voo* |
| Good evening/goodnight<br>**Bonne nuit**<br>*bon nwee* | Fine, thanks<br>**Bien, merci**<br>*byañ mersee* |
| Goodbye<br>**Au revoir**<br>*oh revwar* | And you?<br>**Et vous?**<br>*ay voo* |

## Introductions

| | |
|---|---|
| My name is . . .<br>**Je m'appelle . . .**<br>*juh mapel . . .* | This is my boyfriend/fiancé<br>**Voici mon ami/fiancé**<br>*vwasee mawn amee/fee-oñsay* |
| This is . . .<br>**Voici . . .**<br>*vwasee . . .* | This is my wife/daughter<br>**Voici ma femme/fille**<br>*vwasee ma fam/feey* |
| This is Mr/Mrs Brown<br>**Voici Monsieur/Madame Brown**<br>*vwasee muhsyuh/madam . . .* | This is my girlfriend/fiancée<br>**Voici mon amie/ma fiancée**<br>*vwasee mawn amee/ma fee-oñsay* |
| This is my husband/son<br>**Voici mon mari/fils**<br>*vwasee mawñ maree/fees* | Pleased to meet you<br>**Enchanté(e)**<br>*oñchoñtay* |

## Talking about yourself and your family

(*see* Countries and nationalities, *page 203*)

I am English
**Je suis anglais** (*if you're a man*)
*juh sweez oñglay*
**Je suis anglaise** (*if you're a woman*)
*juh sweez oñglez*

I am Scottish
**Je suis écossais/écossaise**
*juh sweez aykosay/aykosez*

I am Irish
**Je suis irlandais/irlandaise**
*juh sweez eerlanday/eerlandez*

I am Welsh
**Je suis gallois/galloise**
*juh swee galwa/galwaz*

I live in London
**J'habite à Londres**
*jabeet a lawñdr*

We live in Newcastle
**Nous habitons à Newcastle**
*nooz abitawñ a . . .*

I am a student
**Je suis étudiant** (*male*)/
**étudiante** (*female*)
*juh sweez aytewdyoñ/
aytewdyoñt*

I am a nurse
**Je suis infirmière**
*juh swees añfeermyer*

I work in . . .
**Je travaille dans . . .**
*juh traviy doñ . . .*

I work in an office/factory
**Je travaille dans un bureau/
une usine**
*juh traviy doñz uñ bewroh/
ewn ewzeen*

I work for a company that makes computers
**Je travaille dans une
compagnie qui fabrique des
ordinateurs**
*juh traviy doñz ewn
kawmpanyee kee fabreek
dayz ordeenatuhr*

I am unemployed
**Je suis en chômage**
*juh sweez oñ shohmaj*

I am single
**Je suis célibataire**
*juh swee sayleebater*

I am married
**Je suis marié(e)**
*juh swee maree-ay*

We are separated
**Nous sommes séparés**
*noo som sayparay*

I am divorced
**Je suis divorcé(e)**
*juh swee deevorsay*

I am a widower/widow
**Je suis veuf/veuve**
*juh swee vuhf/vuhv*

I have a son/a daughter
**J'ai un fils/une fille**
*jay uñ fees/ewn feey*

I have three children
**J'ai trois enfants**
*jay trwaz oñfoñ*

I don't have any children
**Je n'ai pas d'enfants**
*juh nay pa doñfoñ*

I have one brother
**J'ai un frère**
*jay uñ frer*

I have three sisters
**J'ai trois sœurs**
*jay trwa suhr*

I'm here with my husband/
my wife
**Je suis ici avec mon mari/ma
femme**
*juh sweez eesee avek mawñ
maree/ma fam*

I'm here with my family
**Je suis ici avec ma famille**
*juh sweez eesee avek ma
fameey*

I'm here on holiday
**Je suis ici en vacances**
*juh sweez eesee oñ vakoñs*

I'm here on a business trip
**Je suis ici en voyage d'affaires**
*juh sweez eesee oñ vwiyaj dafer*

I don't speak French very
well
**Je ne parle pas bien le français**
*juh nuh parl pa byañ luh
froñsay*

My husband/My wife is . . .
**Mon mari/Ma femme est . . .**
*mawñ maree/ma fam e . . .*

My husband is a bus-driver
**Mon mari est chauffeur
d'autobus**
*mawñ maree e shofuhr
dohtohbews*

My wife is an accountant
**Ma femme est comptable**
*ma fam e cawñtabl*

My husband/My wife works
in . . .
**Mon mari/Ma femme
travaille dans . . .**
*mawñ maree/ma fam traviy
doñ . . .*

My son is five years old
**Mon fils a cinq ans**
*mawñ fees a sañk oñ*

My daughter is eight years
old
**Ma fille a huit ans**
*ma feey a weet oñ*

## You may hear

**Comment vous appelez-vous?**
*komoñ vooz apuhlay voo*
What is your name?

**D'où êtes-vous?**
*doo et voo*
Where are you from?

**Que faites-vous?**
*kuh fet voo*
What do you do?

**Qu'est-ce que vous étudiez?**
*keskuh vooz aytewdee-ay*
What are you studying?

**Êtes-vous marié(e)?**
*et voo maree-ay*
Are you married?

**Avez-vous des enfants?**
*avay voo dayz oñfoñ*
Do you have any children?

**Quel âge ont-ils?**
*kel aj awñteel*
How old are they?

**Quel âge a-t-il/a-t-elle?**
*kel aj ateel/atel*
How old is he/she?

**Il est très sympathique/beau**
*eel e tre sampateek/boh*
He is very nice/good-looking

**Elle est très sympathique/belle**
*el e tre sampateek/bel*
She is very nice/pretty

**Il/Elle est très mignon/ mignonne**
*eel/el e tre meenyawñ/ meenyon*
He/She is very pretty (sweet)

**Avez-vous des frères et des sœurs?**
*avay voo day frer ay day suhr*
Do you have any brothers and sisters?

**Est-ce que c'est votre mari/ fiancé/ami?**
*eskuh say votr maree/ fee-oñsay/amee*
Is this your husband/ fiancé/boyfriend?

**Est-ce que c'est votre femme/ fiancée/amie?**
*eskuh say votr fam/fee-oñsay/ amee*
Is this your wife/fiancée/ girlfriend?

**Où allez-vous?**
*oo alay voo*
Where are you going?

**Où êtes-vous descendu(e)?**
*oo et voo desoñdew*
Where are you staying?

**Où habitez-vous?**
*oo abeetay voo*
Where do you live?

## Talking about their and your own country

I like France (very much)
**J'aime beaucoup la France**
*jem bohkoo la froñs*

Switzerland is a very
beautiful country
**La Suisse est un très beau
pays**
*la swees et uñ tre boh payee*

It's my first time in Belgium
**C'est la première fois que je
viens en Belgique**
*say la pruhmyer fwa kuh juh
vyañ oñ beljeek*

I've been here a week
**Je suis ici depuis une
semaine**
*juh sweez eesee duhpwee ewn
suhmen*

I come to France a lot
**Je viens beaucoup en France**
*juh vyañ bohkoo oñ froñs*

Are you from here?
**Vous êtes d'ici?**
*vooz et deesee*

Have you ever been to
England?
**Est-ce que vous êtes déjà
allé(e) en Angleterre?**
*eskuh vooz et dayja alay on
oñgluhter*

To Scotland/Ireland
**En Écosse/Irlande**
*on aykos/eerloñd*

To Wales
**Au pays de Galles**
*oh payee de gal*

Did you like it?
**Ça vous a plu?**
*sa vooz a plew*

15

## You may hear

**Est-ce que vous aimez le Luxembourg?**
*eskuh vooz aymay le Lewxomboor*
Do you like Luxembourg?

**Est-ce que c'est la première fois que vous venez en France?**
*eskuh say la pruhmyer fwa kuh voo vuhnay oñ froñs*
Is this the first time you've been to France?

**Combien de temps restez-vous?**
*kawmbyañ duh toñ restay voo*
How long are you here for?

**Est-ce que vous vous plaisez ici?**
*eskuh voo voo playzay eesee*
Are you enjoying it here?

**Qu'est-ce que vous pensez de . . . ?**
*keskuh voo poñsay duh . . .*
What do you think of . . . ?

**Qu'est-ce que vous pensez de la Suisse?**
*keskuh voo poñsay duh la swees*
What do you think of Switzerland?

**Vous parlez très bien le français**
*voo parlay tre byañ luh froñsay*
Your French is very good

16

## Likes and dislikes

I like . . .
**J'aime . . .**
*jem . . .*

I like it
**J'aime ça**
*jem sa*

I like football
**J'aime le football**
*jem le footbol*

I like swimming
**J'aime nager**
*jem najay*

I like strawberries
**J'aime les fraises**
*jem lay frez*

I don't like . . .
**Je n'aime pas . . .**
*juh nem pa . . .*

I don't like it
**Je n'aime pas ça**
*juh nem pa sa*

I don't like beer
**Je n'aime pas la bière**
*juh nem pa la byer*

Do you like it?
**Est-ce que vous aimez ça?**
*eskuh vooz aymay sa*

Do you like ice cream?
**Est-ce que vous aimez les glaces?**
*eskuh vooz aymay lay glas*

## Talking to a child

What's your name?
**Comment tu t'appelles?**
*komoñ tew tapel*

How old are you?
**Quel âge as-tu?**
*kel aj a tew*

Do you have any brothers and sisters?
**Est-ce que tu as des frères et des sœurs?**
*eskuh tew a day frer ay day suhr*

## Invitations and replies

Would you like a drink?
**Voulez-vous prendre un verre?**
*voolay voo proñdr uñ ver*

Yes, please
**Oui, s'il vous plaît**
*wee seelvooplay*

No, thank you
**Non, merci**
*nawñ mersee*

With pleasure/I'd be delighted
**Avec plaisir**
*avek playzeer*

That's very kind of you
**C'est très aimable**
*say trez aymabl*

Please leave me alone
**Laissez-moi tranquille, s'il vous plaît**
*lesay mwa troñkeel seelvooplay*

## You may hear

**Voulez-vous . . . ?**
*voolay voo . . .*
Would you like . . . ?

**Voulez-vous prendre un verre?**
*voolay voo proñdr uñ ver*
Would you like a drink?

**Voulez-vous manger quelque chose?**
*voolay voo moñjay kelkuh shohz*
Would you like something to eat?

**Que faites-vous ce soir?**
*kuh fet voo suh swar*
What are you doing tonight?

**Voulez-vous venir à . . . ?**
*voolay voo vuhneer a . . .*
Would you like to come to . . . ?

**Voulez-vous venir au cinéma avec moi?**
*voolay voo vuhneer oh seenayma avek mwa*
Would you like to come to the cinema with me?

**Voulez-vous dîner avec moi?**
*voolay voo deenay avek mwa*
Would you like to have dinner with me?

**Voulez-vous danser?**
*voolay voo doñsay*
Would you like to go dancing?

**À quelle heure est-ce qu'on se retrouve?**
*a kel uhr eskawñ suh ruhtroov*
What time shall we meet?

**Où est-ce qu'on se retrouve?**
*oo eskawñ suh ruhtroov*
Where shall we meet?

**Avez-vous du feu?**
*avay voo dew fuh*
Have you got a light?

## Good wishes and exclamations

Congratulations!
**Félicitations!**
*fayleeseetasyawñ*

Happy birthday!
**Bon anniversaire!**
*bon aneeverser*

Merry Christmas!
**Joyeux Noël!**
*jwiyuh noh-el*

Happy New Year!
**Bonne année!**
*bon anay*

Good luck!
**Bonne chance!**
*bon shoñs*

Enjoy yourself!
**Amusez-vous bien!**
*amewsay voo byañ*

Have a good journey!
**Bon voyage!**
*bawñ vwiyaj*

Cheers!
**Santé!**
*soñtay*

Enjoy your meal!
**Bon appétit!**
*bon apaytee*

Bless you! (*when someone sneezes*)
**À vos souhaits!**
*a voh sooway*

What a pity!
**Quel dommage!**
*kel domaj*

## Talking about the weather

The weather's very good
**Il fait très beau temps**
*eel fay tre boh toñ*

The weather's very bad
**Il fait très mauvais temps**
*eel fay tre mohvay toñ*

What a lovely day!
**Quelle belle journée!**
*kel bel joornay*

It's hot
**Il fait chaud**
*eel fay shoh*

It's cold
**Il fait froid**
*eel fay frwa*

I like the heat/the cold
**J'aime la chaleur/le froid**
*jem la shaluhr/luh frwa*

I don't like the heat/the cold
**Je n'aime pas la chaleur/le froid**
*juh nem pa la shaluhr/luh frwa*

It's very windy
**Il fait beaucoup de vent**
*eel fay bohkoo duh voñ*

Do you think it's going to rain?
**Vous pensez qu'il va pleuvoir?**
*voo poñsay keel va pluhvwar*

# ARRIVING IN THE COUNTRY

● Whether you arrive by air, road or sea, the formalities (passport control and Customs) are quite straightforward; the only document you need is a valid passport.

● You will probably not need to say anything in French unless you are asked the purpose of your visit, or have something to declare at Customs. If you need to say what you have to declare (rather than just showing it), look up the words in the dictionary. EC duty-free allowances apply to France, Belgium and Luxembourg, though not to Switzerland – you can get a leaflet with the details at your point of departure.

## You may see

| | |
|---|---|
| Articles à déclarer | Goods to declare |
| Autres passeports | Other passports |
| CE (+ Suisse) | EC (and Switzerland) |
| Contrôle de passeports | Passport control |
| Douane | Customs |
| Passeports français/belges/ suisses | French/Belgian/Swiss passports |
| Rien à déclarer | Nothing to declare |

## You may want to say

I am here on holiday
**Je suis ici en vacances**
*juh sweez eesee oñ vakañs*

I am here on a business trip
**Je suis ici en voyage
d'affaires**
*juh sweez eesee oñ vwiyaj
dafer*

It's a joint passport
**C'est un passeport familial**
*set uñ paspor fameelyal*

I have something to declare
**J'ai quelque chose à déclarer**
*jay kelkuh shohz a dayklaray*

I have this
**J'ai ça**
*jay sa*

I have two bottles of whisky
**J'ai deux bouteilles de whisky**
*jay duh bootay duh weeskee*

I have two cartons of
cigarettes
**J'ai deux cartouches de
cigarettes**
*jay duh kartoosh duh seegaret*

I have the receipt
**J'ai le reçu**
*jay luh ruhsew*

## You may hear

**Votre passeport, s'il vous plaît**
*votr paspor seelvooplay*
Your passport, please

**Vos documents, s'il vous plaît**
*voh dokewmoñ seelvooplay*
Your documents, please

**Quel est l'objet de votre visite?**
*kel e lobjay duh votr veezeet*
What is the purpose of your visit?

**Êtes-vous en vacances ou en voyage d'affaires?**
*et voo oñ vakoñs oo oñ vwiyaj dafer*
Are you here on holiday or business?

**Combien de temps pensez-vous rester en France?**
*kawmbyañ duh toñ poñsay voo restay oñ froñs*
How long are you planning to stay in France?

**Pourriez-vous ouvrir ce sac/ cette valise?**
*pooree-ay voo oovreer suh sak/set valeez*
Will you open this bag/this suitcase?

**Pourriez-vous ouvrir le coffre?**
*pooree-ay voo oovreer luh kofr*
Will you open the boot?

**On doit fouiller la voiture**
*awñ dwa foo-eeyay la vwatewr*
We have to search the car

**Est-ce que vous avez d'autres bagages?**
*eskuh vooz avay dohtr bagaj*
Do you have any other luggage?

**Il faut payer des droits de douane sur cet article**
*eel foh payay day drwa duh doo-an sewr set arteekl*
There is duty to pay on this item

**Suivez-moi/nous**
*sweevay mwa/noo*
Come with me/us

# DIRECTIONS

● Some general maps are available from the national Tourist Offices in the UK (addresses, page 214). Local tourist offices can provide town plans and regional maps.

● When you need to ask the way somewhere, the easiest thing is just to name the place you're looking for and add 'please', e.g. **Calais, s'il vous plaît?** Or you can start with 'where is . . .?': **où se trouve . . .?**

● If you're looking for a particular address, have it written down.

● When you're being given directions, listen out for the important bits (such as whether to turn left or right), and try to repeat each bit to make sure you've understood it correctly.

## You may see

| | |
|---|---|
| **À la/Au . . .** | To the . . . |
| **Avenue** | Avenue |
| **Boulevard** | Avenue |
| **Cathédrale** | Cathedral |
| **Château** | Castle |
| **Église** | Church |
| **Interdit aux piétons** | No access for pedestrians |
| **Musée** | Museum |
| **Palais** | Palace |
| **Passage clouté** | Pedestrian crossing |
| **Passage souterrain** | Subway |
| **Piétons** | Pedestrians |
| **Place** | Square |
| **Rue** | Street |
| **Rue piétonnière** | Pedestrian street/precinct |

## You may want to say

Excuse me
**Pardon**
*pardawñ*

Can you repeat that, please?
**Pourriez-vous répéter, s'il vous plaît?**
*pooree-ay voo raypaytay seelvooplay*

More slowly
**Plus lentement**
*plew loñtuhmoñ*

Again, please
**Encore une fois, s'il vous plaît**
*oñkor ewn fwa seelvooplay*

I am lost
**Je me suis perdu(e)**
*juh muh swee perdew*

Where are we?
**Où sommes-nous?**
*oo som noo*

Where does this road lead to?
**Où conduit cette route?**
*oo kawñdwee set root*

Is this the right way to the castle?
**Est-ce que c'est le bon chemin pour le château?**
*eskuh say luh bawñ shuhmañ poor luh shatoh*

Can you show me on the map?
**Pourriez-vous me le montrer sur la carte?**
*pooree-ay voo muh luh mawñtray sewr la kart*

The station, please?
**La gare, s'il vous plaît?**
*la gar seelvooplay*

The town centre, please?
**Le centre-ville, s'il vous plaît?**
*luh soñtre veel seelvooplay*

The road to Nice, please?
**La route de Nice, s'il vous plaît?**
*la root duh nees seelvooplay*

How do I/we get to . . . ?
**Pour aller à . . . ?**
*poor alay a . . .*

How do I/we get to St Tropez?
**Pour aller à St Tropez?**
*poor alay a sañ tropay*

How do I/we get to the airport?
**Pour aller à l'aéroport?**
*poor alay a la-ayropor*

How do I/we get to the beach?
**Pour aller à la plage?**
*poor alay a la plaj*

24

Where is/are . . . ?
**Où se trouve(nt) . . . ?**
*oo suh troov . . .*

Where is the tourist office?
**Où se trouve le syndicat d'initiative?**
*oo suh troov luh sañdeeka deeneesyateev*

Where is the post office?
**Où se trouve le bureau de poste?**
*oo suh troov luh bewroh duh post*

Where is this office/this room?
**Où se trouve ce bureau/cette chambre?**
*oo suh troov suh bewroh/set shombr*

Where are the toilets?
**Où se trouvent les toilettes?**
*oo se troov lay twalet*

Where is this, please? (*if you've got an address written down*)
**Où c'est, s'il vous plaît?**
*oo say seelvooplay*

Is it far?
**Est-ce que c'est loin?**
*eskuh say lwañ*

Is the airport far away?
**Est-ce que l'aéroport est loin?**
*eskuh la-ayropor e lwañ*

How many kilometres away?
**À combien de kilomètres?**
*a kawmbyañ duh keelometr*

How long does it take (on foot/by car)?
**Combien de temps faut-il (à pied/en voiture)?**
*kawmbyañ duh toñ fohteel (a pyay/oñ vwatewr)*

Is there a bus/train?
**Est-ce qu'il y a un bus/train?**
*eskeelya uñ bews/trañ*

Can I/we get there on foot?
**Est-ce qu'on peut y aller à pied?**
*eskawñ puh ee alay a pyay*

Can I/we get there by car?
**Est-ce qu'on peut y aller en voiture?**
*eskawñ puh ee alay oñ vwatewr*

Is there . . . ?
**Est-ce qu'il y a . . . ?**
*eskeelya . . .*

Is there a bank around here?
**Est-ce qu'il y a une banque par ici?**
*eskeelya ewn boñk par eesee*

Is there a supermarket in the village?
**Est-cè qu'il y a un supermarché dans le village?**
*eskeelya uñ sewpermarshay doñ luh veelaj*

## You may hear

**Vous vous êtes trompé(e)**
*voo vooz et trawmpay*
You've made a mistake

**Vous allez du mauvais côté**
*vooz alay dew mohvay kohtay*
You're going the wrong way

**On est ici**
*awn et eesee*
We are here

**Ici**
*eesee*
Here

**Là**
*la*
There

**Par ici**
*par eesee*
This way

**Par là**
*par la*
That way/Along there

**À droite**
*a drwat*
To/On the right

**À gauche**
*a gohsh*
To/On the left

**Tout droit**
*too drwa*
Straight on

**La première (rue)**
*la pruhmyer (rew)*
The first (street/turning)

**La deuxième (rue)**
*la duhzyem (rew)*
The second (street/turning)

**La troisième (rue)**
*la trwazyem (rew)*
The third (street/turning)

**Sur la droite**
*sewr la drwat*
On the right-hand side

**Sur la gauche**
*sewr la gohsh*
On the left-hand side

**Au bout de la rue**
*oh boo duh la rew*
At the end of the street

**De l'autre côté de la place**
*duh lohtr kohtay duh la plas*
On the other side of the square

**Au coin**
*oh kwañ*
On the corner

**En bas**
*oñ ba*
Down/Downstairs

**En haut**
*oñ oh*
Up/Upstairs

**Par-dessous**
*par duhsoo*
Under

**Par-dessus**
*par duhsew*
Over

**Avant les feux**
*avoñ lay fuh*
Before the traffic lights

**Après la cathédrale**
*apray la kataydral*
After/Past the cathedral

**En face de**
*oñ fas duh*
Opposite

**Devant**
*duhvoñ*
In front of

**Derrière**
*deree-er*
Behind

**À côté de**
*a kohtay duh*
Next to

**Près de**
*pre duh*
Near/Close to

**C'est dans la place**
*say doñ la plas*
It's in the square

**Quand vous arrivez rue du Marché**
*koñ vooz areevay rew dew marchay*
When you get to the Rue du Marché

**Vers la cathédrale**
*ver la kataydral*
Towards the cathedral

**Jusqu'au carrefour**
*jewskoh karfor*
As far as the crossroads

**C'est loin**
*say lwañ*
It's far away

**Ce n'est pas loin**
*suh nay pa lwañ*
It's not far away

**Très loin/Assez loin**
*tre lwañ/asay lwañ*
Very far/Quite far

**C'est près**
*say pre*
It's close by

**Très près/Assez près**
*tre pre/asay pre*
Very close/Quite close

**C'est à cinq minutes d'ici**
*set a sañk meenewt deesee*
It's five minutes away from
here

**C'est à vingt kilomètres d'ici**
*set a vañ keelometr deesee*
It's twenty kilometres away
from here

**Il faut prendre le bus/train**
*eel foh proñdre luh bews/trañ*
You have to catch the bus/
train

**C'est au troisième étage**
*set oh trwazyem aytaj*
It's on the third floor

**La première/deuxième porte**
*la pruhmyer/duhzyem port*
The first/second door

**Prenez l'ascenseur**
*pruhnay lasoñsuhr*
Take the lift

You may also hear words like these, with or without **vous** first:

**Allez . . .**
*alay . . .*
Go . . .

**Continuez . . .**
*kawñteenew-ay . . .*
Carry on/Go on . . .

**Descendez . . .**
*desoñday . . .*
Go down . . .

**Montez . . .**
*mawñtay . . .*
Go up . . .

**Tournez . . .**
*toornay . . .*
Turn . . .

**Prenez . . .**
*pruhnay . . .*
Take . . .

**Traversez . . .**
*traversay . . .*
Cross . . .

# ROAD TRAVEL

● Consult the motoring organisations for information on driving in Europe. An international driving licence and Green Card insurance may not be technically necessary, but check their advice. You must carry your vehicle registration document.

● You drive on the right in France, Belgium, Luxembourg and Switzerland. Traffic from the right generally has priority on roads. This does not apply on roundabouts in France, where traffic already on the roundabout has priority, or where there are signs indicating otherwise. Seatbelts are compulsory, as are crash helmets for both drivers and passengers of motorbikes and scooters.

● **Speed limits** France: 60 km per hour in built-up areas, 90 kph on normal roads, 110 kph on dual carriageways, 130 kph on motorways. Belgium and Luxembourg: 60 kph in built-up areas, 90 kph on normal roads, 120 kph on motorways. Switzerland: 50 kph in built-up areas, 80 kph on normal roads, 120 kph on motorways.

● Main roads are labelled as follows:
**A (Autoroute)** – Motorway
**N (Route Nationale)** – National highway
**D (Route Départementale)** – Provincial or secondary road.

● You have to pay a toll (**péage**) on French motorways. In Switzerland you have to buy and display a special sticker (**une vignette**) to be allowed to drive on motorways – it's available in the UK from motoring organisations or the Swiss National Tourist Office (address, page 214).

● The main grades of petrol are 4-star, **super**, and 2-star, **ordinaire** or **normale** (in Switzerland). Unleaded petrol (**essence sans plomb**) is widely available, as is diesel (**gas-oil**).

Credit cards are accepted in petrol stations in large towns and on motorways, except in Switzerland where they are not accepted at all.

● There are Blue Zone parking areas (**Zone Bleue**) in many cities. Parking time is limited and you must display a parking disc to show the time you parked. Discs are available from places such as garages, police stations, tourist offices, some shops, and offices of motoring organisations of the various countries.

A few places have parking meters. In some cities, illegally parked cars may be wheel-clamped; in Paris especially they may be towed away.

● You can arrange car hire in Britain with the large international firms. They also have offices at airports and elsewhere (and there will often be someone who speaks English). There are local companies too in most towns and cities – look for the sign **Location de voitures**. Lists of agencies are also available from local tourist offices. Cars can also be hired from French Railways (**SNCF**) at over 200 railway stations.

● Bicycles can be hired from over 200 French railway stations, and from many stations in Switzerland – look for the sign **Location de vélos**.

● In case of breakdowns, there are emergency phones (painted orange) on many motorways and main roads. If you break down, set up your red warning triangle on the road 50 metres behind your vehicle.

If you have to tell a mechanic what's wrong with your vehicle, the easiest way is to indicate the part affected and say 'this isn't working': **ça ne marche pas**. Otherwise, look up the word for the appropriate part (see page 40).

## You may see

| | |
|---|---|
| **Accôtement non stabilisé** | Soft verge |
| **Allumez vos phares/lanternes** | Use headlights |
| **Attention** | Caution |
| **Autoroute (à péage)** | (Toll) motorway |
| **Bis = Bison futé** | Alternative route (off motorway) |
| **Carrefour dangereux** | Dangerous crossroads |
| **Cédez le passage** | Give way |
| **Centre-ville** | Town/city centre |
| **Chaussée déformée** | Uneven road surface |
| **Chutes de pierres** | Falling rocks |
| **Col (fermé)** | Mountain pass (closed) |
| **Danger** | Danger |
| **Délestage** | Relief route |
| **Déviation** | Diversion |
| **Douane** | Customs |
| **École** | School |
| **Fin d'autoroute** | End of motorway |
| **Fin d'interdiction (de stationner)** | End of (parking) prohibition |
| **Gravillons** | Loose chippings |
| **Halte – Gendarmerie** | Stop – Police checkpoint |
| **Interdiction de doubler** | No overtaking |
| **Interdit aux piétons** | No access for pedestrians |
| **Laissez la voie libre** | Allow free access |
| **Lave-auto** | Car wash |
| **Location de vélos** | Bicycle hire |
| **Location de voitures** | Car hire |
| **Passage à niveau** | Level crossing |
| **Passage clouté** | Pedestrian crossing |
| **Passage interdit** | No entry |
| **Passage protégé** | Priority road |
| **Péage** | Toll |
| **Périphérique** | Ring road |

| | |
|---|---|
| Piétons | Pedestrians |
| Piste réservée aux transports publics | Lane reserved for public transport |
| Poids lourds | Heavy goods vehicles |
| Priorité à droite | Give way to the right |
| Ralentir | Slow down |
| Rappel | Reminder |
| Roulez au pas | Dead slow |
| Route barrée | Road closed |
| Rue piétonnière | Pedestrian street/ precinct |
| | |
| Sens unique | One-way street |
| Serrez à droite | Keep right |
| Sortie | Exit |
| Sortie de camions | Lorry exit |
| Sortie d'usine | Factory exit |
| Stationnement alterné | Parking on alternate sides |
| Stationnement autorisé | Parking allowed |
| Stationnement interdit | No parking |
| Toutes directions | All routes |
| Travaux | Road works |
| Verglas | Black ice |
| Virage dangereux | Dangerous bend |
| Virages sur . . . km | Bends for . . . kilometres |
| Vitesse limitée | Speed limit |
| Vous n'avez pas la priorité | You do not have priority |
| Zone bleue | Blue zone |

## You may want to say

### Petrol

Is there a petrol station around here?
**Est-ce qu'il y a une station-service par ici?**
*eskeelya ewn stasyawñ servees par eesee*

4-star
**Super**
*sewper*

2-star
**Ordinaire/Normale**
*ordeener/normal*

Unleaded petrol
**Essence sans plomb**
*esoñs soñ plawñ*

Diesel
**Gas-oil**
*gaz oyl*

20 litres of 4-star, please
**Vingt litres de super, s'il vous plaît**
*vañ leetr de sewper seelvooplay*

50 francs' worth of unleaded petrol, please
**Pour cinquante francs d'essence sans plomb, s'il vous plaît**
*poor sañkoñt froñ desoñs soñ plawñ seelvooplay*

Fill it up with 4-star/2-star, please
**Le plein de super/d'ordinaire (de normale), s'il vous plaît**
*luh plañ duh sewper/d'ordeener (duh normal) seelvooplay*

A can of oil/petrol, please
**Un bidon d'huile/d'essence, s'il vous plaît**
*uñ beedawñ dweel/desoñs seelvooplay*

Some water, please
**De l'eau, s'il vous plaît**
*duh loh seelvooplay*

33

Can you check the tyre pressures?
**Pourriez-vous vérifier la pression des pneus?**
*pooree-ay voo vayreefyay la presyawñ day pnuh*

Can you change the tyre?
**Pourriez-vous changer le pneu?**
*pooree-ay voo shoñjay luh pnuh*

Can you clean the windscreen?
**Pourriez-vous nettoyer le pare-brise?**
*pooree-ay voo netwiyay luh parbreez*

Where is the air, please?
**Où est la pompe à air, s'il vous plaît?**
*oo e la pawmp a er seelvooplay*

How much is it?
**C'est combien?**
*say kombyañ*

How does the car wash work?
**Comment marche le lave-auto?**
*komoñ marsh luh lavohtoh*

## Parking

Where can I/we park?
**Où est-ce qu'on peut stationner?**
*oo eskawñ puh stasyonay*

How much is it per hour?
**Combien ça coûte de l'heure?**
*kawmbyañ sa koot duh luhr*

Can I/we park here?
**Est-ce qu'on peut stationner ici?**
*eskawñ puh stasyonay eesee*

A parking disc, please
**Un disque de stationnement, s'il vous plaît**
*uñ deesk duh stasyonmoñ seelvooplay*

How long can I/we park here?
**Combien de temps est-ce qu'on peut stationner ici?**
*kawmbyañ duh toñ eskawñ puh stasyonay eesee*

## Hiring a car

(*see* Days, months, dates, *page 198*)

I would like to hire a car
**Je voudrais louer une voiture**
*juh voodray loo-ay ewn vwatewr*

A medium-sized car, please
**Une voiture moyenne, s'il vous plaît**
*ewn vwatewr mwiy-en seelvooplay*

A small car, please
**Une petite voiture, s'il vous plaît**
*ewn puhteet vwatewr seelvooplay*

A large car, please
**Une grande voiture, s'il vous plaît**
*ewn groñd vwatewr seelvooplay*

An automatic car, please
**Une voiture automatique, s'il vous plaît**
*ewn vwatewr ohtohmateek seelvooplay*

For three days
**Pour trois jours**
*poor trwa joor*

For a week
**Pour une semaine**
*poor ewn suhmen*

For a fortnight
**Pour quinze jours**
*poor kañz joor*

From . . . to . . .
**Du . . . au . . .**
*dew . . . oh . . .*

From Monday to Friday
**Du lundi au vendredi**
*dew luñdee oh voñdruhdee*

From 10th August to 17th August
**Du dix août au dix-sept août**
*dew dees oot oh deeset oot*

How much is it?
**C'est combien?**
*say kwambyañ*

Per day/week
**Par jour/semaine**
*par joor/suhmen*

Per kilometre
**Par kilomètre**
*par keelometr*

Is mileage (kilometrage) included?
**Le kilométrage est-il compris?**
*luh keelomaytraj eteel kawmpree*

Is petrol included?
**L'essence est-elle comprise?**
*lesoñs etel kawmpreez*

Is insurance included?
**L'assurance est-elle comprise?**
*lasewroñs etel kawmpreez*

Comprehensive insurance cover
**Assurance tous risques**
*asewroñs too reesk*

My husband/wife is driving too
**Mon mari/Ma femme conduit aussi**
*mawñ maree/ma fam kawñdwee ohsee*

Do you take credit cards?
**Acceptez-vous les cartes de crédit?**
*akseptay voo lay kart duh kraydee*

Do you take traveller's cheques?
**Acceptez-vous les chèques de voyage?**
*akseptay voo lay shek duh vwiyaj*

Can I leave the car in Nancy?
**Puis-je rendre la voiture à Nancy?**
*pweejuh roñdr la vwatewr a noñsee*

Can I leave the car at the airport?
**Puis-je rendre la voiture à l'aéroport?**
*pweejuh roñdr la vwatewr a la-ayropor*

How do the controls work?
**Comment marchent les commandes?**
*komoñ marsh lay komañd*

## Breakdowns and repairs

(*see also list of* Car parts *on page 40*)

My car has broken down
**Ma voiture est en panne**
*ma vwatewr et oñ pan*

Is there a garage around here?
**Est-ce qu'il y a un garage par ici?**
*eskeelya uñ garaj par eesee*

Can you telephone a garage?
**Pourriez-vous téléphoner à un garage?**
*pooree-ay voo taylayfonay a uñ garaj*

Can you send a mechanic?
**Pourriez-vous envoyer un mécanicien?**
*pooree-ay voo oñvwiyay uñ maykaneesyañ*

Can you tow me to a garage?
**Pourriez-vous me remorquer jusqu'à un garage?**
*pooree-ay voo muh ruhmorkay jewska uñ garaj*

Do you do repairs?
**Est-ce que vous faites les réparations?**
*eskuh voo fet lay rayparasyawñ*

I don't know what's wrong
**Je ne sais pas ce qu'il y a**
*juh nuh say pa suh keelya*

I think . . .
**Je crois que . . .**
*juh krwa kuh . . .*

It's the clutch
**C'est l'embrayage**
*say lombrayaj*

It's the radiator
**C'est le radiateur**
*say luh radee-atuhr*

It's the brakes
**Ce sont les freins**
*se sawñ lay frañ*

The car won't start
**La voiture ne démarre pas**
*la vwatewr nuh daymar pa*

The battery is flat
**La batterie est à plat**
*la batuhree et a pla*

The engine is overheating
**Le moteur chauffe**
*luh mohtuhr shohf*

There's a water/oil leak
**Il y a une fuite d'eau/d'huile**
*eelya ewn fweet doh/dweel*

I have a puncture
**J'ai crevé**
*jay kruhvay*

I have run out of petrol
**Je suis en panne d'essence**
*juh sweez oñ pan desoñs*

The . . . doesn't work
**Le/La . . . ne marche pas**
*luh/la . . . nuh marsh pa*

I need a . . .
**J'ai besoin d'un/d'une . . .**
*jay buhswañ duñ/dewn . . .*

Is it serious?
**C'est grave?**
*say grav*

Can you repair it (today)?
**Est-ce que vous pouvez le
    réparer (aujourd'hui)?**
*eskuh voo poovay luh
    rayparay (ohjoordwee)*

How long is it going to take?
**Combien de temps ça va
    prendre?**
*kawmbyañ duh toñ sa va
    proñdr*

When will it be ready?
**Quand est-ce que ce sera prêt?**
*koñt eskuh suh suhra pray*

How much is it going to cost?
**Combien ça va coûter?**
*kawmbyañ sa va kootay*

## You may hear

### Petrol

**Que désirez-vous?**
*kuh dayzeeray voo*
What would you like?

**Combien en voulez-vous?**
*kawmbyañ oñ voolay voo*
How much do you want?

**La clé, s'il vous plaît**
*la klay seelvooplay*
The key, please

### Parking

**On ne peut pas stationner ici**
*awñ nuh puh pa stasyonay eesee*
You can't park here

**C'est dix francs de l'heure**
*say dees froñ duh luhr*
It's 10 francs an hour

**C'est gratuit**
*say gratwee*
It's free

**Il y a un parking par là**
*eelya uñ parkeeng par la*
There's a car park over there

### Hiring a car

**Quel genre de voiture voulez-vous?**
*kel joñr duh vwatewr voolay voo*
What kind of car do you want?

**Pour combien de temps?**
*poor kawmbyañ duh toñ*
For how long?

**Pour combien de jours?**
*poor kawmbyañ duh joor*
For how many days?

**Qui va conduire?**
*kee va kawñdweer*
Who is driving?

**Le tarif est de trois cents/ deux mille francs**
*luh tareef e duh trwa soñ/duh meel froñ*
The rate is 300/2000 francs

**Par jour**
*par joor*
Per day

**Par semaine**
*par suhmen*
Per week

38

**Votre permis de conduire, s'il vous plaît**
*votr permee duh kawñdweer seelvooplay*
Your driving licence, please

**Quelle est votre adresse?**
*kel e votr adres*
What is your address?

**Voici les clés**
*vwasee lay klay*
Here are the keys

**Rendez la voiture après avoir fait le plein, s'il vous plaît**
*roñday la vwatewr aprez avwar fay luh plañ seelvooplay*
Please return the car with a full tank

**Rendez la voiture avant six heures, s'il vous plaît**
*roñday la vwatewr avoñ seez uhr seelvooplay*
Please return the car before six o'clock

**Si le bureau est fermé, vous pouvez laisser les clés dans la boîte aux lettres**
*see luh bewroh e fermay voo poovay lesay lay klay doñ la bwat oh letr*
If the office is closed, you can leave the keys in the letterbox

## Breakdowns and repairs

**Qu'est-ce qui se passe?**
*keskee suh pas*
What's wrong with it?

**Veuillez ouvrir le capot, s'il vous plaît?**
*vuhyay oovreer luh kapoh seelvooplay*
Would you open the bonnet, please?

**Je n'ai pas de pièces de rechange**
*juh nay pa duh pyes duh ruhshoñj*
I don't have the necessary parts

**Il faut que je commande les pièces**
*eel foh kuh juh komoñd lay pyes*
I will have to order the parts

**Ce sera prêt mardi prochain**
*suh suhra pray mardee proshañ*
It will be ready next Tuesday

**Ça va coûter cinq cents francs**
*sa va kootay sañk soñ froñ*
It will cost 500 francs

## Car and bicycle parts

| | | |
|---|---|---|
| Accelerator | **L'accélérateur** | *aksaylayratuhr* |
| Air filter | **Le filtre à air** | *feeltr a er* |
| Alternator | **L'alternateur** | *alternatuhr* |
| Battery | **La batterie** | *batuhree* |
| Bonnet | **Le capot** | *kapo* |
| Boot | **Le coffre** | *kofr* |
| Brake cable | **Le câble de frein** | *kabl duh frañ* |
| Brake fluid | **Le liquide de frein** | *leekeed duh frañ* |
| Brake hose | **Le flexible de frein** | *flexeeble duh frañ* |
| Brakes (front/rear) | **Les freins (avant/arrière)** | *frañ (avoñ/aree-er)* |
| Carburettor | **Le carburateur** | *karbewratuhr* |
| Chain | **La chaîne** | *shen* |

| Choke | **Le starter** | *starter* |
| Clutch | **L'embrayage** | *ombrayaj* |
| Cooling system | **Le système de refroidissement** | *seestem duh ruhfrwadeesmoñ* |
| Disc brakes | **Les freins à disque** | *frañ a deesk* |
| Distributor | **Le distributeur** | *deestreebewtuhr* |
| Electrical system | **Le système électrique** | *seestem aylektreek* |
| Engine | **Le moteur** | *mohtuhr* |
| Exhaust pipe | **Le pot d'échappement** | *poh dayshapmoñ* |
| Fanbelt | **La courroie de ventilateur** | *koorwa duh voñteelatuhr* |
| Frame | **Le cadre** | *kadr* |
| Front fork | **La fourchette avant** | *foorshet avoñ* |
| Fuel gauge | **La jauge d'essence** | *johj desoñs* |
| Fuel pump | **La pompe à essence** | *pawmp a esoñs* |
| Fuse | **Le fusible** | *fewzeebl* |
| Gearbox | **La boîte de vitesses** | *bwat duh veetes* |
| Gear lever | **Le levier de vitesse** | *luhvyay duh veetes* |
| Gears | **Les vitesses** | *veetes* |
| Handbrake | **Le frein à main** | *frañ a mañ* |
| Handlebars | **Le guidon** | *geedawñ* |
| Headlights | **Les phares** | *far* |
| Heater | **Le chauffage** | *shohfaj* |
| Horn | **Le klaxon** | *klaxawñ* |
| Ignition | **L'allumage** | *alewmaj* |
| Ignition key | **La clé de contact** | *klay duh kawñtakt* |
| Indicator | **Le clignoteur** | *kleenyotuhr* |
| Inner tube | **La chambre à air** | *shombr a er* |
| Lights (front/rear) | **Les feux (avant/arrière)** | *fuh (avoñ/aree-er)* |
| Lock | **La serrure** | *serewr* |
| Oil filter | **Le filtre à l'huile** | *feeltr a lweel* |
| Oil gauge | **Le manomètre d'huile** | *manometr dweel* |

| Pedal | **La pédale** | *paydal* |
| Points | **Les contacts** | *kawñtakt* |
| Pump | **La pompe** | *pawmp* |
| Radiator | **Le radiateur** | *radee-atuhr* |
| Radiator hose (top/bottom) | **Le tubulure (supérieure/ inférieure)** | *tewbewlewr (sewpayree-uhr/ añfayree-uhr)* |
| Reversing lights | **Les feux de marche arrière** | *fuh duh marsh aree-er* |
| Rotor arm | **Le bras d'allumeur** | *bra dalewmuhr* |
| Saddle | **La selle** | *sel* |
| Silencer | **Le silencieux** | *seeloñsyuh* |
| Spare wheel | **La roue de secours** | *roo duh suhkoor* |
| Spark plugs | **Les bougies** | *boojee* |
| Speedometer | **Le compteur de vitesse** | *kawñtuhr duh veetes* |
| Spokes | **Les rayons** | *rayawñ* |
| Starter motor | **Le démarreur** | *daymaruhr* |
| Steering | **La direction** | *deereksyawñ* |
| Steering wheel | **Le volant** | *voloñ* |
| Transmission (automatic) | **La transmission (automatique)** | *troñsmeesyawñ (ohtomateek)* |
| Tyre (front/rear) | **Le pneu (avant/ arrière)** | *pnuh (avoñ/ aree-er)* |
| Valve | **La valve** | *valv* |
| Warning light | **Le voyant** | *vwiyoñ* |
| Wheel (front/rear) | **La roue (avant/ arrière)** | *roo (avoñ/ aree-er)* |
| Wheel rim | **La jante** | *joñt* |
| Window | **La vitre** | *veetr* |
| Windscreen | **Le pare-brise** | *parbreez* |
| Windscreen washer | **Le lave-glace** | *lavglas* |
| Windscreen wiper | **L'essuie-glace** | *eswee glas* |

# TAXIS

• You can hail taxis in the street, or find them at a taxi rank (**station de taxi**). Taxis that are free have a light on.

• Taxis have meters, but there may be extras for luggage, airport pick-ups, etc. A tip of 10% or so is usual (in Switzerland it is sometimes included in the fare).

• Write down clearly the address of your destination if it's at all complicated so that you can show it to the taxi driver.

## You may want to say

(*see also* Directions, *page 23*)

Is there a taxi rank around here?
**Est-ce qu'il y a une station de taxi par ici?**
*eskeelya ewn stasyawñ duh taxee par eesee*

I need a taxi
**J'ai besoin d'un taxi**
*jay buhzwañ duñ taxee*

Please call me a taxi
**Appelez-moi un taxi, s'il vous plaît**
*apuhlay mwa uñ taxee seelvooplay*

Immediately
**Tout de suite**
*toot sweet*

For tomorrow at nine o'clock
**Pour demain à neuf heures**
*poor duhmañ a nuhv uhr*

To go to the airport
**Pour aller à l'aéroport**
*poor alay a la-ayropor*

To the airport, please
**À l'aéroport, s'il vous plaît**
*a la-ayropor seelvooplay*

To the station, please
**À la gare, s'il vous plaît**
*a la gar seelvooplay*

To the Hotel de la Gare, please
**À l'Hôtel de la Gare, s'il vous plaît**
*a lohtel duh la gar seelvooplay*

To this address, please
**À cette adresse, s'il vous plaît**
*a set adres seelvooplay*

Is it far?
**Est-ce que c'est loin?**
*eskuh say lwañ*

How much is it going to cost?
**Combien ça va coûter?**
*kawmbyañ sa va kootay*

I am in a hurry
**Je suis pressé(e)**
*juh swee presay*

Stop here, please
**Arrêtez-vous ici, s'il vous plaît**
*aretay voo eesee seelvooplay*

Can you wait (a few minutes), please?
**Pourriez-vous attendre (quelques minutes), s'il vous plaît?**
*pooree-ay voo atoñdr (kelkuh meenewt) seelvooplay*

How much is it?
**C'est combien?**
*say kawmbyañ*

There is a mistake
**Il y a une erreur**
*eelya ewn eruhr*

The meter says 65 francs
**Le compteur indique soixante-cinq francs**
*le kawñtuhr añdeek swasoñt sañk froñ*

Keep the change
**Gardez la monnaie**
*garday la monay*

Can you give me a receipt?
**Pourriez-vous me donner un reçu?**
*pooree-ay voo muh donay uñ ruhsew*

For 100 francs
**Pour cent francs**
*poor soñ froñ*

## You may hear

**C'est à dix kilomètres**
*set a dees keelometr*
It's ten kilometres away

**Ça va coûter à peu près cent dix francs**
*sa va kootay a puh pre soñ dees froñ*
It will cost approximately 110 francs

**C'est soixante-huit francs**
*say swasoñt weet froñ*
That's 68 francs

**Il y a un supplément**
*eelya uñ sewplaymoñ*
There is a supplement

**Pour les bagages**
*poor lay bagaj*
For the luggage

**Pour chaque valise**
*poor shak valeez*
For each suitcase

**Parce que c'est l'aéroport**
*parskuh say la-ayropor*
For the airport

# AIR TRAVEL

● France has over 30 airports, many for international and domestic flights, some for domestic flights only. Switzerland has four airports, Belgium five and Luxembourg one.

● There are bus services to most airports from the nearest town or city centre, and train connections to some. There are helicopter connections between Paris and its two airports and Le Bourget, and between Nice and Monaco.

● Approximate flight times between cities:
Paris–Brussels, 55 mins
Paris–Geneva, 1 hour 5 mins
Paris–Luxembourg, 1 hour
Brussels–Geneva, 1 hour 10 mins
Brussels–Luxembourg, 45 mins
Geneva–Luxembourg, 1 hour 10 mins

● Approximate distances from main airports to city centres:
Paris (Charles de Gaulle) – 23 km (14½ miles)
Paris (Orly) – 14 km (9 miles)
Brussels – 13 km (8 miles)
Luxembourg – 6 km (4 miles)
Geneva – 5 km (3 miles)
Basle/Mulhouse – 12 km (7½ miles) to Basle, 25 km (15½ miles) to Mulhouse
Nice – 6 km (4 miles)
Marseille – 24 km (15 miles)
Toulouse – 10 km (6 miles)
Bordeaux – 12 km (7½ miles)
Lyon – 24 km (15 miles)
Strasbourg – 12 km (7½ miles)
Montpellier – 8 km (5 miles)
Nantes – 11 km (7 miles)

## You may see

| | |
|---|---|
| **Aéroport** | Airport |
| **Arrivées** | Arrivals |
| **Articles à déclarer** | Goods to declare |
| **Attachez votre ceinture** | Fasten your seatbelt |
| **Autobus (vers le centre-ville)** | Buses (to the town centre) |
| **Autres passeports** | Other passports |
| **Autres terminaux** | Other terminals |
| **Bagages (à main)** | (Hand) luggage |
| **Change** | Bureau de change |
| **CE (+ Suisse)** | EC (and Switzerland) |
| **Contrôle des passeports** | Passport control |
| **Correspondance** | Connection |
| **Défense de fumer** | No smoking |
| **Départs** | Departures |
| **Douane** | Customs |
| **Embarquement** | Boarding |
| **Enregistrement (des bagages)** | Check-in |
| **Entrée** | Entrance |
| **Informations** | Information |
| **Issue de secours** | Emergency exit |
| **Location de voitures** | Car hire |
| **Magasin hors-taxe** | Duty-free shop |
| **Navette** | Shuttle; airport bus |
| **Passeports français/belges/ suisses** | French/Belgian/Swiss passports |
| **Porte** | Gate |
| **Renseignements** | Information |
| **Retard** | Delay |
| **Retrait des bagages** | Luggage reclaim |
| **Rien à déclarer** | Nothing to declare |
| **Salle d'arrivée** | Arrival hall |
| **Salle des départs** | Departure lounge |
| **Sortie (de secours)** | (Emergency) exit |
| **Toilettes** | Toilets |
| **Vol** | Flight |

## You may want to say

(*see also* Numbers, *page 218;* Days, months, dates, *page 198;* Time, *page 201*)

Is there a flight from Paris to Nice?
**Est-ce qu'il y a un vol Paris–Nice?**
*eskeelya uñ vol paree nees*

Is there a flight to Marseille?
**Est-ce qu'il y a un vol pour Marseille?**
*eskeelya uñ vol poor marsay*

Today
**Aujourd'hui**
*ohjoordwee*

This morning
**Ce matin**
*suh matañ*

This afternoon
**Cet après-midi**
*set apremeedee*

Tomorrow (morning/afternoon)
**Demain (matin/après-midi)**
*duhmañ (matañ/apremeedee)*

Do you have a timetable of flights to Geneva?
**Est-ce que vous avez un horaire des vols en direction de Genève?**
*eskuh vooz avay uñ orer day vol oñ deereksyawñ duh juhnev*

What time is the first flight to Geneva?
**À quelle heure part le premier vol pour Genève?**
*a kel uhr par luh pruhmyay vol poor juhnev*

The next flight
**Le prochain vol**
*luh proshañ vol*

The last flight
**Le dernier vol**
*luh dernyay vol*

What time does it arrive (at Geneva)?
**À quelle heure arrive-t-il (à Genève)?**
*a kel uhr areevteel (a juhnev)*

A ticket/Two tickets to Brussels, please
**Un billet/Deux billets pour Bruxelles, s'il vous plaît**
*uñ beeyay/duh beeyay poor brewsel seelvooplay*

Single
**Aller simple**
*alay sampl*

Return
**Aller-retour**
*alay ruhtoor*

48

1st class/Business class
**En première classe/En classe affaires**
*oñ pruhmyer klas/oñ klas afer*

For the eleven o'clock flight
**Pour le vol de onze heures**
*poor luh vol duh awñz uhr*

I want to change/cancel my reservation
**Je voudrais changer/annuler ma réservation**
*juh voodray shoñjay/anewlay ma rayzervasyawñ*

What is the number of the flight?
**Quel est le numéro du vol?**
*kel e luh newmayro dew vol*

What time do I/we have to check in?
**À quelle heure est-ce qu'il faut enregistrer ses bagages?**
*a kel uhr eskeel foh oñruhjeestray say bagaj*

Which gate is it?
**Quelle porte est-ce?**
*kel port es*

Is there a delay?
**Est-ce qu'il y a du retard?**
*eskeelya dew ruhtar*

Where is the luggage from the flight from London?
**Où sont les bagages du vol en provenance de Londres?**
*oo sawñ lay bagaj dew vol oñ provuhnoñs duh lawñdr*

My luggage is not here
**Mes bagages ne sont pas là**
*may bagaj nuh sawñ pa la*

My suitcase is not here
**Ma valise n'est pas là**
*ma valeez ne pa la*

Is there a bus to the centre of town?
**Est-ce qu'il y a un bus pour le centre-ville?**
*eskeelya uñ bews poor luh soñtr veel*

## You may hear

**Vous voulez un coin-fenêtre?**
*voo voolay uñ kwañ fuhnetr*
Would you like a window seat?

**Vous voulez un coin-couloir?**
*voo voolay uñ kwañ koolwar*
Would you like an aisle seat?

**En fumeurs ou en non fumeurs?**
*oñ fewmuhr oo oñ nawñ fewmuhr*
Smoking or non-smoking?

**Embarquement à . . .**
*ombarkmoñ a . . .*
The flight will be called/
board at . . . (time)

**Porte numéro sept**
*port newmayro set*
Gate number seven

**Votre billet, s'il vous plaît**
*votr beeyay seelvooplay*
Your ticket, please

**Votre passeport, s'il vous plaît**
*votr paspor seelvooplay*
Your passport, please

**Votre carte d'embarquement,
s'il vous plaît**
*votr kart dombarkmoñ
seelvooplay*
Your boarding card, please

**Comment sont vos bagages?**
*komoñ sawñ voh bagaj*
What does your luggage
look like?

**Vous avez le ticket?**
*vooz avay luh teekay*
Do you have the reclaim tag?

## Announcements you may hear over the public address system

*Words to listen for include:*

| | | |
|---|---|---|
| **Votre attention, s'il vous plaît** | *votr atonsyawñ seelvooplay* | Your attention please |
| **Départ** | *daypar* | Departure |
| **Embarquement (immédiat)** | *ombarkmoñ (eemaydya)* | Boarding (now) |
| **Le vol** | *vol* | Flight |
| **Passager(s)** | *pasajay* | Passenger(s) |
| **Porte** | *port* | Gate |
| **Retard/Retardé** | *ruhtar/ruhtarday* | Delay/Delayed |

# BRITTANY
# FERRIES

# QUIBERON

PLYMOUTH/ROSCOFF
26/05/91  08H00

LE KIOSQUE
NEWSPAPERS

| JOURNAUX ANGLAIS | 2,50 |
| --- | --- |

**TOTAL** GBP     2,50

ESPECES     2,50

T1  NC:23 TCK:0436 CAISSE:22
26.05.91   07.41

MERCI
*****
BON VOYAGE

----0-----

BRITTANY
FERRIES

QUIBERON

PLYMOUTH-ROSCOFF

JOURNAUX ANGLAIS        2.50
_____

ESPECES                 2.50

26.05.91  07.41

BON VOYAGE

---O---

# TRAVELLING BY TRAIN

● French, Belgian and Swiss Railways have offices in London (addresses, page 215) where you can get information and tickets. You can also get information from national Tourist Offices (addresses, page 214) or from British Rail.

In the countries, you can get information and buy tickets at many travel agents as well as at stations.

● France has very high-speed **TGV** (**train à grande vitesse**) trains running between Paris and the south-east and Paris and Brittany. Other fast trains are the **Trans Europ Express** (**TEE**), **Eurocity**, **Intercité** and **Corail**. The **rapide** is a long-distance express.

The **express** in France and **direct** are ordinary long-distance trains. The **omnibus** in France and Belgium and the Swiss **train régional** are local stopping trains, and the **autorail** is a small diesel used over short distances.

● There is a car–train service (**train autos-couchettes**) available which allows you to take a car or motorbike on a number of trains in France, and between Belgium and Luxembourg and other countries.

● You can take a bicycle on some trains (indeed all trains in Luxembourg). Both French and Swiss Railways operate a bicycle-hire service at a large number of their stations – look for the sign **Location de vélos**.

● Some trains in France and Switzerland are specially designated for family use – there are family carriages or compartments and a children's play area (**espace enfants**).

• There are two classes, first and second, on most trains. Children under four travel free, and for half-fare from ages four to twelve. Fares are cheaper on Blue Days (**Période Bleue**), and other discounts include:

**France Vacances Pass** – available only to visitors to France and obtainable only outside France; gives unlimited travel on a number of days within a set period (four days over a period of fifteen days, nine days during a month).

**Carré Jeune** or **Carte Jeune** (young person's railcard) – available to people under 26; entitles the holder to reduced fares.

**Swiss Pass** – available only to visitors to Switzerland; gives unlimited travel over a period (four, eight or fifteen days or one month) on all Swiss trains, boats, post buses, and urban trams and buses.

**Network tickets (Luxembourg)** – give unlimited travel for one day, five days or one month on all Luxembourg trains and buses.

**Belgium** – pass giving seventeen days unlimited travel; also **Go Pass** for students, giving ten single journeys (more than one person can use the same pass).

Information about other European railcards is obtainable from British Rail.

• Seat reservations are compulsory on **TGV** and certain other trains, and are advisable for any long-distance journey, especially at peak holiday times (**Période Rouge**, Red Days, in France). If you're travelling overnight you can book a sleeper (**wagon-lit**) or **couchette**, or in France a semi-reclining berth in a compartment called a **Cabine 8**.

• When you buy a train ticket in France, you have to validate it with a date-stamp before you travel. You do this by using one of the orange machines at the entrance to the platform.

• Work out in advance what you're going to ask for (1st or 2nd class, single or return, adult or child tickets, particular trains, reservations, etc).

## You may see

| | |
|---|---|
| Accès aux quais | To the platforms |
| Accès aux trains | To the trains |
| Arrivées | Arrivals |
| Billets | Tickets |
| CFL (Chemins de Fer Luxembourgeois) | Luxembourg Railways |
| CFS (Chemins de Fer Fédéraux Suisses) | Swiss Railways |
| Chef de gare | Station master |
| Composition du train | Arrangement of train |
| Consigne | Left luggage |
| Consigne automatique | Left luggage lockers |
| Défense de fumer | No smoking |
| Départs | Departures |
| Dimanche et jours fériés | Sundays and holidays |
| Eau non potable | Water not for drinking |
| Entrée | Entrance |
| Fermé | Closed |
| Fumeurs | Smoking |
| Grandes lignes | Main lines |
| Guichet | Ticket office |
| Horaire des trains | Train timetable |
| Il est interdit de se pencher (par la fenêtre) | Do not lean out (of the window) |
| Interdiction de marcher sur la voie | Do not walk on the track |
| Location de vélos | Bicycle hire |
| Location de voitures | Car hire |
| NMBS | Belgian Railways (Flemish name) |
| Non fumeurs | Non-smoking |
| N'oubliez pas de composter votre billet | Do not forget to validate your ticket |
| Objets trouvés | Lost property |

| | |
|---|---|
| **Période bleue** | Cheap travel days |
| **Quai** | Platform |
| **Renseignements** | Information |
| **Réservation à l'avance** | Advance booking |
| **Réservations** | Reservations |
| **Restauration à la place** | Meals served at your seat |
| **Salle d'attente** | Waiting room |
| **SNCB (Société Nationale des Chemins de Fer Belges)** | Belgian Railways |
| **SNCF (Société Nationale des Chemins de Fer Français)** | French Railways |
| **Sonnette d'alarme** | Alarm (communication cord) |
| **Sortie (de secours)** | (Emergency) exit |
| **Toilettes** | Toilets |
| **Tous les jours sauf . . .** | Every day except . . . |
| **Train autos-couchettes** | Car–train |
| **Trains de banlieue** | Suburban trains |
| **Vente pour usage immédiat** | Tickets for immediate use |
| **Wagon-lit** | Sleeping-car |
| **Wagon-restaurant** | Dining-car |

# You may want to say

## Information

(see Time, page 201)

Is there a train to Angers?
**Est-ce qu'il y a un train pour Angers?**
*eskeelya uñ trañ poor oñjay*

Do you have a timetable of trains to Lyon?
**Est-ce que vous avez un horaire de trains en direction de Lyon?**
*eskuh vooz avay un orer duh trañ oñ deereksyawñ duh lyawñ*

What time . . . ?
**À quelle heure . . . ?**
*a kel uhr . . .*

What time is the train to Bruges?
**À quelle heure part le train pour Bruges?**
*a kel uhr par luh trañ poor brewj*

What time is the first train to Strasbourg?
**À quelle heure part le premier train pour Strasbourg?**
*a kel uhr par luh pruhmyay trañ poor strazboor*

The next train
**Le prochain train**
*luh proshañ trañ*

The last train
**Le dernier train**
*luh dernyay trañ*

What time does it arrive (at Strasbourg)?
**À quelle heure arrive-t-il (à Strasbourg)?**
*a kel uhr areevteel (a strazboor)*

What time does the train from Bordeaux arrive?
**À quelle heure arrive le train de Bordeaux?**
*a kel uhr areev luh trañ duh bordoh*

The train to Calais, please?
**Le train pour Calais, s'il vous plaît?**
*luh trañ poor kalay seelvooplay*

Which platform does the train to Calais leave from?
**De quel quai part le train pour Calais?**
*duh kel kay par luh trañ poor kalay*

Does this train go to Toulouse?
**Ce train va a Toulouse?**
*suh trañ va a toolooz*

Do I/we have to change trains?
**Est-ce qu'il faut changer (de train)?**
*eskeel foh shoñjay (duh trañ)*

Where?
**Où ça?**
*oo sa*

## Tickets

(*see* Time, *page 201;* Numbers, *page 218*)

One/two to Grenoble, please
**Un/deux pour Grenoble, s'il vous plaît**
*uñ/duh poor gruhnobl seelvooplay*

One ticket/Two tickets to Cherbourg, please
**Un billet/Deux billets pour Cherbourg, s'il vous plaît**
*uñ beeyay/duh beeyay poor sherboor seelvooplay*

Single
**Aller simple**
*alay sampl*

Return
**Aller-retour**
*alay ruhtoor*

For one adult/two adults
**Pour un adulte/deux adultes**
*poor un adewlt/duhz adewlt*

(And) one child/two children
**(Et) un enfant/deux enfants**
*(ay) un oñfoñ/duhz oñfoñ*

First/second class
**En première/deuxième (classe)**
*oñ pruhmyer/duhzyem (klas)*

For the 10 o'clock train to Avignon
**Pour le train de dix heures en direction d'Avignon**
*poor luh trañ duh deez uhr oñ deereksyawñ daveenyawñ*

For the TGV to Dijon
**Pour le TGV en direction de Dijon**
*pour luh tayjayvay oñ deereksyawñ duh deejawñ*

I want to reserve a seat/two seats
**Je voudrais réserver une place/deux places**
*juh voodray rayzervay ewn plas/duh plas*

I want to reserve a sleeper
**Je voudrais réserver un wagon-lit**
*juh voodray rayzervay uñ vagawñ lee*

I want to reserve a couchette
**Je voudrais réserver une couchette**
*juh voodray rayzervay ewn kooshet*

I want to reserve a 'Cabine 8'
**Je voudrais réserver une Cabine 8**
*juh voodray rayzervay ewn kabeen weet*

I want to book tickets on the car-train to Nice

**Je voudrais réserver des billets de train autos-couchettes pour Nice**

*juh voodray rayzervay day beeyay duh trañ ohtoh kooshet poor nees*

For a car and two passengers

**Pour une voiture et deux passagers**

*poor ewn vwatewr ay duh pasajay*

My car is a Renault 5

**Ma voiture est une Renault 5**

*ma vwatewr et ewn ruhnoh sañk*

Can I take my bicycle on the train?

**Est-ce que je peux emporter mon vélo dans le train?**

*eskuh juh puh omportay mawñ vayloh doñ luh trañ*

How much is it?

**C'est combien?**

*say kawmbyañ*

Is there a supplement?

**Est-ce qu'il y a un supplément?**

*eskeelya uñ sewplaymoñ*

## Left luggage

Can I leave this?

**Est-ce que je peux laisser ça?**

*eskuh juh puh lesay sa*

Can I leave these two suitcases?

**Est-ce que je peux laisser ces deux valises?**

*eskuh juh puh lesay say duh valeez*

Until three o'clock

**Jusqu'à trois heures**

*jewska trwaz uhr*

What time do you close?

**À quelle heure est-ce que vous fermez?**

*a kel uhr eskuh voo fermay*

How much is it?

**C'est combien?**

*say kawmbyañ*

## On the train

I have reserved a seat
**J'ai réservé une place**
*jay rayzervay ewn plas*

I have reserved a sleeper
**J'ai réservé un wagon-lit**
*jay rayzervay uñ vagawñ lee*

I have reserved a couchette
**J'ai réservé une couchette**
*jay rayzervay ewn kooshet*

Is this seat taken?
**Est-ce que cette place est occupée?**
*eskuh set plas et okewpay*

Excuse me, may I get by?
**Pardon, est-ce que je peux passer?**
*pardawñ eskuh juh puh pasay*

Where is the restaurant-car?
**Où est le wagon-restaurant?**
*oo e luh vagawñ restohroñ*

Where is the sleeping-car?
**Où est le wagon-lit?**
*oo e luh vagawñ lee*

May I open the window?
**Est-ce que je peux ouvrir la fenêtre?**
*eskuh juh puh oovreer la fuhnetr*

May I smoke?
**Est-ce que je peux fumer?**
*eskuh juh puh fewmay*

Where are we?
**Où on est?**
*oo awn e*

Are we at Liège?
**On est à Liège?**
*awn et a lyej*

How long does the train stop here?
**Combien de temps est-ce que le train s'arrête ici?**
*kawmbyañ duh toñ eskuh luh trañ saret eesee*

Can you tell me when we get to Toulon?
**Pourriez-vous m'avertir quand nous arriverons à Toulon?**
*pooree-ay voo maverteer koñ nooz areevuhrawñ a toolawñ*

## You may hear

### Information

**Il part à dix heures trente**
*eel par a deez uhr troñt*
It leaves at 10.30

**Il arrive à quatre heures
moins dix**
*eel areev a katr uhr mwañ
dees*
It arrives at ten to four

**Il faut changer de train à
Strasbourg**
*eel foh shoñjay duh trañ a
strazboor*
You have to change trains
at Strasbourg

**C'est le quai numéro quatre**
*say luh kay newmayroh katr*
It's platform number four

### Tickets

**Pour quand voulez-vous
le billet?**
*poor koñ voolay voo luh
beeyay*
When do you want the
ticket for?

**Quand voulez-vous voyager?**
*koñ voolay voo vwiyajay*
When do you want to travel?

**Aller simple ou aller-retour?**
*alay sampl oo alay ruhtoor*
Single or return?

**Pour quand le retour?**
*poor koñ luh ruhtoor*
When do you want to return?

**En fumeurs ou non fumeurs?**
*oñ fewmuhr oo nawñ fewmuhr*
Smoking or non-smoking?

**Dans le sens de la marche?**
*doñ luh soñs duh la marsh*
Facing (forward)?

**Le sens contraire**
*luh soñs kawñtrer*
Back

**Il n'y a que des places de
première**
*eelnya kuh day plas duh
pruhmyer*
There are only seats in first
class

**C'est cent quatre-vingts francs**
*say soñ katr vañ froñ*
That's 180 francs

**Il y a un supplément**
*eelya uñ sewplaymoñ*
There is a supplement

# BUSES AND COACHES

● On the whole, buses operate on the pay-as-you-enter system. Some cities have machines at bus stops where you buy a ticket or date-stamp a pre-paid ticket.

● If you intend to use the buses a lot in a town or city, you can buy multiple or rover tickets. **Un carnet** is a book of ten tickets, and there are tourist tickets (**billet touristique**), valid for several days, and other season tickets (**abonnement** or **carte**) to cover other periods, e.g. one day, a week or a month.

● In Paris you can buy a **Paris-Sésame** pass which allows unlimited bus and underground travel over two, four or seven days. You can buy this at underground (**métro**) stations and bus terminals.

● There are no real long-distance coach services in France, though there are regional and local services, and some **SNCF** (French Railways) services.

● In Switzerland you can buy a **Swiss Pass**: it's available only to visitors to Switzerland and gives unlimited travel over a period (four, eight or fifteen days or one month) on all urban trams and buses, as well as all Swiss trains, boats and post buses.

● In Luxembourg there are **Network tickets** giving unlimited travel for one day, five days or one month on all buses and trains.

## You may see

| | |
|---|---|
| Arrêt (d'autobus) | Bus stop |
| Arrêt fixe | Obligatory bus stop |
| Arrêt sur demande | Bus stops on request |
| Conservez votre ticket | Keep your ticket |
| Défense de cracher | No spitting |
| Défense de fumer | No smoking |
| Entrée | Entrance |
| Entrez par la porte de devant/ derrière | Enter by the front/rear door |
| Gare routière | Coach station |
| Interdiction de parler au conducteur | Do not talk to the driver |
| Introduire ici | Insert here |
| Itinéraire | Route |
| Pièces rejetées | Rejected coins |
| Préparez la monnaie | Have the correct money ready |
| Sortie (de secours) | (Emergency) exit |
| Sortie par la porte centrale | Exit by the centre door |
| Trajet | Route |

## You may want to say

(*for sightseeing bus tours, see* Sightseeing, *page 148*)

## Information

Where is the bus stop?
**Où est l'arrêt d'autobus?**
*oo e laray dohtohbews*

Where is the coach station?
**Où est la gare routière?**
*oo e la gar rootyer*

Is there a bus to the beach?
**Est-ce qu'il y a un bus qui va à la plage?**
*eskeelya uñ bews kee va a la plaj*

Which bus goes to the station?
**Quel bus va à la gare?**
*kel bews va a la gar*

Do they go often?
**Est-ce qu'ils sont fréquents?**
*eskeel sawñ fraykoñ*

What time is the coach to Orléans?
**À quelle heure part le car pour Orléans?**
*a kel uhr par luh kar poor orlayoñ*

What time is the first coach to Arles?
**À quelle heure part le premier car pour Arles?**
*a kel uhr par luh pruhmyay kar poor arl*

The next/last bus
**Le prochain/dernier car**
*luh proshañ/dernyay kar*

What time does it arrive?
**À quelle heure arrive-t-il?**
*a kel uhr areevteel*

Where can I buy a book of tickets?
**Où est-ce que je peux acheter un carnet?**
*oo eskuh juh puh ashtay uñ karnay*

Where does the bus to the town centre leave from?
**D'où part le bus pour le centre-ville?**
*doo par luh bews poor luh soñtr veel*

Does the bus to the airport leave from here?
**Est-ce que le bus pour l'aéroport part d'ici?**
*eskuh luh bews poor la-ayropor par deesee*

Does this coach go to La Rochelle?
**Ce car va à La Rochelle?**
*suh kar va a la roshel*

I want to get off at the Louvre
**Je voudrais descendre au Louvre**
*juh voodray desoñdr oh loovr*

Can you tell me where to get off?
**Pourriez-vous me dire où descendre?**
*pooree-ay voo muh deer oo desoñdr*

Is this the stop for the cathedral?
**C'est ici pour la cathédrale?**
*set eesee pour la kataydral*

The next stop, please
**Le prochain arrêt, s'il vous plaît**
*luh proshen aray seelvooplay*

Can you open the door, please?
**Pourriez-vous ouvrir la porte, s'il vous plaît?**
*pooree-ay voo oovreer la port seelvooplay*

Excuse me, may I get by?
**Pardon, est-ce que je peux passer?**
*pardawñ eskuh juh puh pasay*

## Tickets

One/Two to the town centre, please
**Un ticket/Deux tickets pour le centre-ville, s'il vous plaît**
*uñ teekay/duh teekay poor luh soñtr veel seelvooplay*

A book of tickets, please
**Un carnet, s'il vous plaît**
*uñ karnay seelvooplay*

A Paris-Sésame ticket, please
**Un Paris-Sésame, s'il vous plaît**
*uñ paree sayzam seelvooplay*

How much is it?
**C'est combien?**
*say kawmbyañ*

## You may hear

**Le bus pour le centre-ville part de cet arrêt là**
*luh bews poor luh soñtr veel par duh set aray la*
The bus to the centre leaves from that stop there

**Le cinquante-sept va à la gare**
*luh sañkoñt set va a la gar*
The 57 goes to the station

**Il y en a un toutes les dix minutes**
*eelee on a uñ toot lay dees meenewt*
There's one every ten minutes

**Il part à dix heures et demie**
*eel par a deez uhr ay duhmee*
It leaves at half past ten

**Il arrive à trois heures vingt**
*eel areev a trwaz uhr vañ*
It arrives at twenty past three

**Vous pourriez acheter un carnet dans le métro**
*voo pooree-ayz ashtay uñ karnay doñ luh maytro*
You can buy a book of tickets in the underground

**Vous descendez?**
*voo desoñday*
Are you getting off?

**Vous descendez au prochain arrêt/à la prochaine**
*voo desoñday oh proshen aray/a la proshen*
You get off at the next stop

**Vous auriez dû descendre avant**
*vooz ohree-ay dew desoñdr avoñ*
You should have got off before

# UNDERGROUND TRAVEL

● The underground is called **le métro**, and there are systems in Paris, Lyon and Brussels.

● Tickets are one price, but you may need to use more than one if you're travelling through more than one fare zone. You can buy a book of ten tickets (**un carnet**) at any **métro** ticket office, and there are tourist tickets (**billet touristique**) valid for several days.

● In Paris you can buy a **Paris-Sésame** pass which allows unlimited underground and bus travel over two, four or seven days. You can buy this at **métro** stations and bus terminals.

● In Lyon you can get a book of six **métro** tickets. There is also a 'Freedom Ticket' (**Ticket Liberté**) giving unlimited **métro** and bus travel over two or three days.

● In Brussels you can get a one-day card for the **métro** and buses, or a travelcard for ten journeys on **métro**, buses and trams.

## You may see

| | |
|---|---|
| **Défense de cracher** | No spitting |
| **Défense de fumer** | No smoking |
| **Entrée** | Entrance |
| **Métro** | Underground |
| **RATP (Régie Autonome des Transports Parisiens)** | Paris Transport Authority |
| **RER (Réseau Express Régional)** | Suburban **métro** network |
| **Sortie (de secours)** | (Emergency) exit |

## You may want to say

Where is the (nearest) underground station?
**Où est la station de métro (la plus proche)?**
*oo e la stasyawñ duh maytroh (la plew prosh)*

Do you have a map of the underground, please?
**Est-ce que vous avez un plan du métro, s'il vous plaît?**
*eskuh vooz avay uñ ploñ dew maytroh seelvooplay*

One ticket/Two tickets, please
**Un ticket/Deux tickets, s'il vous plaît**
*uñ teekay/duh teekay seelvooplay*

A 'Freedom Ticket', please
**Un Ticket Liberté, s'il vous plaît**
*uñ teekay leebertay seelvooplay*

Which direction is it for the Gare du Nord station?
**C'est quelle direction pour la Gare du Nord?**
*say kel deereksyawñ poor la gar dew nor*

Which stop is it for Notre Dame?
**C'est quelle station pour Notre Dame?**
*say kel stasyawñ poor notr dam*

Does this train go to Montparnasse?
**Est-ce que cette rame va à Montparnasse?**
*eskuh set ram va a mawñparnas*

Where are we?
**Où on est?**
*oo on e*

Is this the stop for the Arc de Triomphe?
**C'est ici pour l'Arc de Triomphe?**
*set eesee poor lark duh tree-awmf*

## You may hear

**C'est la direction de Neuilly**
*say la deereeksyawñ duh nuhyee*
It's the Neuilly direction/train

**C'est la prochaine station/le prochain arrêt**
*say la proshen stasyawñ/luh proshen aray*
It's the next stop

**Vous auriez dû descendre avant**
*vooz ohree-ay dew desoñdr avoñ*
You should have got off before

# BOATS AND FERRIES

● As well as car ferry and hovercraft services across the Channel, there are ferries and hydrofoils to and from the Channel Islands.

● There are car ferry services to Corsica (**la Corse**) from Marseille, Nice and Toulon.

● Other opportunities for boat travel include trips on the Seine in Paris in a **bateau-mouche**, down the Meuse and Moselle rivers, around the canals in Bruges, and cruises on the Swiss Lakes.

## You may see

| | |
|---|---|
| **Aéroglisseur** | Hovercraft |
| **Bateau-mouche** | Riverboat/pleasure boat |
| **Bateaux** | Boats |
| **Cabines** | Cabins |
| **Canot de sauvetage** | Lifeboat |
| **Ceinture de sauvetage** | Lifebelt |
| **Croisières du lac** | Cruises on the lake |
| **Embarcadère** | Pier |
| **Ferry** | (Car) ferry |
| **Hydroptère** | Hydrofoil |
| **Pont** | Deck |
| **Pont autos** | Car deck |
| **Port** | Port/harbour |

## You may want to say

### Information

(*see* Time, *page 201*)

Is there a boat to Lausanne (today)?
**Est-ce qu'il y a un bateau pour Lausanne (aujourd'hui)?**
*eskeelya uñ batoh poor lohzan (ohjoordwee)*

Is there a car ferry to Ajaccio?
**Est-ce qu'il y a un ferry pour Ajaccio?**
*eskeelya uñ feree poor ajaksyoh*

Are there any boat trips?
**Est-ce qu'il y a des excursions en bateau?**
*eskeelya dayz exkewrsyawñ oñ batoh*

What cruises are there?
**Quelles croisières il y a?**
*kel krwazyer eelya*

What time is the boat to Dover?
**À quelle heure part le bateau pour Douvres?**
*a kel uhr par luh batoh poor doovr*

What time is the first hovercraft?
**À quelle heure part le premier aéroglisseur?**
*a kel uhr par luh pruhmyay a-ayrohgleesuhr*

The next hovercraft
**Le prochain aéroglisseur**
*luh proshen a-ayrohgleesuhr*

The last hovercraft
**Le dernier aéroglisseur**
*luh dernyay a-ayrohgleesuhr*

What time does it arrive?
**À quelle heure arrive-t-il?**
*a kel uhr areevteel*

What time does it return?
**À quelle heure est le retour?**
*a kel uhr e luh ruhtoor*

How long does the crossing take?
**Combien de temps dure la traversée?**
*kawmbyañ duh toñ dewr la traversay*

What times do the cruises leave?
**Quelles sont les horaires des croisières?**
*kel sawñ layz orer day krwazyer*

How long does the cruise last?
**Combien de temps dure la croisière?**
*kawmbyañ duh toñ dewr la krwazyer*

Where does the boat to Bastia leave from?
**D'où part le bateau pour Bastia?**
*doo par luh batoh poor bastya*

Where do the riverboats leave from?
**D'où partent les bateaux-mouches?**
*doo part lay batoh moosh*

Where can I buy tickets?
**Où est-ce que je peux acheter des billets?**
*oo eskuh juh puh ashtay day beeyay*

What is the sea like today?
**Comment est la mer aujourd'hui?**
*komoñ e la mer ohjoordwee*

# Tickets

(*see* Numbers, *page 218*)

Four tickets for the ten
o'clock cruise, please
**Quatre billets pour la
croisière de dix heures, s'il
vous plaît**
*katr beeyay poor la krwazyer
duh deez uhr seelvooplay*

Two adults and two
children
**Deux adultes et deux enfants**
*duhz adewlt ay duhz oñfoñ*

Single
**Aller simple**
*alay sampl*

Return
**Aller-retour**
*alay ruhtoor*

I want to book tickets for
the ferry to Dover
**Je voudrais réserver des
billets pour le ferry à
Douvres**
*juh voodray rayzervay day
beeyay poor luh feree a
doovr*

For a car and two passengers
**Pour une voiture et deux
passagers**
*poor ewn vwatewr ay duh pasajay*

My car is a Renault 16
**Ma voiture est une Renault seize**
*ma vwatewr et ewn ruhnoh sez*

I want to book a cabin
**Je voudrais réserver une cabine**
*juh voudray rayzervay ewn
kabeen*

For one person
**Pour une personne**
*poor ewn person*

For two people
**Pour deux personnes**
*poor duh person*

How much is it?
**C'est combien?**
*say kawmbyañ*

## On board

I have reserved a cabin
**J'ai réservé une cabine**
*jay rayzervay ewn kabeen*

I have reserved two berths
**J'ai réservé deux couchettes**
*jay rayzervay duh kooshet*

Where are the cabins?
**Où sont les cabines?**
*oo sawñ lay kabeen*

Where is cabin number 20?
**Où est la cabine numéro vingt?**
*oo e la kabeen newmayroh vañ*

Can I/we go out on deck?
**Est-ce qu'on peut sortir sur le pont?**
*eskawñ puh sorteer sewr luh pawñ*

## You may hear

### Information

(*see* Time, *page 201*)

(*see* Time, *page 201*)

**Il y a des bateaux le mardi et le vendredi**
*eelya day batoh luh mardee ay luh voñdruhdee*
There are boats on Tuesdays and Fridays

**Le bateau pour Lausanne part à neuf heures**
*luh batoh poor lohzan par a nuhv uhr*
The boat to Lausanne leaves at nine o'clock

**Le retour est à quatre heures et demie**
*luh ruhtoor et a katr uhr ay duhmee*
It returns at half past four

**Il y a des croisières à dix heures et à deux heures et demie**
*eelya day krwazyer a deez uhr ay a duhz uhr ay demee*
There are cruises at ten o'clock and half past two

**Le bateau pour Ajaccio part de l'embarcadère numéro deux**
*le batoh poor ajaksyo par duh lombarkader newmayro duh*
The boat to Ajaccio leaves from pier number two

**Les bateaux-mouches partent du Pont-Neuf**
*lay batoh moosh part dew pawñ nuhf*
The riverboats leave from the Pont Neuf

**La mer est calme**
*la mer e kalm*
The sea is calm

**La mer est grosse**
*la mer e gros*
The sea is rough

## Tickets

**Quel genre de voiture avez-vous?**
*kel joñr duh vwatewr avay voo*
What type of car do you have?

**Pour combien de personnes?**
*poor kawmbyañ duh person*
For how many people?

## On board

**Les cabines sont sur le pont inférieur**
*lay kabeen sawñ sewr luh pawñ añfayree-uhr*
The cabins are on the lower deck

**La cabine numéro vingt est à l'avant**
*la kabeen newmayroh vañ et a lavoñ*
Cabin number twenty is in the bow

**À l'arrière**
*a laree-er*
In the stern/aft

# AT THE TOURIST OFFICE

● All the French-speaking countries have local tourist offices in towns and cities – France alone has 5,000 or so. In France they are mostly called **le syndicat d'initiative**; elsewhere they will be **l'office du tourisme** or **la maison du tourisme**. There will often be someone who speaks English.

● Tourist offices have leaflets about sights worth seeing, sightseeing excursions, lists of hotels, town plans and regional maps, and can supply information about opening times and local transport. They may also be able to book hotel rooms for you.

## You may see

| | |
|---|---|
| **Accueil de France, Loisir-Accueil** | Hotel booking services |
| **Maison/Office du tourisme** | Tourist office |
| **Syndicat d'initiative** | Tourist office |

## You may want to say

(*see* Directions, *page 23;* Sightseeing, *page 148;* Time, *page 201*)

Where is the tourist office?
**Où se trouve le syndicat d'initiative?**
*oo suh troov luh sañdeeka deeneesyateev*
**Où se trouve l'office du tourisme?**
*oo suh troov lofees dew tooreezm*

Do you have . . . ?
**Est-ce que vous avez . . . ?**
*eskuh vooz avay . . .*

Do you have a plan of the town?
**Est-ce que vouz avez un plan de la ville?**
*eskuh vooz avay uñ ploñ duh la veel*

Do you have a map of the area?
**Est-ce que vous avez une carte de la région?**
*eskuh vooz avay ewn kart duh la rayjawñ*

Do you have a list of hotels?
**Est-ce que vous avez une liste d'hôtels?**
*eskuh vooz avay ewn leest dohtel*

Do you have a list of campsites?
**Est-ce que vous avez une liste de campings?**
*eskuh vooz avay ewn leest duh kompeeng*

Could you recommend an inexpensive hotel?
**Pourriez-vous me recommander un hôtel pas trop cher?**
*pooree-ay voo muh ruhkomoñday un ohtel pa troh sher*

Could you book me a hotel room, please?
**Pourriez-vous me réserver une chambre d'hôtel, s'il vous plaît?**
*pooree-ay voo muh rayzervay ewn shombr dohtel seelvooplay*

Could you recommend a good restaurant?
**Pourriez-vous me recommander un bon restaurant?**
*pooree-ay voo muh ruhkomoñday uñ bawñ restohroñ*

Where can I/we hire a car?
**Où est-ce qu'on peut louer une voiture?**
*oo eskawñ puh looay ewn vwatewr*

What is there to see here?
**Qu'est-ce qu'il y a à voir ici?**
*keskeelya a vwar eesee*

Do you have any leaflets?
**Est-ce que vous avez des brochures?**
*eskuh vooz avay day brohshewr*

Can you give me some information about . . . ?
**Pourriez-vous me donner des informations sur . . . ?**
*pooree-ay voo muh donay dayz añformasyawñ sewr . . .*

Where is the archaeological museum?
**Où est le musée archéologique?**
*oo e luh mewzay arshayolojeek*

Can you show me on the map?
**Pourriez-vous me le montrer sur la carte?**
*pooree-ay voo muh luh mawñtray sewr la kart*

What are the opening hours of the museum?
**Quelles sont les heures d'ouverture du musée?**
*kel sawñ layz uhr doovertewr dew mewzay*

Are there any excursions/guided tours?
**Est-ce qu'il y a des visites guidées?**
*eskeelya day veezeet geeday*

## You may hear

**Vous désirez?**
*voo dayzeeray*
Can I help you?

**Vous êtes anglais/anglaise?**
*vooz et oñglay/oñglez*
Are you English?

**Allemand/Allemande?**
*almoñ/almoñd*
German?

**D'où êtes-vous?**
*doo et voo*
Where are you from?

**Combien de temps restez-vous?**
*kawmbyañ duh toñ restay voo*
How long are you going to be here?

**Où êtes-vous descendu(e)?**
*oo et voo desoñdew*
Where are you staying?

**Quelle sorte d'hôtel voulez-vous?**
*kel sort dohtel voolay voo*
What kind of hotel do you want?

**C'est dans la vieille ville**
*say doñ la vyey veel*
It's in the old part of town

# ACCOMMODATION

● France, Belgium, Switzerland and Luxembourg all have a wide range of places to stay – hotels, guest houses, campsites, youth hostels, and a variety of farmhouse, cottage, chalet and other self-catering accommodation. Information and lists are available from the national Tourist Offices (addresses, page 214).

The national Tourist Offices cannot generally make bookings, but can give information about centralized reservation services.

● **Logis de France** and **Auberges de France** are small, family-run hotels, mainly one- or two-star. There are over 5,000 of them all over France. A guide to these is available from the French Government Tourist Office.

● **Gîtes** are a type of self-catering accommodation in rural areas of France, in country cottages, parts of farmhouses, mills, etc. They can be booked via **Gîtes de France Ltd** (same address as the French Government Tourist Office).

● If you're travelling round, you can get accommodation lists from local tourist offices – they may also be able to make a booking for you.

In France, many regions (**départements**) have a service called **Loisir-Accueil** that can book hotels, campsites, **gîtes** and specialist holidays in their areas. This service is free. There are also **Accueil de France** offices in some towns – these provide hotel booking facilities for a small fee.

● Campsites in France are often quite luxurious – like hotels, they are rated from one to four stars according to facilities. Many have tents and caravans on site.

In all the countries, it is advisable to book places at campsites in advance, especially during the summer.

● When you book in somewhere you will usually be asked for your passport and to fill in a registration card.

## Information requested on a registration card:

| | |
|---|---|
| **Prénom** | First name |
| **Nom** | Surname |
| **Lieu de domicile/N°/Rue** | Home address/Number/Street |
| **Nationalité** | Nationality |
| **Profession** | Occupation |
| **Date de naissance** | Date of birth |
| **Lieu de naissance** | Place of birth |
| **N° de passeport** | Passport number |
| **Délivré à** | Issued at |
| **Date** | Date |
| **Signature** | Signature |

## You may see

| | |
|---|---|
| **Ascenseur** | Lift |
| **Auberge (rurale)** | Country inn, small hotel |
| **Auberge de jeunesse** | Youth hostel |
| **Blanchisserie** | Laundry |
| **Camping** | Campsite |
| **Centre de naturisme** | Naturist/nudist centre |
| **Chambre d'hôte** | Bed and breakfast, often in private homes |
| **Chambres (à louer)** | Rooms (to let) |
| **Château-Hôtel** | Hotel in a castle/mansion |
| **Complet** | Full up |
| **Demi-pension** | Half board |
| **Douches** | Showers |
| **Eau non potable** | Water not for drinking |

| | |
|---|---|
| Eau potable | Drinking water |
| Électricité | Electricity |
| Entrée | Entrance |
| 1er étage | 1st floor |
| 2ème étage | 2nd floor |
| Gîte (rurale) | Country cottage/farmhouse |
| Interdiction de faire du feu | Do not light fires |
| Issue de secours | Emergency exit |
| Logis | Type of small hotel in France |
| Motel (de tourisme) | Motel |
| Ordures | Rubbish |
| Pension | Boarding-house |
| Pension complète | Full board |
| Piscine | Swimming pool |
| Prière de ne pas jeter d'ordures | Do not dump rubbish |
| Réception | Reception |
| Relais | Inn |
| Relais de campagne | Country hotel |
| Rez-de-chaussée | Ground floor |
| Salle à manger | Dining-room |
| Salle de bains | Bathroom |
| Salle de télévision | Television room |
| Salon | Lounge |
| Sanitaires | Toilets/showers |
| Service en chambre | Room service |
| Sonnez, s'il vous plaît | Please ring the bell |
| Sortie (de secours) | (Emergency) exit |
| Sous-sol | Basement |
| Toilettes | Toilets |
| Videz les WC chimiques ici | Empty chemical toilets here |

82

## You may want to say

### Booking in and out

I've reserved a room
**J'ai réservé une chambre**
*jay rayzervay ewn shombr*

I've reserved two rooms
**J'ai réservé deux chambres**
*jay rayzervay duh shombr*

I've reserved a place/space
**J'ai réservé un emplacement**
*jay rayzervay un omplasmoñ*

My name is . . .
**Je m'appelle . . .**
*juh mapel . . .*

Do you have a room?
**Est-ce que vous avez une chambre?**
*eskuh vooz avay ewn shombr*

A single room
**Une chambre pour une personne**
*ewn shombr poor ewn person*

A room with twin beds
**Une chambre avec lits jumeaux**
*ewn shombr avek lee jewmoh*

A room with a double bed
**Une chambre avec un grand lit**
*ewn shombr avek uñ groñ lee*

For one night
**Pour une nuit**
*poor ewn nwee*

For two nights
**Pour deux nuits**
*poor duh nwee*

With bathroom/shower
**Avec salle de bains/douche**
*avek sal duh bañ/doosh*

Do you have space for a tent?
**Est-ce que vous avez de la place pour une tente?**
*eskuh vooz avay duh la plas poor ewn toñt*

Do you have space for a caravan?
**Est-ce que vous avez de la place pour une caravane?**
*eskuh vooz avay duh la plas poor ewn karavan*

How much is it?
**C'est combien?**
*say kawmbyañ*

Per night
**Par nuit**
*par nwee*

Per week
**Par semaine**
*par suhmen*

Is there a reduction for children?
**Est-ce qu'il y a une réduction pour les enfants?**
*eskeelya ewn raydewksyawñ poor layz oñfoñ*

Is breakfast included?
**Le petit déjeuner est compris?**
*luh puhtee dayjuhnay e kawmpree*

Can I see the room?
**Est-ce que je peux voir la chambre?**
*eskuh juh puh vwar la shombr*

It's too expensive
**C'est trop cher**
*say troh sher*

Do you have anything cheaper?
**Est-ce que vous avez quelque chose de meilleur marché?**
*eskuh vooz avay kelkuh shohz duh mayuhr marshay*

Do you have anything bigger/smaller?
**Est-ce que vous avez quelque chose de plus grand/petit?**
*eskuh vooz avay kelkuh shohz duh plew groñ/puhtee*

I'd like to stay another night
**Je voudrais rester encore une nuit**
*juh voodray restay oñkor ewn nwee*

I'm leaving tomorrow morning
**Je pars demain matin**
*juh par duhmañ matañ*

The bill, please
**La note, s'il vous plaît**
*la not seelvooplay*

Do you take credit cards?
**Vous acceptez les cartes de crédit?**
*vooz akseptay lay kart duh kraydee*

Do you take traveller's cheques?
**Vous acceptez les chèques de voyage?**
*vooz akseptay lay shek duh vwiyaj*

Could you recommend a hotel in Bruges?
**Pourriez-vous me recommander un hôtel à Bruges?**
*pooree-ay voo muh rukhomoñday un ohtel a brewj*

Could you phone them to make a booking?
**Pourriez-vous les appeler pour faire une réservation?**
*pooree-ay voo layz apuhlay poor fer ewn rayzervasyawñ*

# In hotels

(see Problems and complaints, *page 179;* Time, *page 201*)

Where can I/we park?
**Où est-ce qu'on peut stationner?**
*oo eskawñ puh stasyonay*

Do you have a cot for the baby?
**Est-ce que vous avez un berceau pour le bébé?**
*eskuh vooz avay uñ bersoh poor luh baybay*

Do you have facilities for the disabled?
**Est-ce que vous avez des installations spéciales pour les handicapés?**
*eskuh vooz avay dayz añstalasyawñ spaysyal poor layz oñdeekapay*

What time do you serve breakfast?
**À quelle heure vous servez le petit déjeuner?**
*a kel uhr voo servay luh puhtee dayjuhnay*

Can I/we have breakfast in the room?
**Est-ce qu'on peut prendre le petit déjeuner dans la chambre?**
*eskawñ puh proñdr luh puhtee dayjuhnay doñ la shombr*

What time do you serve dinner?
**À quelle heure vous servez le dîner?**
*a kel uhr voo servay luh deenay*

What time does the hotel close?
**À quelle heure ferme l'hôtel?**
*a kel uhr ferm lohtel*

I'm going to be back (very) late
**Je vais rentrer (très) tard**
*juh vay roñtray (tre) tar*

(Key) number 42, please
**(La clé) numéro quarante-deux, s'il vous plaît**
*(la klay) newmayro karoñt duh seelvooplay*

Are there any messages for me?
**Est-ce qu'il y a des messages pour moi?**
*eskeelya day mesaj poor mwa*

Where is the bathroom?
**Où se trouve la salle de bains?**
*oo suh troov la sal duh bañ*

Where is the dining-room?
**Où se trouve la salle à manger?**
*oo suh troov la sal a moñjay*

Can I leave this in the safe?
**Est-ce que je peux laisser ça dans le coffre?**
*eskuh juh puh lesay sa doñ luh kofr*

Can you get my things from the safe?
**Pourriez-vous retirer mes affaires du coffre?**
*pooree-ay voo ruhteeray mayz afer dew kofr*

Could you call me at eight o'clock?
**Pourriez-vous m'appeler à huit heures?**
*pooree-ay voo mapuhlay a weet uhr*

Could you order me a taxi?
**Pourriez-vous m'appeler un taxi?**
*pooree-ay voo mapuhlay uñ taxee*

For right now
**C'est pour tout de suite**
*say poor toot sweet*

For tomorrow at nine o'clock
**Pour demain à neuf heures**
*poor duhmañ a nuhv uhr*

Could you have my suit cleaned?
**Pourriez-vous me faire nettoyer mon complet?**
*pooree-ay voo muh fer netwiyay mawñ kawmplay*

Could you find me a babysitter?
**Pourriez-vous me trouver une babysitter?**
*pooree-ay voo muh troovay ewn babeeseeter*

Could you put it on the bill?
**Pourriez-vous le mettre sur ma note?**
*pooree-ay voo luh metr sewr ma not*

It's room number 21
**C'est la chambre numéro vingt et un**
*say la shombr newmayro vañtayuñ*

I need another pillow
**J'ai besoin d'encore un oreiller**
*jay buhzwañ doñkor uñ orayay*

I need a bath towel
**J'ai besoin d'une serviette de bain**
*jay buhzwañ dewn servyet duh bañ*

## At campsites

Is there a campsite around here?
**Est-ce qu'il y a un camping par ici?**
*eskeelya uñ kompeeng par eesee*

Can I/we camp here?
**Est-ce qu'on peut camper ici?**
*eskawñ puh kompay eesee*

Where can I park?
**Où est-ce que je peux stationner?**
*oo eskuh juh puh stasyonay*

Where are the showers?
**Où se trouvent les douches?**
*oo suh troov lay doosh*

Where are the toilets?
**Où se trouvent les toilettes?**
*oo suh troov lay twalet*

Where are the dustbins?
**Où se trouvent les poubelles?**
*oo suh troov lay poobel*

Is the water drinkable?
**Est-ce que l'eau est potable?**
*eskuh loh e potabl*

Where is the laundry-room?
**Où se trouve la blanchisserie?**
*oo suh troov la bloñsheesuhree*

Where is the electric point?
**Où se trouve la prise électrique?**
*oo suh troov la preez aylektreek*

## Self-catering accommodation

*(see Directions, page 23; Problems and complaints, page 179)*

My name is . . .
**Je m'appelle . . .**
*juh mapel . . .*

I have rented an apartment
**J'ai loué un appartement**
*jay looay un apartuhmoñ*

It's number 11
**C'est le numéro onze**
*say luh newmayro awñz*

What is the address?
**Quelle est l'adresse?**
*kel e ladres*

How do I/we get there?
**Comment est-ce qu'on y va?**
*komoñ eskawn ee va*

The key, please?
**La clé, s'il vous plaît?**
*la klay seelvooplay*

Where is . . .
**Où se trouve . . . ?**
*oo suh troov . . .*

Where is the stopcock?
**Où se trouve le robinet
d'arrêt?**
*oo suh troov luh robeenay
daray*

Where is the fusebox?
**Où se trouve la boîte à
fusibles?**
*oo su troov la bwat a fewzeebl*

How does the cooker work?
**Comment marche la cuisinière?**
*komoñ marsh la kweezeenyer*

How does the water-heater work?
**Comment marche le chauffeeau?**
*komoñ marsh luh shohfoh*

Is there air conditioning?
**Est-ce qu'il y a l'air conditionné?**
*eskeelya ler kawñdeesyonay*

Is there any spare bedding?
**Est-ce qu'il y a encore des
draps et des couvertures?**
*eskeelya oñkor day dra ay day
koovertewr*

What day do they come to
clean?
**Quel jour est-ce qu'on vient
pour nettoyer?**
*kel joor eskawñ vyañ poor
netwiyay*

When do they come to
collect the rubbish?
**Quand a lieu le ramassage
des ordures?**
*koñt a lyuh luh ramasaj dayz
ordewr*

Where can I contact you?
**Où est-ce que je peux vous
contacter?**
*oo eskuh juh puh voo
kawñtaktay*

## You may hear

**Vous désirez?**
*voo dayzeeray*
Can I help you?

**Votre nom, s'il vous plaît?**
*votr nawñ seelvooplay*
Your name, please?

**Pour combien de nuits?**
*poor kawmbyañ duh nwee*
For how many nights?

**Pour combien de personnes?**
*poor kawmbyañ duh person*
For how many people?

**Avec bains ou sans bains?**
*avek bañ oo soñ bañ*
With bath or without bath?

**Est-ce que c'est une tente grande ou petite?**
*eskuh set ewn toñt groñd oo puhteet*
Is it a large or small tent?

**Je suis désolé(e), nous sommes complets**
*juh swee dayzolay noo som kawmplay*
I'm sorry, we're full

**Votre passeport, s'il vous plaît**
*votr paspor seelvooplay*
Your passport, please

**Signez ici, s'il vous plaît**
*seenyay eesee seelvooplay*
Sign here, please

**Vous allumez comme ça**
*vooz alewmay kom sa*
You switch it on like this

**Vous éteignez comme ça**
*vooz aytenyay kom sa*
You switch it off like this

**On vient tous les jours**
*awñ vyañ too lay joor*
They come every day

**On vient le vendredi**
*awñ vyañ luh voñdruhdee*
They come on Fridays

# TELEPHONES

● You can make both local and international calls from telephone booths in the street. Many bars and cafés also have public phones.

● You can also make calls from post or telephone offices, where there will be someone to assist you if necessary. French post offices have the sign **Postes et Télécommunications (P & T)**; Swiss ones have a **PTT** sign. In Belgium, look for **Téléphone/Télégraphe**.

● Public telephones take different coins in the various countries. There will be instructions on the phone. To operate a public telephone, lift the receiver, insert a coin or coins, wait for the dialling tone, and then dial the number.

● There are also telephones operated by card (**télécarte**) in France and Belgium. Cards are obtainable from post offices, railway ticket counters and shops showing a **Télécarte** sign.

## Instructions for using a telephone card:

| | |
|---|---|
| **Décrochez** | Lift receiver |
| **Introduire la carte ou faire le nº d'urgence** | Insert card or dial emergency number |
| **Fermez le volet** | Close the flap |
| **Patientez, s.v.p.** | Please wait |
| **Crédit** | Amount left on card |
| **Numérotez** | Dial/Key in number |
| **Numéro appelé** | Number dialled |
| **Retirez votre carte** | Take your card |

● To call abroad, first dial the international access number –
**19** in France (and you then wait for a second dialling tone), or
**00** in Belgium, Switzerland and Luxembourg. Then dial the
code for the country – for the UK it's **44**. Follow this with the
town code minus the 0, and then the number you want. For
example: for a Central London number, dial **19** (or **00**) **44 71**,
then the number.

● If you want to make a reverse charge call to the UK from
France, you can get straight through to the UK operator by
dialling **19 00 44** (wait for a second dialling tone after dialling
**19**).

● Telephone numbers for emergencies are:

|  | *Police* | *Fire brigade* | *Ambulance* |
|---|---|---|---|
| France | **17** | **18** | **18** |
| Switzerland | **117** | **118** | **144** |
| Belgium | **101** | **100** | **100** |
| Luxembourg | **012** | **012** | **012** |

● In French, telephone numbers are given in groups of two.
For example, the number 65 43 21 would be **soixante-cinq,
quarante-trois, vingt et un** (sixty-five, forty-three, twenty-one).

## You may see

| | |
|---|---|
| **Postes** | Post office |
| **Postes et Télécommunications (P & T)** | Post and Telecommunications office |
| **Télécarte** | Telephone card |
| **Téléphone** | Telephone |
| **Téléphone/Télégraphe** | Telephone office |

## You may want to say

Is there a telephone?
**Est-ce qu'il y a un téléphone?**
*eskeelya uñ taylayfon*

Where is the telephone?
**Où est le téléphone?**
*oo e luh taylayfon*

Do you have change for the telephone, please?
**Est-ce que vous auriez de la monnaie pour le téléphone,
    s'il vous plaît?**
*eskuh vooz ohree-ay duh la monay poor luh taylayfon
    seelvooplay*

A telephone card, please
**Une télécarte, s'il vous plaît**
*ewn taylaykart seelvooplay*

I want to call England
**Je voudrais téléphoner en Angleterre**
*juh voodray taylayfonay oñ oñgluhter*

Mr Dupont, please
**Monsieur Dupont, s'il vous plaît**
*muhsyuh dewpawñ seelvooplay*

Extension number 121, please
**Le poste cent vingt et un, s'il vous plaît**
*luh post soñ vañtayuñ seelvooplay*

My name is . . .
**Je m'appelle . . .**
*juh mapel . . .*

It's . . . speaking
**C'est . . .**
*say . . .*

When will he be back?
**Quand est-ce qu'il sera de retour?**
*koñt eskeel suhra duh ruhtoor*

When will she be back?
**Quand est-ce qu'elle sera de retour?**
*koñt eskel suhra duh ruhtoor*

I'll call back later
**Je rappelerai plus tard**
*juh rapeluhray plew tar*

Can I leave a message?
**Est-ce que je peux laisser un message?**
*eskuh juh puh lesay uñ mesaj*

Please tell him/her that I called
**Veuillez lui dire que j'ai appelé**
*vuhyay lwee deer kuh jay apuhlay*

I am in the Hotel Victor-Hugo
**Je suis à l'Hôtel Victor-Hugo**
*juh sweez a lohtel veektor ewgoh*

My telephone number is . . .
**Mon numéro de téléphone est le . . .**
*mawñ newmayroh duh taylayfon e luh . . .*

Could you ask him/her to call me?
**Pourriez-vous lui demander de me rappeler?**
*pooree-ay voo lwee duhmoñday duh muh rapuhlay*

Could you repeat that, please?
**Pourriez-vous répéter, s'il vous plaît?**
*pooree-ay voo raypaytay seelvooplay*

We were cut off
**Nous avons été coupés**
*nooz avawnz aytay koopay*

Sorry, I've got the wrong number
**Excusez-moi, je me suis trompé(e) de numéro**
*exkewsay mwa juh muh swee trawmpay duh newmayroh*

How much is the call?
**Combien coûte la communication?**
*kawmbyañ koot la komewneekasyawñ*

Could you give me a number to call a taxi?
**Pourriez-vous me donner un numéro pour appeler un taxi?**
*pooree-ay voo muh donay uñ newmayroh poor apuhlay uñ taxee*

## You may hear

**Allô**
*aloh*
Hello (*said by person answering phone*)

**Lui-même/Elle-même/J'écoute**
*lweemem/elmem/jaykoot*
Speaking

**Qui est à l'appareil?**
*kee et a laparay*
Who's calling?

**Un instant, s'il vous plaît**
*un añstoñ seelvooplay*
One moment, please

**Ne quittez pas, s'il vous plaît**
*nuh keetay pa seelvooplay*
Hold on, please

**Vous êtes en ligne**
*vooz etz oñ leenyuh*
I'm putting you through

**La ligne est occupée**
*la leenyuh et okewpay*
The line's engaged

**Vous voulez attendre?**
*voo voolayz atoñdr*
Do you want to hold on?

**Il n'y a personne**
*eelnya person*
There's no answer

**Il/Elle n'est pas là**
*eel/el ne pa la*
He/She is not in

**Vous vous êtes trompé(e) de numéro**
*voo vooz et trompay duh newmayroh*
You've got the wrong number

# CHANGING MONEY

● All French-speaking countries in Europe have the **franc** (abbreviated to **Fr** or **F**) as the unit of currency, though it has different values in different countries. The **franc** is divided into 100 **centimes**.

● In France, there are coins of 5, 10, 20 and 50 centimes, and 1, 2, 5 and 10 francs; and banknotes of 20, 50, 100, 200 and 500 francs.

● In Switzerland, there are coins of 5, 10, 20 and 50 centimes, and 1, 2 and 5 francs; and banknotes of 10, 20, 50, 100, 500 and 1,000 francs.

● In Belgium, there are coins of 50 centimes, and 1, 5, 20 and 50 francs; and banknotes of 50, 100, 500, 1,000 and 5,000 francs.

● In Luxembourg, the Luxembourg and Belgian franc are both used, and are worth the same.

● To change money in a bank, go to the counter marked **Change**.

● Banking hours vary from country to country. They are generally as follows:
France: 9 a.m.–12 noon and 2 p.m.–4 p.m., Mondays to Fridays
Switzerland: 7.30 a.m.–12 noon and 1.45 p.m.–6 p.m., Mondays to Fridays; 7.30 a.m.–11 a.m., Saturdays
Belgium: 9 a.m.–6 p.m., Mondays to Fridays; 9 a.m.–12 noon, Saturdays
Luxembourg: 8.30 a.m.–12 noon and 1.30 p.m.–4 p.m., Mondays to Fridays

● There are also currency exchange offices (**bureau de change**) which generally open longer hours.

● You can obtain francs by exchanging cash or traveller's cheques, cashing Eurocheques and with a credit card. You can also pay with any of these in many hotels and shops.

● There is an extensive network of cash dispensers outside banks, many of which can be operated with credit cards or Eurocheque cards – check with British banks for details.

## You may see the following instructions when using a cash dispenser:

| | |
|---|---|
| Introduisez votre carte | Insert your card |
| Veuillez patienter quelques instants | Please wait |
| Veuillez composer votre numéro confidentiel | Please key in your PIN number |
| Composez le montant désiré | Enter amount required |
| Retrait | Withdrawal |
| Tapez 'fin' ou choisissez une autre opération | Press 'fin' (end) or choose another transaction |
| Retirez votre carte | Take your card |
| Retirez le reçu et l'argent | Take your receipt and cash |

## You may see

| | |
|---|---|
| Banque | Bank |
| Caisse | Cashier |
| Caisse d'épargne | Savings bank |
| Change | Exchange |
| Distributeur automatique de billets | Cash dispenser |
| Entrée | Entrance |
| Fermé | Closed |
| Ouvert | Open |
| Sortie | Exit |

## You may want to say

I'd like to change some pounds (sterling)
**Je voudrais changer des livres (sterling)**
*juh voodray shoñjay day leevr (sterleeng)*

I'd like to change some traveller's cheques
**Je voudrais changer des chèques de voyage**
*juh voodray shoñjay day shek duh vwiyaj*

I'd like to change a Eurocheque
**Je voudrais changer un Eurochèque**
*juh voodray shoñjay un uhroshek*

I'd like to get some money with this credit card
**Je voudrais retirer de l'argent avec cette carte de crédit**
*juh voodray ruhteeray duh larjoñ avek set kart duh kraydee*

What's the exchange rate today?
**Quel est le cours du change aujourd'hui?**
*kel e luh koor dew shoñj ohjoordwee*

Can you give me some change, please?
**Pourriez-vous me faire de la monnaie, s'il vous plaît?**
*pooree-ay voo muh fer duh la monay seelvooplay*

Can you give me five fifty-franc notes?
**Pourriez-vous me donner cinq billets de cinquante francs?**
*pooree-ay voo muh donay sañk beeyay duh sañkoñt froñ*

I'm at the Hotel Victor-Hugo
**Je suis à l'Hôtel Victor-Hugo**
*juh sweez a lohtel veektor ewgoh*

I'm staying with friends
**Je suis chez des amis**
*juh swee shay dayz amee*

The address is 25 Rue de la Gare
**L'adresse est vingt-cinq rue de la Gare**
*ladres e vañsañk rew duh la gar*

## You may hear

**Votre passeport, s'il vous plaît**
*votr paspor seelvooplay*
Your passport, please

**Combien vous voulez changer?**
*kawmbyañ voo voolay shoñjay*
How much do you want to change?

**Votre adresse, s'il vous plaît?**
*votr adres seelvooplay*
Your address, please?

**Votre hôtel, s'il vous plaît?**
*votr ohtel seelvooplay*
The name of your hotel, please?

**Signez ici, s'il vous plaît**
*seenyay eesee seelvooplay*
Sign here, please

**Veuillez passer à la caisse, s'il vous plaît**
*vuhyay pasay a la kes seelvooplay*
Please go to the cashier

# EATING AND DRINKING

- To order something, all you need do is name it, and say 'please', adding 'for me', 'for him' or 'for her' if you're ordering for several people to show who wants what.

- Bars, open all day, serve alcoholic and non-alcoholic drinks, coffee, tea etc., and also snacks such as croissants and sandwiches; some serve complete meals. Cafés generally have a list of dishes on the wall, often illustrated. There are no age restrictions for going into bars, only for being served alcohol.

- Lunch is generally served between 12 and 2 p.m., and dinner from 7 p.m. to 9 or 10 p.m.

- If you're looking for gastronomic experiences, consult a restaurant guide. You'll also find very good, but cheaper, food at restaurants designed mainly for people like lorry drivers (**restaurants de routiers**), and also at motorway restaurants.

Restaurants often have a set menu (**menu à prix fixe** or **menu touristique**), as well as **à la carte**. Some have a **menu gastronomique** featuring local specialities.

In France especially, Sunday lunch is a traditional time for families to eat out, so booking is advisable if you want to eat out then. Many restaurants are not open on Sunday evenings.

- A service charge is usually included in the bill (**service compris**), so there is no need to leave a tip.

- If you want to try the local wine wherever you are, ask for **vin du pays**. You will find opportunities for wine-tasting in many areas – look out for the sign **Dégustation de vins**.

- Beer is virtually the national drink in Luxembourg and Belgium, and there is a huge variety to choose from, ranging from the very dark to the very light.

● Cider (**le cidre**) is a speciality of Normandy.

● Coffee is usually served black, unless you say you want it white (**café au lait** or **café crème**). You also need to say if you want milk or lemon with tea. Herbal teas like **camomille** (camomile), **menthe** (mint) and **verveine** (verbena) are very popular.

● Sandwiches (**sandwiches**) are made with chunks of French bread. A **croque-monsieur** is a toasted ham and cheese sandwich. A **croque-madame** is the same with a fried egg on top.

● **Crêpes** are a speciality of Brittany – they are thin, rolled pancakes, which can be filled with jam or chocolate or just sprinkled with sugar. **Galettes** are savoury pancakes, typically filled with ham, cheese or mushrooms.

● Chips (**frites**) with mayonnaise are very popular in Belgium.

● French food is too vast a subject to go into in detail, but every region has its own cuisine. Regional specialities include **bouillabaisse**, a fish soup from the South; **cassoulet**, a stew of beans, pork and sausage from the South West; **choucroute**, sauerkraut with ham and sausage, from Alsace; and many dishes based on cream, apples, cider and **calvados** (apple brandy) in Normandy. You'll also come across **couscous** in North African restaurants in France – it's steamed semolina with meat and vegetables.

The other French-speaking countries have their own specialities too: for instance, Switzerland has **fondues** and **raclette** (dishes based on melted cheese); Luxembourg and Belgium have Ardennes ham, sausages and other pork products.

In restaurants you'll usually have only one vegetable with your main course. It's also quite common to have a small green salad before the cheese.

In many places a basket of bread is automatically put on the table when you sit down and can be refilled several times during the meal.

## You may see

| | |
|---|---|
| **Auberge** | Inn |
| **Bar à café** | Coffee shop (with light meals) |
| **Bistrot/Bistro** | Bar serving a limited range of food |
| **Brasserie** | Large café |
| **Buffet** | Station restaurant |
| **Buffet-express** | Snack-bar |
| **Carnotzet** | Cellar restaurant found in Switzerland serving local dishes and cheese specialities |
| **Cave (viticole)** | Wine cellar |
| **Cuisine** | Kitchen; cooking |
| **Dégustation de vins (gratuite)** | (Free) wine-tasting |
| **Hostellerie** | Traditional country restaurant |
| **Libre-service** | Self-service |
| **Menu à prix fixe** | Set menu |
| **Menu gastronomique** | Gastronomic menu, with regional specialities |
| **Menu touristique** | Tourist menu |
| **Plat du jour** | Dish of the day |
| **Plats à emporter** | Take-away meals |
| **Relais (de campagne)** | Country inn |
| **Restaurant de routiers** | Roadside diner |
| **Restoroute** | Motorway restaurant |
| **Rôtisserie** | Restaurant, grill |
| **Salle à manger** | Dining-room |
| **Salon de thé** | Tea-room |
| **Spécialités locales** | Local specialities |
| **Toilettes** | Toilets |
| **Vestiaire** | Cloakroom |

## You may want to say

### General phrases

Are there any cheap
restaurants around here?
**Est-ce qu'il y a des
restaurants bon marché par
ici?**
*eskeelya day restohroñ bawñ
marshay par eesee*

A (one) . . . , please
**Un/Une . . . , s'il vous plaît**
*uñ/ewn . . . seelvooplay*

Another . . . , please
**Encore un/une . . . , s'il vous
plaît**
*oñkor uñ/ewn . . . seelvooplay*

More . . . , please
**Encore de . . . , s'il vous plaît**
*oñkor duh . . . seelvooplay*

For me
**Pour moi**
*poor mwa*

For him/her/them
**Pour lui/elle/eux**
*poor lwee/el/uh*

I'd like this, please
**Je voudrais ça, s'il vous plaît**
*juh voodray sa seelvooplay*

Two of these, please
**Deux comme ça, s'il vous plaît**
*duh kom sa seelvooplay*

Do you have . . . ?
**Est-ce que vous avez . . . ?**
*eskuh vooz avay . . .*

Is/Are there any . . . ?
**Est-ce qu'il y a . . . ?**
*eskeelya . . .*

What is there to eat?
**Qu'est-ce qu'il y a à manger?**
*keskeelya a moñjay*

What is there for dessert?
**Qu'est-ce qu'il y a comme
dessert?**
*keskeelya kom deser*

What do you recommend?
**Qu'est-ce que vous
recommandez?**
*keskuh voo ruhkomoñday*

Do you have any typical
local dishes?
**Est-ce que vous avez des
plats typiques de la région?**
*eskuh vooz avay day pla
teepeek duh la rayjawñ*

What is this?
**Qu'est-ce que c'est?**
*keskuh say*

How do you eat this?
**Ça se mange comment?**
*sa suh moñj komoñ*

Cheers!
**Santé!/À la vôtre!**
*soñtay/a la vohtr*

Enjoy your meal!
**Bon appétit!**
*bon apaytee*

Where are the toilets?
**Où se trouvent les toilettes?**
*oo suh troov lay twalet*

That's all, thanks
**C'est tout, merci**
*say too mersee*

The bill, please
**L'addition, s'il vous plaît**
*ladeesyawñ seelvooplay*

## Bars and cafés

A (black) coffee, please
**Un café (noir), s'il vous plaît**
*uñ kafay (nwar) seelvooplay*

Two white coffees, please
**Deux cafés au lait,
s'il vous plaît**
*duh kafay oh lay seelvooplay*

A coffee with cream, please
**Un café crème, s'il vous plaît**
*uñ kafay krem seelvooplay*

A tea with milk/lemon, please
**Un thé au lait/citron, s'il
vous plaît**
*uñ tay oh lay/seetrawñ
seelvooplay*

A camomile tea, please
**Une camomille, s'il vous plaît**
*ewn kamomeel seelvooplay*

A fizzy orange, please
**Une orangeade, s'il vous plaît**
*ewn oroñjad seelvooplay*

Mineral water, please
**De l'eau minérale, s'il vous plaît**
*duh loh meenayral
seelvooplay*

Fizzy/Still
**Gazeuse/Non gazeuse**
*gazuhz/nawñ gazuhz*

What fruit juices do you have?
**Quels jus de fruits vous avez?**
*kel jew duh frwee vooz avay*

An orange juice, please
**Un jus d'orange, s'il vous plaît**
*uñ jew doroñj seelvooplay*

A beer, please
**Une bière, s'il vous plaît**
*ewn byer seelvooplay*

A dark/light beer, please
**Une bière brune/blonde, s'il
vous plaît**
*ewn byer brewn/blawñd
seelvooplay*

Two draught beers, please
**Deux bières pression, s'il vous plaît**
*duh byer presyawñ seelvooplay*

A glass of red/white wine, please
**Un verre de vin rouge/blanc, s'il vous plaît**
*uñ ver duh vañ rooj/bloñ seelvooplay*

A gin and tonic, please
**Un gin-tonic, s'il vous plaît**
*uñ jeen toneek seelvooplay*

With ice
**Avec des glaçons**
*avek day glasawñ*

A croissant, please
**Un croissant, s'il vous plaît**
*uñ krwasoñ seelvooplay*

Some crisps, please
**Des chips, s'il vous plaît**
*day sheep seelvooplay*

What sandwiches do you have?
**Quels sandwiches vous avez?**
*kel soñdweesh vooz avay*

A ham sandwich, please
**Un sandwich au jambon, s'il vous plaît**
*uñ soñdweesh oh jombawñ seelvooplay*

Two cheese sandwiches
**Deux sandwiches au fromage**
*duh soñdweesh oh fromaj*

A toasted ham and cheese sandwich, please
**Un croque-monsieur, s'il vous plaît**
*uñ krok muhsyuh seelvooplay*

A pancake with ham, please
**Une galette au jambon, s'il vous plaît**
*ewn galet oh jombawñ seelvooplay*

A pancake with jam, please
**Une crêpe à la confiture, s'il vous plaît**
*ewn krep a la kawñfeetewr seelvooplay*

Do you have ice creams?
**Est-ce que vous avez des glaces?**
*eskuh vooz avay day glas*

What flavours do you have?
**Quels parfums vous avez?**
*kel parfuñ vooz avay*

A chocolate cone, please
**Un cornet au chocolat, s'il vous plaît**
*uñ kornay oh shokola seelvooplay*

A vanilla ice cream, please
**Une glace à la vanille, s'il vous plaît**
*ewn glas a la vaneey seelvooplay*

An (orange) ice-lolly
**Un Esquimau (à l'orange)**
*un eskeemoh (a loroñj)*

## Booking a table

I want to reserve a table for
two people
**Je voudrais réserver une table
pour deux personnes**
*juh voodray rayzervay ewn
tabl poor duh person*

For seven o'clock
**Pour sept heures**
*poor set uhr*

For tomorrow at quarter to
eight
**Pour demain à huit heures
moins le quart**
*poor demañ a weet uhr mwañ
luh kar*

I have booked a table
**J'ai réservé une table**
*jay rayzervay ewn tabl*

My name is . . .
**Je m'appelle . . .**
*juh mapel . . .*

## In restaurants

A table for four, please
**Une table pour quatre
personnes, s'il vous plaît**
*ewn tabl poor katr person
seelvooplay*

Outside/On the terrace, if
possible
**Dehors/Sur la terrasse, si
c'est possible**
*duh-or/sewr la teras see say
poseebl*

Waiter!
**Garçon!**
*garsawñ*

Waitress!/Miss!
**Mademoiselle!**
*madmwazel*

The menu, please
**Le menu/La carte,
s'il vous plaît**
*luh muhnew/la kart seelvooplay*

The wine list, please
**La carte des vins, s'il vous plaît**
*la kart day vañ seelvooplay*

Do you have a set menu?
**Est-ce que vous avez un menu
du jour/touristique?**
*eskuh vooz avay uñ muhnew
dew joor/tooreesteek*

Do you have vegetarian dishes?
**Est-ce que vous avez des
plats végétariens?**
*eskuh vooz avay day pla
vayjaytaree-añ*

The set menu (at 80 francs),
please
**Le menu (à quatre-vingts
francs), s'il vous plaît**
*luh muhnew (a katr vañ froñ)
seelvooplay*

For the first course . . .
**Comme entrée . . .**
*kom oñtray . . .*

Fish soup, please
**Une soupe de poissons, s'il
vous plaît**
*ewn soop duh pwasawñ
seelvooplay*

Two mixed hors-d'œuvres,
please
**Deux hors-d'œuvre variés, s'il
vous plaît**
*duhz orduhvr varee-ay
seelvooplay*

And to follow . . .
**Et ensuite . . .**
*ay oñsweet . . .*

Pork chop, please
**Une côte de porc, s'il vous plaît**
*ewn koht duh por seelvooplay*

Lobster, please
**Un homard, s'il vous plaît**
*un ohmar seelvooplay*

Are vegetables included?
**Est-ce que les légumes sont
compris?**
*eskuh lay laygewm sawñ
kawmpree*

With chips
**Avec des frites**
*avek day freet*

And a mixed/green salad
**Et une salade composée/
verte**
*ay ewn salad kawmpohzay/
vert*

For dessert . . .
**Comme dessert . . .**
*kom deser . . .*

Apple tart, please
**Une tarte aux pommes, s'il
vous plaît**
*ewn tart oh pom seelvooplay*

A peach, please
**Une pêche, s'il vous plaît**
*ewn pesh seelvooplay*

Some cheese, please
**Du fromage, s'il vous plaît**
*dew fromaj seelvooplay*

What cheeses do you have?
**Qu'est-ce que vous avez
comme fromages?**
*keskuh vooz avay kom fromaj*

Is this cheese strong or mild?
**Ce fromage, est-il fort ou doux?**
*suh fromaj eteel for oo doo*

Excuse me, where is my
steak and chips?
**Pardon, où est mon steack-
frites?**
*pardawñ oo e mawñ staykfreet*

Some bread, please
**Du pain, s'il vous plaît**
*dew pañ seelvooplay*

More chips, please
**Encore des frites, s'il vous plaît**
*oñkor day freet seelvooplay*

A glass/A jug of water
**Un verre/Une carafe d'eau**
*uñ ver/ewn karaf doh*

A bottle of the local red wine
**Une bouteille de vin rouge du pays**
*ewn bootay duh vañ rooj dew payee*

Half a bottle of white house wine
**Une demi-bouteille de vin blanc cuvée maison**
*ewn duhmee bootay duh vañ bloñ kewvay mayzawñ*

*(for ordering coffee, see page 103)*

It's very good
**C'est très bon**
*say tre bawñ*

It's really delicious
**C'est vraiment délicieux**
*say vraymoñ dayleesyuh*

This is overcooked
**C'est trop cuit**
*say tro kwee*

This is not cooked
**Ce n'est pas assez cuit**
*suh ne paz asay kwee*

No, I ordered the chicken
**Non, j'ai commandé du poulet**
*nawñ jay komoñday dew poolay*

The bill, please
**L'addition, s'il vous plaît**
*ladeesyawñ seelvooplay*

Do you accept credit cards?
**Vous acceptez les cartes de crédit?**
*vooz akseptay lay kart duh kraydee*

Do you accept traveller's cheques?
**Vous acceptez les chèques de voyage?**
*vooz akseptay lay shek duh vwiyaj*

Excuse me, I think there's a mistake
**Pardon, je crois qu'il y a une erreur**
*pardawñ juh krwa keelya ewn eruhr*

## You may hear

### Bars and cafés

**Qu'est-ce que vous prenez/désirez?**
*keskuh voo pruhnay/dayzeeray*
What would you like?

**Qu'est-ce que vous voulez prendre?**
*keskuh voo voolay proñdr*
What would you like?

**Vous voulez des glaçons?**
*voo voolay day glasawñ*
Would you like some ice?

**Gazeuse ou non gazeuse?**
*gazuhz oo nawñ gazuhz*
Fizzy or still?

### Restaurants

**Vous êtes combien?**
*vooz et kawmbyañ*
How many are you?

**Pour combien de personnes?**
*poor kawmbyañ duh person*
For how many people?

**Un instant, s'il vous plaît**
*un añstoñ seelvooplay*
Just a moment, please

**Est-ce que vous avez réservé (une table)?**
*eskuh vooz avay rayzervay (ewn tabl)*
Have you booked (a table)?

**Grand ou petit?/Grande ou petite?**
*groñ oo puhtee/groñd oo puhteet*
Large or small?

**Lequel/Laquelle préférez-vous?**
*luhkel/lakel prafayray voo*
Which do you prefer?

**D'accord**
*dakor*
Very good, fine

**Tout de suite**
*toot sweet*
Right away

**Nous avons . . .**
*nooz avawñ . . .*
We have . . .

**Il y une attente de dix minutes**
*eelya ewn atoñt duh dees meenewt*
You will have to wait ten minutes

**Voudriez-vous attendre?**
*voodree-ay vooz atoñdr*
Would you like to wait?

**Qu'est-ce que vous prenez/
désirez?**
*keskuh voo pruhnay/dayzeeray*
What would you like?

**Vous voulez prendre un apéritif?**
*voo voolay proñdr un apayreeteef*
Would you like an aperitif?

**Vous avez choisi?**
*vooz avay shwazee*
Have you chosen?

**Nous vous recommandons . . .**
*noo voo ruhkomoñdawñ*
We recommend . . .

**Comme entrée?**
*kom oñtray*
For the first course?

**Et ensuite?**
*ay oñsweet*
And to follow?

**Comme viande?**
*kom vyoñd*
For the main/meat course?

**Comme boisson?**
*kom bwasawñ*
To drink?

**C'est pour qui le/la . . . ?**
*say poor kee luh/la . . .*
Who is the . . . for?

**Vous prenez un dessert, ou
du café?**
*voo pruhnay uñ deser oo dew
kafay*
Would you like dessert, or
coffee?

**Le plateau de fromages?**
*luh platoh duh fromaj*
The cheese board?

**Vous désirez autre chose?**
*voo dayzeeray ohtr shohz*
Would you like anything
else?

**Vous avez terminé?**
*vooz avay termeenay*
Have you finished?

# MENU READER

## General Phrases

| | |
|---|---|
| Boisson comprise | Drink included |
| Boissons alcoolisées | Alcoholic drinks |
| Boissons sans alcool | Non-alcoholic drinks |
| Carte | Menu |
| Carte des vins | Wine list |
| Couvert | Cover charge |
| Crustacés | Shellfish |
| En saison | In season |
| En supplément, En sus | Extra |
| Entrée | First course |
| Entremets | Sweet dish, dessert |
| Fromages | Cheeses |
| Fruits | Fruit |
| Fruits de mer | Seafood |
| Garniture au choix | Choice of vegetables |
| Gibier et volaille | Game and poultry |
| Grillades | Grills |
| Hors-d'œuvre | Starters |
| Légumes | Vegetables |
| Menu à prix fixe | Set menu |
| Menu gastronomique | Gastronomic menu, with regional specialities |
| Menu touristique | Tourist menu |
| Omelettes | Omelettes |
| Pâtes | Pasta, noodles |
| Pâtisseries | Pastries |
| Plat du jour | Dish of the day |
| Plat principal | Main course |
| Plats à emporter | Take-away meals |
| Poissons | Fish |
| Potages et soupes | Soups |

| | |
|---|---|
| **Salades** | Salads |
| **Selon arrivage** | When available |
| **Selon grosseur/grandeur (SG)** | According to size |
| **Service compris** | Service included |
| **Spécialités locales** | Local specialities |
| **Supplément** | Extra charge |
| **Sur commande** | To order |
| **Tous nos plats sont garnis** | All dishes served with vegetables |
| **Viandes** | Meat dishes |
| **Vins** | Wines |
| **Volonté, à volonté** | At no extra charge |

## Drinks

| | |
|---|---|
| **Appellation d'origine contrôlée (AOC)** | Guarantee of origin and quality of wine |
| **Armagnac** | Brandy from Armagnac region |
| **Bière** | Beer |
|   **blonde** | light, lager |
|   **brune** | dark, bitter |
|   **pression** | draught |
|   **sans alcool** | alcohol-free |
| **Blanc de blancs** | White wine made from white grapes |
| **Bouteille** | Bottle |
| **Brut** | Very dry |
| **Cacao** | Cocoa |
| **Café** | Coffee |
|   **au lait** | white |
|   **complet** | Continental breakfast |
|   **crème** | with cream |
|   **décaféiné** | decaffeinated |
|   **filtre** | filtered |
|   **frappé** | iced |
|   **noir** | black |

| | |
|---|---|
| Calvados | Apple brandy |
| Camomille | Camomile tea |
| Carafe | Carafe, jug |
| Cassis | Blackcurrant liqueur |
| Chambré(e) | At room temperature |
| Champagne | Champagne |
| Chocolat (chaud/froid) | Chocolate (hot/cold) |
|   grande tasse |   large hot chocolate |
| Cidre (brut/doux) | Cider (dry/sweet) |
| Citron pressé | Freshly squeezed lemon drink |
| Cognac | Cognac, brandy |
| Cru: Grand cru, Premier cru | Vintage wine |
| Diabolo-menthe | Mint cordial and lemonade |
| Demi | Draught beer (France); half litre of wine (Switzerland) |
| Doux/Douce | Sweet |
| Eau | Water |
| Eau de Seltz | Soda water |
| Eau-de-vie | Brandy |
| Eau minérale (gazeuse/ non gazeuse) | Mineral water (fizzy/still) |
| Frappé | Iced; milkshake |
| Gin | Gin |
|   gin-tonic |   gin and tonic |
| Grand crème | Large white coffee |
| Infusion | Herbal tea |
| Jus de fruits | Fruit juice |
| Kir | White wine and blackcurrant liqueur (cassis) |
| Kirsch | Cherry brandy |
| Lait (chaud/froid) | Milk (hot/cold) |
| Limonade | Lemonade |
| Madère | Madeira |
| Marc | Grape brandy |
| Menthe | Mint tea; peppermint cordial |
| Mirabelle | Plum brandy |

| | |
|---|---|
| **Muscat** | Sweet white wine |
| **Orange pressée** | Freshly squeezed orange juice |
| **Panaché** | Shandy |
| **Pastis** | Aniseed-flavoured apéritif, drunk with water |
| **Pichet** | Jug, pitcher |
| **Porto** | Port |
| **Pression** | Draught beer |
| **Quetsche** | Plum brandy |
| **Réserve du patron** | House wine |
| **Rhum** | Rum |
| **Schweppes** | Tonic water |
| **Sec/Sèche** | Dry |
| **Sirop** | Cordial, syrup |
| **Soda** | Fizzy drink |
| à l'orange | fizzy orange, orangeade |
| **Thé** | Tea |
| à la menthe | mint tea |
| au lait/citron | with milk/lemon |
| glacé | iced |
| **Tilleul** | Lime tea |
| **Tisane** | Herb tea |
| **Vermouth** | Vermouth |
| **Verveine** | Verbena tea |
| **Vin** | Wine |
| blanc | white |
| de table | table |
| du pays | local |
| mousseux | sparkling |
| ordinaire | ordinary |
| rosé | rosé |
| rouge | red |
| **Vodka** | Vodka |
| **Whisky (soda)** | Whisky (and soda) |
| **Xérès** | Sherry |

# Food

| | |
|---|---|
| **Abricot** | Apricot |
| **Agneau** | Lamb |
| **Aiglefin** | Haddock |
| **Aigre** | Sour, bitter |
| à l'aigre-doux | sweet and sour |
| **Ail** | Garlic |
| à l'ail | with garlic |
| **Aïoli** | Garlic mayonnaise |
| **Amandes** | Almonds |
| **Ananas** | Pineapple |
| **Anchois** | Anchovies |
| **Andouille, Andouillette** (smaller) | Chitterling sausage |
| **Anguille** | Eel |
| **À point** | Medium (steak) |
| **Arachides** | Peanuts |
| **Asperges** | Asparagus |
| **Assiette de . . .** | Plate of . . . |
| **Assiette anglaise** | Assorted cold roast meats |
| **Artichaut** | Artichoke |
| **Aubergine** | Aubergine |
| **Avocat** | Avocado |
| **Baba au rhum** | Rum baba |
| **Banane** | Banana |
| **Bar** | Bass |
| **Barbue** | Brill |
| **Barquette** | Small boat-shaped pastry |
| **Basilic** | Basil |
| **Bavaroise** | Type of light mousse |
| **Bavette à l'échalote** | Beef with shallots |
| **Beignet** | Type of doughnut or fritter |
| **Betterave** | Beetroot |
| **Beurre** | Butter |
| maître d'hôtel | parsley butter |
| noir | black butter |

| | |
|---|---|
| **Bien cuit** | Well done (steak) |
| **Bifteck** | Steak |
|   **tartare** | minced raw steak with raw egg, onion, tartare or Worcester sauce |
| **Biscuit de Savoie** | Sponge cake |
| **Bisque** | Seafood soup, chowder |
| **Blanquette de veau** | Stewed veal in white sauce |
| **Bleu** | Very rare (steak) |
| **Bœuf** | Beef |
|   **à la mode** | braised with red wine and vegetables |
|   **bourguignon/à la bourguignonne** | stew with red wine |
|   **miroton** | stewed with onions |
| **Bois: des bois** | Wild |
| **Bolets** | Boletus mushrooms |
| **Bouchée à la reine** | Chicken vol-au-vent |
| **Boudin blanc** | White pudding |
| **Boudin noir** | Black pudding |
| **Bouillabaisse** | Fish soup, speciality of the South of France |
| **Bouilli(e)** | Boiled |
| **Bouillon** | Broth |
| **Boulettes** | Meatballs |
| **Bouquet rose** | Prawn |
| **Bourride** | Fish stew |
| **Braisé(e)** | Braised |
| **Brandade (de morue)** | Poached cod with cream, parsley and garlic |
| **Brioche** | Type of bun |
| **Broche: à la broche** | Spit-roasted |
| **Brochet** | Pike |
| **Brochette** | Kebab |
| **Brugnon** | Nectarine |
| **Cabillaud** | Cod |

| | |
|---|---|
| **Cabri** | Kid |
| **Cacahouètes** | Peanuts |
| **Caille** | Quail |
| **Calmar** | Squid |
| **Campagne: de campagne** | Country-style |
| **Canard** | Duck |
| à l'orange | in orange sauce |
| sauvage | wild |
| **Caneton** | Duckling |
| **Cannelle** | Cinnamon |
| **Câpres** | Capers |
| **Carbonnade de bœuf** | Beef stewed in beer with onions |
| **Carottes** | Carrots |
| râpées | grated carrots with vinaigrette |
| Vichy | cooked with butter and sugar |
| **Carpe** | Carp |
| **Carré d'agneau** | Rack of lamb |
| **Carrelet** | Plaice |
| **Cassis** | Blackcurrant |
| **Cassoulet** | Casserole of haricot beans, mutton, pork, goose and sausage, speciality of the Toulouse area |
| **Céléri** | Celeriac; celery |
| remoulade | celeriac in mustard dressing |
| **Cèpes** | Boletus mushrooms |
| **Cerises** | Cherries |
| **Cervelas** | Type of sausage |
| **Cervelle** | Brains |
| **Champignons** | Mushrooms |
| à la grecque | in olive oil, herbs and tomato |

| | |
|---|---|
| Charcuterie | Assorted cold meats |
| Charlotte | Dessert of cream with fruit and biscuits |
| Chateaubriand | Large fillet steak |
| Chaud(e) | Hot |
| Chausson aux pommes | Apple turnover |
| Chef: du chef | Chef's own/special |
| Chevreuil | Venison |
| Chicorée | Endive |
| Chips | Crisps |
| Chocolat | Chocolate |
| Chou | Cabbage |
| Chou à la crème | Cream puff |
| Choucroute (garnie) | Sauerkraut served with smoked ham, sausages etc. |
| Chou-fleur | Cauliflower |
| Chou-rave | Kohlrabi |
| Choux de Bruxelles | Brussels sprouts |
| Citron | Lemon |
| Civet de lapin/lièvre | Jugged rabbit/hare |
| Clafoutis | Fruit (usually black cherries) cooked in batter |
| Cochon de lait | Sucking pig |
| Cocotte: en cocotte | Casseroled |
| Cœurs d'artichaut | Artichoke hearts |
| Coing | Quince |
| Colin | Hake |
| Compote | Stewed fruit |
| Concombre | Cucumber |
| Confit d'oie | Goose preserved in fat |
| Confiture | Jam |
| Consommé | Consommé, clear soup |
| à l'œuf | with raw egg |
| au porto | with port |
| Coq au vin | Chicken in red wine, bacon, onions and mushrooms |

| | |
|---|---|
| Coque | Cockle |
| Coque: à la coque | Soft-boiled (egg) |
| Coquilles St-Jacques | Scallops, served in a cream sauce in their shells |
| Corbeille | Basket |
| Cornichon | Gherkin |
| Côte | Chop, cutlet |
|   de bœuf |   rib of beef |
| Côtelette | Chop, cutlet |
| Coulis | Sauce |
| Coupe | Cup |
|   de fruits |   fruit salad |
|   glacée |   ice-cream sundae |
| Courgette | Courgette |
| Court-bouillon | Stock |
| Couscous | North African speciality, steamed semolina served with meat and vegetables |
| Crabe | Crab |
| Crème | Cream; cream soup |
|   à la crème |   in cream sauce |
|   anglaise |   custard |
|   caramel |   cream caramel |
|   Chantilly |   whipped cream |
|   Dubarry |   cream of cauliflower soup |
|   patissière |   confectioner's custard |
|   renversée |   moulded cream dessert |
|   vichyssoise |   cream of leek and potato soup, served cold |
| Crêpe | Thin pancake |
|   à la confiture |   with jam |
|   au sucre |   sprinkled with sugar |
|   Suzette |   with orange sauce and flamed with brandy or liqueur |
| Cresson | Watercress |

| | |
|---|---|
| Crevettes | Prawns, shrimps |
| Croque-madame | Toasted ham and cheese sandwich with a fried egg on top |
| Croque-monsieur | Toasted ham and cheese sandwich |
| Croustade | Pastry shell |
| Croûte: en croûte | In a pastry crust |
| Crudités | Assorted raw vegetables |
| Cuisses de grenouille | Frogs' legs |
| Darne | Thick fish steak |
| Dattes | Dates |
| Daube: en daube | Casseroled |
| Daurade | Sea bream |
| Diable: à la diable | Devilled |
| Dinde | Turkey |
| Douzaine | Dozen |
| Échalotes | Shallots |
| Écrevisses | Crayfish |
| Endives | Chicory |
| Entrecôte | Entrecote (rib) steak |
| Épaule d'agneau | Shoulder of lamb |
| Épinards | Spinach |
| Escalope | Escalope |
|   de veau |   veal |
|   milanaise |   breaded veal with tomato sauce |
|   panée/viennoise |   breaded |
| Escargots | Snails |
|   à la bourguignonne |   in garlic butter |
| Estragon | Tarragon |
| Faisan | Pheasant |
| Farci(e) | Stuffed |
| Faux-filet | Sirloin |
| Fenouil | Fennel |
| Féra | Type of freshwater salmon |

| | |
|---|---|
| **Fèves** | Broad beans |
| **Figue** | Fig |
| **Filet** | Fillet |
|   mignon | small fillet |
| **Fines herbes** | Herbs |
| **Flageolets** | Small kidney beans |
| **Flambé(e)** | Sprinkled with brandy or other spirit and ignited |
| **Flan** | Crème caramel |
| **Flétan** | Halibut |
| **Foie** | Liver |
|   de volaille | chicken |
|   gras | goose (or duck) liver pâté |
| **Fondue** | Pot of melted cheese with white wine, into which diners dip pieces of bread on a fork |
|   bourguignonne | meat fondue: pieces of raw meat on forks cooked by diners in pot of hot oil |
| **Fouetté(e)** | Whipped |
| **Four: au four** | Baked |
| **Frais, Fraîche** | Fresh |
| **Fraise** | Strawberry |
| **Framboise** | Raspberry |
| **Francfort** | Frankfurter |
| **Fricassé(e)** | Stewed |
| **Frisée** | Curly endive |
| **Frit(e)** | Fried |
| **Frites** | Chips |
| **Froid(e)** | Cold |
| **Fromage** | Cheese |
|   blanc | soft cream cheese |
|   de chèvre | goat's cheese |
|   demi-sel | soft cream cheese. slightly salted |
| **Fumé(e)** | Smoked |

| | |
|---|---|
| **Galantine** | Cold poultry or game in aspic or gelatine |
| **Galette** | Pancake made with buckwheat flour |
| **Garbure** | Thick cabbage soup |
| **Garni(e)** | Garnished, with vegetables |
| **Gâteau** | Cake, gateau |
| **Gaufre** | Wafer, waffle |
| **Gelée** | Jelly |
| en gelée | in aspic, jellied |
| **Germes de soja** | Beansprouts |
| **Gigot (d'agneau)** | Leg of lamb |
| **Gingembre** | Ginger |
| **Girolle** | Chanterelle mushroom |
| **Glace** | Ice cream |
| au praliné | with crushed almonds and burnt sugar |
| **Goujon** | Gudgeon |
| **Granité** | Water-ice |
| **Gras-double** | Tripe |
| à la lyonnaise | with onions and wine |
| **Gratin: au gratin** | With cheese topping, in cheese sauce |
| **Gratin dauphinois** | Sliced potatoes baked with milk, cream and cheese |
| **Grillé(e)** | Grilled |
| **Groseilles (blanches/rouges)** | Currants (white/red) |
| à maquereau | gooseberries |
| **Hachis** | Minced meat, hash |
| Parmentier | type of cottage pie |
| **Hareng** | Herring |
| **Haricot de mouton** | Mutton stew with haricot beans |
| **Haricots** | Beans |
| blancs | haricot beans |
| rouges | red kidney beans |
| verts | green/French beans |

| | |
|---|---|
| **Herbes** | Herbs |
| **Homard** | Lobster |
| **à l'américaine/armoricaine** | in wine, tomatoes, shallots and brandy |
| **Thermidor** | with white wine, mushrooms and spices, flamed with brandy |
| **Hors d'œuvre variés** | Mixed hors d'œuvres |
| **Huile** | Oil |
| **d'arachide** | groundnut |
| **d'olive** | olive |
| **Huîtres** | Oysters |
| **Îles flottantes** | Floating islands: whisked egg whites floating in custard |
| **Jambon** | Ham |
| **cru** | raw cured |
| **cuit** | cooked |
| **de Bayonne** | type of raw cured ham |
| **Jardinière: à la jardinière** | With mixed vegetables |
| **Jarret** | Knuckle, shin |
| **Jour: du jour** | Of the day |
| **Julienne** | Soup of shredded vegetables |
| **Laitue** | Lettuce |
| **Langouste** | Crayfish |
| **Langoustines** | Scampi |
| **Langue** | Tongue |
| **Lapin** | Rabbit |
| **aux pruneaux** | casseroled in red wine with prunes |
| **chasseur** | with white wine and herbs |
| **Lard** | Bacon; fat |
| **Lardons** | Strips of bacon |
| **Légume** | Vegetable |
| **Lentilles** | Lentils |
| **en salade** | in vinaigrette |

| | |
|---|---|
| **Lièvre** | Hare |
| **Limande** | Lemon sole |
| **Longe** | Loin |
| **Lotte** | Burbot |
| **Lotte de mer** | Angler fish |
| **Loup** | Sea bass |
| **Macédoine de fruits** | Fruit salad |
| **Macédoine de légumes** | Mixed vegetables |
| **Magret de canard** | Breast of duck |
| **Maïs** | Sweet corn |
| **Maison (eg Tarte Maison)** | House speciality, home-made |
| **Maquereau** | Mackerel |
| **Marchand de vin** | Red wine sauce with shallots |
| **Mariné(e)** | Marinated |
| **Marrons** | Chestnuts |
| glacés | candied |
| **Massepain** | Marzipan |
| **Matelote d'anguilles** | Eel stew with wine |
| **Médaillons** | Medallions, tenderloin steak |
| **Melon** | Melon |
| **Menthe** | Mint |
| **Merguez** | Spicy sausage, from North Africa |
| **Merlan** | Whiting |
| **Meunière, à la meunière** | Fried in butter, with lemon juice and parsley |
| **Miel** | Honey |
| **Millefeuille** | Cream slice |
| **Morilles** | Morel mushrooms |
| **Mortadelle** | Mortadella, Bologna sausage |
| **Morue** | Salt cod |
| **Moules** | Mussels |
| marinière | in their shells with white wine, shallots and parsley |
| **Mousse** | Mousse |
| au chocolat | chocolate mousse |
| au jambon | light ham mousse |

123

| | |
|---|---|
| **Moutarde** | Mustard |
| à la moutarde | in mustard sauce |
| **Mouton** | Mutton |
| **Mûres** | Blackberries |
| **Myrtilles** | Bilberries, blueberries |
| **Nature, au naturel** | Plain |
| **Navarin d'agneau** | Lamb stew with vegetables |
| **Navet** | Turnip |
| **Noisette d'agneau** | Small boneless round of lamb |
| **Noisettes** | Hazelnuts |
| **Noix** | Walnuts |
| **Noix de coco** | Coconut |
| **Normande: à la normande** | In cream sauce |
| **Nouilles** | Noodles |
| **Oeuf(s)** | Egg(s) |
| à la coque | soft-boiled |
| à la neige | floating islands, whisked |
| | egg whites floating in custard |
| au/sur le plat | fried |
| brouillés | scrambled |
| dur | hard-boiled |
| dur mayonnaise | egg mayonnaise |
| (dur) mimosa | stuffed hard-boiled egg |
| **Oie** | Goose |
| **Oignon** | Onion |
| **Olive** | Olive |
| farcie | stuffed |
| noire | black |
| verte | green |
| **Omelette** | Omelette |
| fines herbes | with herbs |
| norvégienne | baked Alaska |
| paysanne | with potatoes and bacon |
| **Orange** | Orange |
| givrée | orange sorbet served in |
| | scooped-out orange |

| | |
|---|---|
| **Oseille** | Sorrel |
| **Oursin** | Sea urchin |
| **Pain** | Bread |
|    **d'épices** |    gingerbread |
|    **grillé** |    toast |
| **Palourdes** | Clams |
| **Pamplemousse** | Grapefruit |
| **Pané(e)** | Breaded |
| **Papillote: en papillote** | Baked in paper or foil |
| **Passé(e) au four** | Finished in the oven |
| **Pastèque** | Water melon |
| **Pâté** | Pâté |
|    **de campagne** |    coarse pork pâté |
|    **de foie** |    liver pâté |
| **Paupiettes de veau** | Rolled and stuffed slices of veal |
| **Pêche** | Peach |
|    **Melba** |    with vanilla ice cream, raspberry sauce and whipped cream |
| **Perche** | Perch |
| **Perdrix** | Partridge |
| **Persil** | Parsley |
| **Petit pain** | Roll |
| **Petit suisse** | Fresh cream cheese |
| **Petite friture** | Whitebait |
| **Petits pois** | Peas |
| **Pieds de porc** | Pig's trotters |
| **Pigeon** | Pigeon |
| **Pintade** | Guinea fowl |
| **Piperade** | Egg dish with tomatoes and peppers |
| **Pissaladière** | Onion tart with black olives and anchovies |
| **Pistache** | Pistachio |
| **Plateau de fromages** | Cheese board |

125

| | |
|---|---|
| **Poché(e)** | Poached |
| **Pointes d'asperges** | Asparagus tips |
| **Poire** | Pear |
| **belle Hélène** | pear with vanilla ice cream and chocolate sauce |
| **Poireau** | Leek |
| **Pois chiches** | Chickpeas |
| **Poisson** | Fish |
| **Poivre** | Pepper |
| **noir** | black |
| **vert** | green |
| **Poivron** | Sweet pepper |
| **Pomme** | Apple |
| **bonne femme** | baked |
| **Pommes (de terre)** | Potatoes |
| **à l'huile** | fried |
| **allumettes** | matchstick |
| **dauphine** | croquettes of potato mashed with butter and egg yolks and deep-fried |
| **duchesse** | mashed with butter and egg yolks |
| **en robe de chambre/des champs** | jacket |
| **frites** | chips |
| **mousseline** | mashed |
| **nature, vapeur** | boiled, steamed |
| **Porc** | Pork |
| **Pot: au pot** | Stewed |
| **Pot-au-feu** | Beef and vegetable stew |
| **Potage** | Thick vegetable soup |
| **bonne femme** | potato and leek |
| **Crécy** | carrot |
| **Parmentier** | potato |
| **printanier** | mixed vegetable |
| **Potée** | Hotpot |

| | |
|---|---|
| **Poule** | Chicken |
| **au pot** | boiled with vegetables |
| **Poulet** | Chicken |
| **à la basquaise** | Basque-style, in sauce of ham, tomatoes, onions and peppers |
| **à l'estragon** | in tarragon sauce |
| **au sang** | jugged |
| **chasseur** | in wine, mushroom and tomato sauce |
| **frites** | and chips |
| **Marengo** | with white wine, tomatoes, garlic, shallots and mushrooms |
| **Poulpe** | Octopus |
| **Poussin** | Spring chicken |
| **Praline** | Burnt-sugar almond |
| **Pressé(e) (eg orange pressée)** | Freshly-squeezed juice |
| **Profiteroles** | Small choux pastry puffs filled with cream or confectioner's custard |
| **Provençale: à la provençale** | With tomatoes, garlic and herbs |
| **Prune** | Plum |
| **Pruneau** | Prune |
| **Purée** | Mashed potatoes |
| **Quenelle** | Type of fish or meat dumpling |
| **Queue de bœuf** | Oxtail |
| **Quiche lorraine** | Bacon, egg and cheese flan |
| **Raclette** | Swiss speciality, hot melted cheese eaten with potatoes and pickles |
| **Radis** | Radish |
| **Ragoût** | Meat stew |
| **Raie** | Skate |

| | |
|---|---|
| **Raisins** | Grapes |
| secs | raisins |
| **Rascasse** | Scorpion fish (used in **bouillabaisse**) |
| **Ratatouille** | Mixture of courgettes, peppers, aubergine and tomatoes cooked in olive oil |
| **Reine-claude** | Greengage |
| **Rillettes (de porc)** | Potted pork |
| **Rillettes de saumon** | Potted salmon |
| **Ris de veau** | Veal sweetbreads |
| **Riz** | Rice |
| au lait | pudding |
| **Rognons** | Kidneys |
| **Romarin** | Rosemary |
| **Rosbif** | Roast beef |
| **Rôti(e)** | Roast |
| **Rouget** | Red mullet |
| **Sabayon** | Dessert of whipped egg yolks with wine and sugar |
| **Saignant** | Rare (steak) |
| **Saint-Honoré** | Gateau of choux pastry puffs and cream |
| **Saison: de saison** | In season |
| **Salade** | Salad |
| composée | mixed |
| de tomates | tomatoes with oil and vinegar and sometimes garlic |
| en salade | in vinaigrette |
| mixte | mixed |
| Niçoise | green beans, tuna, anchovies, tomatoes and black olives |
| russe | Russian salad, diced cooked vegetables in mayonnaise |
| verte | green |

| | |
|---|---|
| **Salmis** | Ragout of game in wine and vegetable sauce |
| **Sandwich** | Sandwich, made with French bread |
| **Sanglier** | Wild boar |
| **Sardine** | Sardine |
| **Sauce** | Sauce |
| aurore | white sauce with tomato purée |
| béarnaise | butter, egg yolks, shallots, vinegar and herbs |
| béchamel | white |
| bigarade | brown sauce with oranges |
| blanche | white |
| bordelaise | mushrooms, red wine and shallots |
| chasseur | white wine, shallots, tomatoes and mushrooms |
| gribiche | vinaigrette with hard-boiled eggs and capers |
| hollandaise | egg yolks, butter and vinegar |
| Mornay | cheese |
| provençale | tomatoes, garlic and herbs |
| rémoulade | mayonnaise with mustard and herbs |
| **Saucisse** | Sausage |
| **Saucisson** | Cold sausage, salami |
| à l'ail | garlic sausage |
| sec | dried |
| **Saumon** | Salmon |
| **Sauté(e)** | Sautéed |
| **Savarin** | Type of rum baba |
| **Sel** | Salt |
| **Selle d'agneau** | Saddle of lamb |
| **Sole** | Sole |
| bonne femme | in white wine with mushrooms |

| | |
|---|---|
| **Sorbet** | Sorbet, water-ice |
| **Soufflé** | Soufflé |
| au Grand Marnier | with orange liqueur |
| **Soupe** | Soup |
| à l'oignon | French onion soup, topped with slice of bread with cheese on |
| au pistou | thick soup of potatoes, courgettes, beans and herbs, from Provence |
| **Spaghettis** | Spaghetti |
| à la bolognaise | bolognese |
| à l'italienne | with tomato sauce |
| **Stea(c)k** | Steak |
| au poivre | with peppercorns |
| frites | steak and chips |
| haché | minced meat, hamburger |
| tartare | raw minced steak with a raw egg |
| **Sucre** | Sugar |
| **Suprême de volaille** | Chicken breast in cream sauce |
| **Tarte** | Tart, flan |
| frangipane | almond cream tart |
| Tatin | apple tart |
| **Tartelette** | Small tart |
| **Tartine** | Slice of bread and butter |
| **Terrine** | Terrine, pâté |
| **Tête de veau** | Calf's head |
| **Thon** | Tuna |
| **Tomate** | Tomato |
| **Topinambour** | Jerusalem artichoke |
| **Tournedos** | Thick fillet steak |
| Rossini | with foie gras and truffles, in Madeira sauce |
| **Tourte** | Layer cake |

| | |
|---|---|
| **Tranche** | Slice |
| **Tripes** | Tripe |
| **à la mode de Caen** | cooked in cider and Calvados with vegetables and herbs |
| **Truffe** | Truffle |
| **Truffé(e)** | With truffles |
| **Truite** | Trout |
| **au bleu** | poached |
| **aux amandes** | with butter and almonds |
| **Turbot** | Turbot |
| **Vacherin glacé** | Ice cream and meringue gateau |
| **Vanille** | Vanilla |
| **Vapeur, (cuit) à la vapeur** | Steamed, boiled |
| **Veau** | Veal |
| **Velouté** | Cream (soup) |
| **Vinaigre** | Vinegar |
| **Vinaigrette** | French dressing |
| **Volaille** | Poultry, chicken |
| **Waterzoi de poulet** | Chicken in wine and cream sauce with vegetables |
| **Yaourt** | Yoghurt (plain, eaten as part of cheese course) |

# SHOPPING

● In France, Belgium, Luxembourg and Switzerland, shop opening hours are fairly similar: from around 9 a.m. to somewhere between 6 and 7.30 p.m. (6 p.m. in Belgium, 6.30 p.m. in Switzerland – earlier on Saturdays). These hours apply to weekdays and Saturdays; shops are generally closed on Sundays, except for some food shops (especially bakers). Most shops in France (though not in Paris), most in Switzerland, and some in Belgium, close for an hour or two at midday. In France most shops (though again not in Paris, except for food shops and hairdressers) are closed on Mondays, all day or just for the morning. In Switzerland shops are often closed on Monday mornings.

Large stores may not close for lunch, and shops in large cities may open late one night a week. French hypermarkets generally stay open until 9 or 10 p.m. six days a week, but are closed on Monday mornings.

● Chemists (**pharmacie**) have a green cross sign outside. They sell mainly medicines, baby products and health foods. For toiletries and cosmetics go to a **parfumerie** or **droguerie**.

List of duty chemists that are open outside normal shop hours are displayed on the shop door or window.

● In France, cigarettes and tobacco are a State monopoly – you can buy them where you see the sign **Tabac** and/or a red symbol. Tobacconists also sell stamps.

● Post offices in the various countries are open all day Mondays to Fridays, and also Saturday mornings. Hours are: France, 8 a.m.–12, 2 p.m.–6.30 p.m.; Switzerland, 7.30 a.m.–12, 1.45 p.m.–6.30 p.m. (Saturday till 11 a.m.); Belgium, 9 a.m.–12, 2 p.m.–5 p.m.; Luxembourg, 8 a.m.–12, 2 p.m.–5 p.m.

Letterboxes are painted yellow in France, Switzerland and Luxembourg, and red in Belgium. There may be separate slots for mail within the country and abroad (**l'étranger**), or for letters (**lettres**) and postcards (**cartes postales**).

If you want to receive mail at a post office, have it addressed c/o **Poste Restante** at the town or village you're staying in.

● When buying food by weight in France, you can ask for so many kilos, or so many grams. For half a kilo, you can either say **cinq cents grammes** (500 grams) or **une livre** (a pound). 250 grams is **deux cent cinquante grammes** or **une demi-livre**.

● To ask for something in a shop, all you need do is name it and add 'please' – or just point and say 'some of this, please' or 'two of those, please'.

Before you go shopping, try to make a list of what you need – in French. If you're looking for clothes or shoes, work out what size to ask for and other things like colour, material and so on.

## You may see

| | |
|---|---|
| **Alimentation** | Groceries |
| **Antiquaire/Antiquités** | Antiques |
| **Appareils électriques/ ménagers** | Electrical/household appliances |
| **Articles de cuir** | Leather goods |
| **Articles de sport** | Sports goods |
| **Bijouterie** | Jeweller's |
| **Blanchisserie** | Laundry |
| **Boucherie** | Butcher's |
| **Boulangerie** | Baker's |
| **Bureau de poste** | Post office |
| **Cabines d'essayage** | Fitting rooms |
| **Caddy obligatoire** | Please take a trolley |
| **Caisse** | Cashier |
| **Cave** | Wine merchant |

| | |
|---|---|
| **Centre commercial** | Shopping centre |
| **Charcuterie** | Delicatessen |
| **Chaussures** | Shoes |
| **Coiffeur** | Hairdresser's |
| **Confiserie** | Confectioner's |
| **Diététique** | Health food shop |
| **Disquaire/Disques** | Records |
| **Droguerie** | Toiletries and household articles |
| **Entrée** | Entrance |
| **Entrée gratuite/libre** | Free admission (no obligation to buy) |
| **Épicerie** | Grocer's |
| **Épicerie fine** | Delicatessen |
| **Fermé** | Closed |
| **Fermeture hebdomadaire** | Weekly closing day |
| **Fruits et légumes** | Fruit and vegetables |
| **Horlogerie–Bijouterie** | Watchmaker's–Jeweller's |
| **Hypermarché** | Hypermarket |
| **Jouets** | Toys |
| **Journaux** | Newspapers |
| **Laiterie** | Dairy |
| **Lavanderie automatique** | Laundrette |
| **Librairie** | Bookshop |
| **Marchand de vin** | Wine merchant |
| **Marché** | Market |
| **Meubles** | Furniture |
| **Opticien** | Optician's |
| **Ouvert** | Open |
| **Papeterie** | Stationer's |
| **Parfumerie** | Drugstore/Perfumery |
| **Pâtisserie** | Cake shop |
| **Pharmacie** | Chemist's |
| **Pharmacie de service** | Duty chemist |
| **Poissonnerie** | Fishmonger's |
| **Postes (et Télécommunications) (P & T)** | Post office |

| | |
|---|---|
| **Prenez un panier s.v.p.** | Please take a basket |
| **Primeurs** | Greengrocer's |
| **Prix (réduit/spécial)** | (Reduced/Special) price |
| **PTT** | Post office |
| **Quincaillerie** | Ironmonger's/Hardware |
| **Soldes** | Sales/Reductions |
| **Sortie (de secours)** | (Emergency) exit |
| **Supermarché** | Supermarket |
| **Tabac** | Tobacconist's |
| **Teinturerie** | Dry-cleaner's |
| **Timbres** | Stamps |
| **Vêtements (enfants/ femmes/hommes)** | Clothes (children's/ women's/men's) |

## You may want to say

### General phrases

(*see also* Directions, *page 23;* Problems and complaints, *page 179*)

Where is the main shopping area?
**Où se trouve le centre commercial?**
*oo suh troov luh soñtr komersyal*

Where is the chemist's?
**Où se trouve la pharmacie?**
*oo suh troov la farmasee*

Is there a grocer's shop around here?
**Est-ce qu'il y a une épicerie par ici?**
*eskeelya ewn aypeesuhree par eesee*

Where can I buy batteries?
**Où est-ce que je peux acheter des piles?**
*oo eskuh juh puh ashtay day peel*

What time does the baker's open?
**À quelle heure ouvre la boulangerie?**
*a kel uhr oovr la booloñjuhree*

What time does the post office close?
**À quelle heure ferme le bureau de poste?**
*a kel uhr ferm luh bewroh duh post*

What time do you open in the morning?

**À quelle heure vous ouvrez le matin?**

_a kel uhr vooz oovray luh matañ_

What time do you close this evening?

**À quelle heure vous fermez ce soir?**

_a kel uhr voo fermay suh swar_

Do you have . . . ?

**Est-ce que vous avez . . . ?**

_eskuh vooz avay . . ._

Do you have stamps?

**Est-ce que vous avez des timbres?**

_eskuh vooz avay day tambr_

Do you have any wholemeal bread?

**Est-ce que vous avez du pain complet?**

_eskuh vooz avay dew pañ kawmplay_

How much is it?

**C'est combien?**

_say kawmbyañ_

How much does this cost?

**Combien ça coûte?**

_kawmbyañ sa koot_

I don't understand

**Je ne comprends pas**

_juh nuh kawmproñ pa_

Can you write it down, please?

**Pourriez-vous me l'écrire, s'il vous plaît?**

_pooree-ay voo muh laykreer seelvooplay_

It's too expensive

**C'est trop cher**

_say troh sher_

Have you got anything less expensive?

**Est-ce que vous auriez quelque chose de moins cher?**

_eskuh vooz ohree-ay kelkuh shohz duh mwañ sher_

I don't have enough money

**Je n'ai pas assez d'argent**

_juh nay paz asay darjoñ_

Can you keep it for me?

**Pourriez-vous me le mettre de côté?**

_pooree-ay voo muh luh metr duh kohtay_

I'm just looking

**Je regarde seulement**

_juh ruhgard suhlmoñ_

This one, please

**Ça, s'il vous plaît**

_sa seelvooplay_

That one, please

**Celui-là, s'il vous plaît**

_suhlweela seelvooplay_

Three of these, please
**Trois, s'il vous plaît** (*and point to what you want*)
*trwa seelvooplay*

Not that one – this one
**Celui-là, non – celui-ci**
*suhlweela nawñ – suhlweesee*

There's one in the window
**Il y en a une dans la vitrine**
*eelyona ewn doñ la veetreen*

That's fine
**Ça ira**
*sa eera*

That's all, thank you
**C'est tout, merci**
*say too mersee*

I'll take it
**Je vais le prendre**
*juh vay luh proñdr*

I'll think about it
**Je vais voir**
*juh vay vwar*

Do you have a bag, please?
**Est-ce que vous auriez un sac, s'il vous plaît?**
*eskuh vooz ohree-ay uñ sak seelvooplay*

Can you wrap it, please?
**Pourriez-vous me l'emballer, s'il vous plaît?**
*pooree-ay voo muh lombalay seelvooplay*

With plenty of paper
**Avec beaucoup de papier**
*avek bohkoo duh papyay*

I'm taking it to England
**Je l'emporte en Angleterre**
*juh lomport on oñgluhter*

It's a gift
**C'est pour un cadeau**
*say poor uñ kadoh*

Where do I/we pay?
**Où est-ce qu'on paie?**
*oo eskawñ pay*

Do you take credit cards?
**Vous acceptez les cartes de crédit?**
*vooz akseptay lay kart duh kraydee*

Do you take traveller's cheques?
**Vous acceptez les chèques de voyage?**
*vooz akseptay lay shek duh vwiyaj*

I'm sorry, I don't have any change
**Désolé(e), je n'ai pas de monnaie**
*dayzolay juh nay pa duh monay*

Can you give me a receipt please?
**Pourriez-vous me donner un reçu, s'il vous plaît?**
*pooree-ay voo muh donay uñ ruhsew seelvooplay*

## Buying food and drink

A kilo of . . .
**Un kilo de . . .**
*uñ keeloh duh . . .*

A kilo of cherries, please
**Un kilo de cerises, s'il vous plaît**
*uñ keeloh duh suhreez seelvooplay*

Two kilos of oranges, please
**Deux kilos d'oranges, s'il vous plaît**
*duh keeloh doroñj seelvooplay*

500 grams (half a kilo) of tomatoes, please
**Cinq cents grammes de tomates, s'il vous plaît**
*sañk soñ gram duh tomat seelvooplay*
or
**Une livre de . . .**
*ewn leevr duh . . .*

A hundred grams of . . .
**Cent grammes de . . .**
*soñ gram duh . . .*

A hundred grams of butter
**Cent grammes de beurre**
*soñ gram duh buhr*

Two hundred grams of sausage, please
**Deux cents grammes de saucisson, s'il vous plaît**
*duh soñ gram duh sohseesawñ seelvooplay*

Sliced
**En tranches**
*oñ troñsh*

A piece of cheese, please
**Un morceau de fromage, s'il vous plaît**
*uñ morsoh duh fromaj seelvooplay*

Five slices of ham, please
**Cinq tranches de jambon, s'il vous plaît**
*sañk troñsh duh jombawñ seelvooplay*

A loaf of bread, please (French stick)
**Une baguette, s'il vous plaît**
*ewn baget seelvooplay*

A bottle of water, please
**Une bouteille d'eau, s'il vous plaît**
*ewn bootay doh seelvooplay*

A litre of white wine, please
**Un litre de vin blanc, s'il vous plaît**
*uñ leetr duh vañ bloñ seelvooplay*

Half a litre of milk, please
**Un demi-litre de lait, s'il vous plaît**
*uñ duhmee leetr duh lay seelvooplay*

Two cans of peaches
**Deux boîtes de pêches**
*duh bwat duh pesh*

A bit of that, please
**Un peu de ça, s'il vous plaît**
*uñ puh duh sa seelvooplay*

A bit more
**Encore un peu**
*oñkor uñ puh*

A bit less
**Un peu moins**
*uñ puh mwañ*

What is this?
**Qu'est-ce que c'est que ça?**
*keskuh say kuh sa*

What is there in this?
**Qu'est-ce qu'il y a dedans?**
*keskeelya duhdoñ*

Can I try it?
**Est-ce que je peux l'essayer?**
*eskuh juh puh lesayay*

## At the chemist's

Some aspirins, please
**De l'aspirine, s'il vous plaît**
*duh laspeereen seelvooplay*

Some plasters, please
**Du sparadrap, s'il vous plaît**
*dew sparadra seelvooplay*

I want something for . . .
**Je voudrais quelque chose
contre . . .**
*juh voodray kelkuh shohz
kawñtr . . .*

I want something for
diarrhoea
**Je voudrais quelque chose
contre la diarrhée**
*juh voodray kelkuh shohz
kawñtr la dee-aray*

I want something for insect
bites
**Je voudrais quelque chose
contre les piqûres
d'insectes**
*juh voodray kelkuh shohz
kawñtr lay peekewr dañsekt*

I want something for period
pains
**Je voudrais quelque chose
contre les douleurs de
règles**
*juh voodray kelkuh shohz
kawñtr lay dooluhr duh regl*

## Buying clothes and shoes

I want a skirt/a shirt
**Je voudrais une jupe/une chemise**
*juh voodray ewn jewp/ewn shuhmeez*

I want a pair of sandals
**Je voudrais une paire de sandales**
*juh voodray ewn per duh soñdal*

I take a (size) 40
**Je porte un quarante**
*juh port uñ karoñt*

Could you measure me?
**Pourriez-vous prendre mes mesures?**
*pooree-ay voo proñdr may muhzewr*

Can I try it on?
**Est-ce que je peux l'essayer?**
*eskuh juh puh lesayay*

Is there a mirror?
**Est-ce qu'il y a un miroir?**
*eskeelya uñ meerwar*

I like it/them
**Ça me plaît**
*sa muh play*

I don't like it/them
**Ça ne me plaît pas**
*sa nuh muh play pa*

I don't like the colour
**Je n'aime pas la couleur**
*juh nem pa la kooluhr*

Do you have it in another colour?
**Est-ce que vous avez ça dans une autre couleur?**
*eskuh vooz avay sa doñz ewn ohtr kooluhr*

It's/They're too big
**C'est trop grand**
*say trop groñ*

It's/They're too small
**C'est trop petit**
*say troh puhtee*

Do you have a smaller size? (clothing)
**Est-ce que vous avez la taille au-dessous?**
*eskuh vooz avay la tiy ohduhsoo*

Do you have a bigger size? (shoes)
**Est-ce que vous avez la pointure au-dessus?**
*eskuh vooz avay la pwañtewr ohdesew*

## Miscellaneous

Five stamps for England,
please
**Cinq timbres pour
l'Angleterre, s'il vous plaît**
*sañk tambr poor loñgluhter
seelvooplay*

For postcards
**Pour cartes postales**
*poor kart postal*

For letters
**Pour lettres**
*poor letr*

Three postcards, please
**Trois cartes postales, s'il
vous plaît**
*trwa kart postal seelvooplay*

Matches, please
**Des allumettes, s'il vous plaît**
*dayz alewmet seelvooplay*

A film like this, please
**Une pellicule comme ça,
s'il vous plaît**
*ewn pelikewl kom sa
seelvooplay*

For this camera
**Pour cet appareil**
*poor set aparay*

Do you have any English
newspapers?
**Est-ce que vous avez des
journaux anglais?**
*eskuh vooz avay day joornoh
oñglay*

## You may hear

**Est-ce que je peux vous être utile?**
*eskuh juh puh vooz etr ewteel*
May I help you?

**Qu'est-ce que vous désirez?**
*keskuh voo dayzeeray*
What would you like?

**Combien voulez-vous?**
*kawmbyañ voolay voo*
How much/many would you like?

**Ça vous va comme ça?**
*sa voo va kom sa*
Is that all right?

**Je regrette, notre stock est épuisé**
*juh ruhgret notr stok et aypweezay*
I'm sorry, we're sold out

**Je regrette, on est fermé**
*juh ruhgret awn e fermay*
I'm sorry, we're closed

**Vous voulez que je l'emballe?**
*voo voolay kuh juh lombal*
Shall I wrap it for you?

**Veuillez passer à la caisse, s'il vous plaît**
*vuhyay pasay a la kes seelvooplay*
Please go to the cashier

**Vous avez de la monnaie?**
*vooz avay duh la monay*
Do you have any change?

**Il vous faut une ordonnance**
*eel voo foh ewn ordonoñs*
You need a prescription

**Quelle taille portez-vous?**
*kel tiy portay voo*
What size are you? (*clothing*)

**Quelle pointure portez-vous?**
*kel pwañtewr portay voo*
What size are you? (*shoes*)

**Pour carte postale ou lettre?**
*poor kart postal oo letr*
For postcard or letter?

**Quel genre de . . . ?**
*kel joñr duh . . .*
What sort of . . . ?

**Quel genre d'appareil avez-vous?**
*kel joñr daparay avay voo*
What sort of camera do you have?

**Quel genre de pellicule voulez-vous?**
*kel joñr duh peleekewl voolay voo*
What sort of film do you want?

142

# BUSINESS TRIPS

● You'll probably be doing business with the help of interpreters or in a language everyone speaks, but you may need a few French phrases to cope at a company's reception desk.

● When you arrive for an appointment, all you need do is say who you've come to see and give your name or hand over your business card. However, if you're not expected you may need to make an appointment or leave a message.

## You may see

| | |
|---|---|
| Ascenseur | Lift |
| Cie. = Compagnie | Company |
| Entrée | Entrance |
| Entrée interdite | No entry |
| Escalier | Stairs |
| 1er étage | 1st floor |
| 2ème étage | 2nd floor |
| Issue de secours | Emergency exit |
| Interdit aux personnes non autorisées | No entry to unauthorised persons |
| Réception | Reception |
| Rez-de-chaussée | Ground floor |
| Sortie (de secours) | (Emergency) exit |
| SA = Société Anonyme | Limited company/PLC |

## You may want to say

(see also Days, months, dates, *page 198*, Time, *page 201*)

Mr Dupont, please
**Monsieur Dupont, s'il vous plaît**
*muhsyuh dewpawñ seelvooplay*

Mrs Lebrun, please
**Madame Lebrun, s'il vous plaît**
*madam luhbruñ seelvooplay*

Miss Legros, please
**Mademoiselle Legros, s'il vous plaît**
*madmwazel luhgroh seelvooplay*

The manager, please
**Le directeur, s'il vous plaît**
*luh deerektuhr seelvooplay*

My name is . . .
**Je m'appelle . . .**
*juh mapel . . .*

I have an appointment with Mr Pierre Dupont
**J'ai rendez-vous avec Monsieur Pierre Dupont**
*jay roñdayvoo avek muhsyuh pyer dewpawñ*

I don't have an appointment
**Je n'ai pas pris rendez-vous**
*juh nay pa pree roñdayvoo*

I'd like to make an appointment with Miss Legros
**Je voudrais prendre rendez-vous avec Mademoiselle Legros**
*juh voodray proñdr roñdayvoo avek madmwazel luhgroh*

I am free this afternoon at three o'clock
**Je suis libre cet après-midi à trois heures**
*juh swee leebr set apremeedee a trwaz uhr*

I'd like to talk to the export manager
**Je voudrais parler avec le directeur d'exportations**
*juh voodray parlay avek luh deerektuhr dexportasyawñ*

What is his name?
**Comment s'appelle-t-il?**
*komoñ sapelteel*

What is her name?
**Comment s'appelle-t-elle?**
*komoñ sapeltel*

When will he be back?
**Quand est-ce qu'il doit revenir?**
*koñt eskeel dwa ruhvuhneer*

When will she be back?
**Quand est-ce qu'elle doit revenir?**
*koñt eskel dwa ruhvuhneer*

Can I leave a message?
**Est-ce que je peux laisser un message?**
*eskuh juh puh lesay uñ mesaj*

Can you ask him/her to call me?
**Pourriez-vous lui demander de m'appeler?**
*pooree-ay voo lwee duhmoñday duh mapuhlay*

My telephone number is . . .
**Mon numéro de téléphone est . . .**
*mawñ newmayroh duh taylayfon e . . .*

I am staying at the Hôtel du Commerce
**Je suis à l'Hôtel du Commerce**
*juh sweez a lohtel dew komers*

Where is his/her office?
**Où se trouve son bureau?**
*oo suh troov sawñ bewroh*

I am here for the exhibition
**Je suis ici pour l'exposition**
*juh sweez eesee poor lexpozeesyawñ*

I am here for the trade fair
**Je suis ici pour la foire**
*juh sweez eesee poor la fwar*

I am attending the conference
**Je prends part au congrès**
*juh proñ par oh kawñgray*

I have to make a phone call (to Britain)
**Il faut que je téléphone (en Grande Bretagne)**
*eel foh kuh juh taylayfon (oñ groñd bruhtanyuh)*

I have to send a telex
**Il faut que j'envoie un télex**
*eel foh kuh juh joñvwa uñ taylex*

I have to send this by fax
**Il faut que j'envoie ça par télécopie**
*eel foh kuh juh joñvwa sa par taylaykopee*

I want to send this by post/ by courier
**Je voudrais envoyer ça par la poste/par messager**
*juh voodray oñvwiyay sa par la post/par mesajay*

I need someone to type a letter for me
**J'aurais besoin que quelqu'un me tape cette lettre**
*johray buhzwañ kuh kelkuñ muh tap set letr*

I need a photocopy (of this)
**J'aurais besoin d'une photocopie (de ça)**
*johray buhzwañ dewn fohtokopee (duh sa)*

I need an interpreter
**J'aurais besoin d'un interprète**
*johray buhzwañ dun añterpret*

## You may hear

**Votre nom, s'il vous plaît?**
*votr nawñ seelvooplay*
Your name, please?

**Comment vous appelez-vous?**
*komoñ vooz apuhlay voo*
What is your name?

**Le nom de votre compagnie,
s'il vous plaît?**
*luh nawñ duh votr
kawmpanyee seelvooplay*
The name of your company,
please?

**Vous avez pris rendez-vous?**
*vooz avay pree roñdayvoo*
Do you have an appointment?

**Vous avez une carte?**
*vooz avay ewn kart*
Do you have a card?

**Est-ce qu'il/qu'elle vous attend?**
*eskeel/eskel vooz atoñ*
Is he/she expecting you?

**(Attendez) un instant, s'il
vous plaît**
*(atoñday) un añstoñ seelvooplay*
(Wait) one moment, please

**Je vais lui dire que vous êtes ici**
*juh vay lwee deer kuh vooz et
eesee*
I'll tell him/her you're here

**Il/Elle arrive**
*eel/el areev*
He/She is just coming

**Asseyez-vous, s'il vous plaît**
*asayay voo seelvooplay*
Please sit down

**Voulez-vous vous asseoir, s'il
vous plaît**
*voolayvoo vooz aswar seelvooplay*
Would you sit down, please

**Entrez, s'il vous plaît**
*oñtray seelvooplay*
Go in, please

**Par ici, s'il vous plaît**
*par eesee seelvooplay*
This way, please

**Monsieur Dupont n'est pas là**
*muhsyuh dewpawñ ne pa la*
Mr Dupont is not in

**Mademoiselle Legros est sortie**
*madmwazel luhgroh e sortee*
Miss Legros is out

**Madame Lebrun sera de
retour à onze heures**
*madam luhbruñ suhra duh
ruhtoor a awñz uhr*
Mrs Lebrun will be back at
eleven o'clock

**Dans une demi-heure/
une heure**
*doñz ewn duhmee-uhr/ewn uhr*
In half an hour/an hour

**Prenez l'ascenseur jusqu'au
troisième étage**
*pruhnay lasoñsuhr jewskoh
trwazyem aytaj*
Take the lift to the third floor

**Continuez dans le couloir**
*kawñteenew-ay doñ luh
koolwar*
Go along the corridor

**C'est la deuxième/troisième
porte**
*say la duhzyem/trwazyem port*
It's the second/third door

**À gauche/À droite**
*a gohsh/a drwat*
On the left/On the right

**C'est le bureau numéro trois
cent vingt**
*say luh bewroh newmayroh
trwa soñ vañ*
It's room number 320

**Entrez!**
*oñtray*
Come in!

147

# SIGHTSEEING

● You can get information about sights worth seeing from national Tourist Offices (addresses, page 214) or local ones (see At the Tourist Office, page 76).

● Sightseeing tours by coach and on foot, with English-speaking guides, are available in many cities and tourist areas.

● Most museums in France, and some in other countries, are closed on Mondays – though French *national* museums are closed on Tuesdays.

● In Paris you can get a museum card (**Carte Musées**) which gives free admission over one, three or five days to most museums and monuments in the Paris area. You can buy the card at the places covered or at underground stations.

## You may see

| | |
|---|---|
| Défense de marcher sur le gazon | Keep off the grass |
| Défense de toucher | Do not touch |
| Entrée gratuite/libre | Free admission |
| Entrée interdite | No entry |
| Fermé (pour travaux) | Closed (for restoration) |
| Horaire de visites | Visiting hours |
| Interdiction de prendre des photos | No photography |
| Ouvert | Open |
| Privé | Private |
| Visites guidées | Guided tours |

## You may want to say

(*see* At the Tourist Office, *page 76, for asking for information, brochures, etc.*)

## Opening times

(*see* Time, *page 201*)

When is the museum open?
**Quelles sont les heures d'ouverture du musée?**
*kel sawñ layz uhr doovertewr dew mewzay*

What time does the castle open?
**À quelle heure ouvre le château?**
*a kel uhr oovr luh shatoh*

What time does the palace close?
**À quelle heure ferme le palais?**
*a kel uhr ferm luh palay*

Is it open on Sundays?
**Est-ce qu'il est ouvert le dimanche?**
*eskeel et oover luh deemoñsh*

Can I/we visit the monastery?
**Est-ce qu'on peut visiter le monastère?**
*eskawñ puh veezeetay luh monaster*

Is it open to the public?
**Est-ce qu'il est ouvert au public?**
*eskeel et oover oh pewbleek*

## Visiting places

One/Two, please
**Un/Deux, s'il vous plaît**
*uñ/duh seelvooplay*

Two adults and one child
**Deux adultes et un enfant**
*duhz adewlt ay un oñfoñ*

Are there reductions for
children?
**Est-ce qu'il y a des
réductions pour les enfants?**
*eskeelya day raydewksyawñ
poor layz oñfoñ*

For students
**Pour les étudiants**
*poor layz aytewdyoñ*

For pensioners
**Pour les retraités**
*poor lay ruhtretay*

For the disabled
**Pour les handicapés**
*poor layz oñdeekapay*

For groups
**Pour les groupes**
*poor lay groop*

A museum card for three
days, please
**Une Carte Musées pour trois
jours, s'il vous plaît**
*ewn kart mewzay poor trwa
joor seelvooplay*

Are there guided tours (in
English)?
**Est-ce qu'il y a des visites
guidées (en anglais)?**
*eskeelya day veezeet geeday
(on oñglay)*

Can I/we take photos?
**Est-ce qu'on peut prendre
des photos?**
*eskawñ puh proñdr day fohtoh*

Who is that painting by?
**De qui est ce tableau?**
*duh kee e suh tabloh*

When was it built?
**Quand est-ce que ç'a été
construit?**
*koñt eskuh sa aytay
kawñstrwee*

In what year? (*see* Days,
months, dates, *page 198*)
**En quelle année?**
*oñ kel anay*

What time is mass/the
service?
**À quelle heure est la messe/
l'office?**
*a kel uhr e la mess/lofees*

Is there a priest who speaks
English?
**Est-ce qu'il y a un prêtre qui
parle l'anglais?**
*eskeelya uñ pretr kee parl
loñglay*

What is this flower called?
**Comment s'appelle cette fleur?**
*komoñ sapel set fluhr*

What is that bird called?
**Comment s'appelle cet oiseau?**
*komoñ sapel set wazoh*

## Sightseeing excursions

What excursions are there?
**Qu'est qu'il y a comme excursions?**
*keskeelya kom exkewrsyawñ*

Are there any excursions to Thoiry?
**Est-ce qu'il y a des excursions à Thoiry?**
*eskeelya dayz exkewrsyawñ a twary*

What time does it leave?
**À quelle heure est-ce qu'on part?**
*a kel uhr eskawñ par*

How long does the excursion last?
**Combien de temps dure l'excursion?**
*kawmbyañ duh toñ dewr lexkewrsyawñ*

Can you take a photo of me/us, please?
**Pourriez-vous prendre une photo de moi/nous, s'il vous plaît?**
*pooree-ay voo proñdr ewn fohtoh duh mwa/noo seelvooplay*

What time does it get back?
**À quelle heure est le retour?**
*a kel uhr e luh ruhtoor*

Where does it leave from?
**D'où est-ce qu'on part?**
*doo eskawñ par*

Does the guide speak English?
**Est-ce que le guide parle l'anglais?**
*eskuh luh geed parl loñglay*

How much is it?
**C'est combien?**
*say kawmbyañ*

## You may hear

**Le musée est ouvert tous les jours sauf le lundi**
*luh mewzay et oover too lay joor sohf luh luñdee*
The museum is open every day except Mondays

**Il est fermé le dimanche**
*eel e fermay luh deemañsh*
It is closed on Sundays

**Le château a été construit au quatorzième siècle**
*luh shatoh a aytay kawñstrwee oh katorzyem syekl*
The castle was built in the fourteenth century

**Ce tableau est de Delacroix**
*suh tabloh e duh duhlakrwa*
That painting is by Delacroix

**Il y a des excursions le mardi et le jeudi**
*eelya dayz exkewrsyawñ luh mardee ay luh juhdee*
There are excursions on Tuesdays and Thursdays

**Le car part à dix heures de la place du marché**
*luh kar par a deez uhr duh la plas dew marshay*
The coach leaves at ten o'clock from the market square

# ENTERTAINMENTS

● Films are categorised according to age. Some are labelled as unsuitable for under-13s, some for under-18s.

Many American and British films are shown, sometimes sub-titled (**sous-titré**) but mostly dubbed (**doublé**). Unless a foreign film is labelled **VO (version originale)** it is dubbed.

● It is usual to give a small tip to cinema and theatre usherettes in France and Belgium.

● A popular attraction during the summer in France are sound-and-light shows (**son et lumière**) held at historic buildings – you can get information from tourist offices.

● Popular spectator sports include football, horse racing, cycling and tennis. Sports fixtures generally take place on Sundays.

## You may see

| | |
|---|---|
| **Balcon** | Circle |
| **Champ de courses** | Racecourse |
| **Cinéma** | Cinema |
| **Cirque** | Circus |
| **Complet** | Sold out |
| **Dancing** | Dance hall |
| **Doublé** | Dubbed |
| **Hippodrome** | Racecourse |
| **Interdit aux moins de 13/18 ans** | Under-13s/18s not allowed |
| **Les spectateurs ne sont pas admis après le début de la séance/représentation** | No entry once the performance has begun |
| **Loges** | Boxes |

| | |
|---|---|
| **Matinée** | Matinee |
| **Opéra** | Opera house |
| **Orchestre** | Stalls |
| **Permanent** | Continuous screening |
| **Porte** | Door |
| **Rang** | Row, tier |
| **Réservations** | Reservations |
| **Salle de concerts** | Concert hall |
| **Sans entracte** | No interval |
| **Séances à . . .** | Separate screenings at . . . |
| **Soirée** | Evening performance |
| **Son et lumière** | Sound-and-light show |
| **Sous-titré** | Subtitled |
| **Stade** | Stadium |
| **Théâtre** | Theatre |
| **Tribune** | Stand, grandstand |
| **Vestiaire** | Cloakroom |
| **VF = version française** | French version, i.e. dubbed in French |
| **VO = version originale** | Original version, i.e. in the original language |

## You may want to say

### What's on

(*see* Time, *page 201*)

What is there to do in the evenings?
**Qu'est-ce qu'il y a à faire le soir?**
*keskeelya a fer luh swar*

Is there a disco around here?
**Est-ce qu'il y a une discothèque par ici?**
*eskeelya ewn deeskohtek par eesee*

Is there any entertainment for children?
**Est-ce qu'il y a des divertissements pour les enfants?**
*eskeelya day deeverteesmoñ poor layz oñfoñ*

What's on tonight?
**Qu'est-ce qu'on joue ce soir?**
*keskawñ joo suh swar*

What's on tomorrow?
**Qu'est-ce qu'on joue demain?**
*keskawñ joo demañ*

At the cinema
**Au cinéma**
*oh seenayma*

At the theatre
**Au théâtre**
*oh tay-atr*

Who is playing? (*music*)
**Qui joue?**
*kee joo*

Who is singing?
**Qui chante?**
*kee shoñt*

Who is dancing?
**Qui danse?**
*kee doñs*

Is the film dubbed or subtitled?
**Est-ce que le film est doublé ou sous-titré?**
*eskuh luh feelm e dooblay oo sooteetray*

Is there a floor show?
**Est-ce qu'il y a un spectacle de cabaret?**
*eskeelya uñ spektakl duh kabaray*

Is there a sound-and-light show?
**Est-ce qu'il y a un son et lumière?**
*eskeelya uñ sawñ ay lewmyer*

Is there a football match next Sunday?
**Est-ce qu'il y a un match de football dimanche prochain?**
*eskeelya uñ mach duh footbol deemoñsh proshañ*

Who are the teams?
**Quelles sont les équipes?**
*kel sawñ lays aykeep*

What time does the show start?
**À quelle heure commence le spectacle?**
*a kel uhr komoñs luh spektakl*

What time does the concert start?
**À quelle heure commence le concert?**
*a kel uhr komoñs luh kawñser*

How long does the performance last?
**Combien de temps dure la représentation?**
*kawmbyañ duh toñ dewr la ruhprayszoñtasyawñ*

When does it end?
**À quelle heure est-ce qu'il se termine?**
*a kel uhr eskeel suh termeen*

## Tickets

Where can I/we buy tickets?
**Où est-ce qu'on peut acheter des billets?**
*oo eskawñ puh ashtay day beeyay*

Can you get me tickets for the football match?
**Pourriez-vous m'acheter des billets pour le match de football?**
*pooree-ay voo mashtay day beeyay poor le mach duh footbol*

For the theatre
**Pour le théâtre**
*poor luh tay-atr*

Two, please
**Deux, s'il vous plaît**
*duh seelvooplay*

Two for tonight, please
**Deux pour ce soir, s'il vous plaît**
*duh poor se swar seelvooplay*

Two for the eight o'clock screening, please
**Deux pour la séance de huit heures, s'il vous plaît**
*duh poor la sayoñs duh weet uhr seelvooplay*

Are there any seats left for Saturday?
**Est-ce qu'il y a des places pour samedi?**
*eskeelya day plas poor samdee*

I want to book a box for four people
**Je voudrais réserver une loge pour quatre personnes**
*juh voodray rayzervay ewn loj poor katr person*

I want to book two seats
**Je voudrais réserver deux places**
*juh voodray rayzervay duh plas*

For Friday
**Pour vendredi**
*poor voñdruhdee*

In the stalls
**À l'orchestre**
*a lorkestr*

In the circle
**Au balcon**
*oh balkawñ*

How much are the seats?
**Combien coûtent les places?**
*kawmbyañ koot lay plas*

Do you have anything less expensive?
**Est-ce que vous avez quelque chose de moins cher?**
*eskuh vooz avay kelkuh shohz duh mwañ sher*

That's fine
**Ça ira**
*sa eera*

## At the show/game

Where is this, please?
(*showing your ticket*)
**Où est-ce que c'est, s'il vous plaît?**
*oo eskuh say seelvooplay*

Where is the cloakroom?
**Où se trouve le vestiaire?**
*oo suh troov luh vestyer*

Where is the bar?
**Où se trouve le bar?**
*oo suh troov luh bar*

Where are the toilets?
**Où se trouvent les toilettes?**
*oo suh troov lay twalet*

A programme, please
**Un programme, s'il vous plaît**
*uñ program seelvooplay*

Where can I/we get a programme?
**Où est-ce que je peux trouver un programme?**
*oo eskuh juh puh troovay uñ program*

Is there an interval?
**Est-ce qu'il y a un entracte?**
*eskeelya un oñtrakt*

## You may hear

**Vous pourriez acheter les billets ici à l'hôtel**
*voo pooree-ay ashtay lay beeyay eesee a lohtel*
You can get tickets here in the hotel

**Au stade**
*oh stad*
At the stadium

**Ça commence à sept heures**
*sa komoñs a set uhr*
It begins at seven o'clock

**Ça dure deux heures et quart**
*sa dewr duhz uhr ay kar*
It lasts two and a quarter hours

**Ça termine à neuf heures et demie**
*sa termeen a nuhv uhr ay duhmee*
It ends at half past nine

**Il y a un entracte d'un quart d'heure**
*eelya un oñtrakt duñ kar duhr*
There is a fifteen-minute interval

**Pour quand les voulez-vous?**
*poor koñ lay voolay voo*
When would you like them for?

**À l'orchestre, au balcon?**
*a lorkestr, oh balkawñ*
In the stalls, in the circle?

**Il y en a deux ici, à l'orchestre**
*eelyona duh eesee a lorkestr*
There are two here, in the stalls (*indicating on seating plan*)

**Je regrette, c'est complet**
*juh ruhgret say kawmplay*
I'm sorry, we're sold out

**Votre billet/Vos billets, s'il vous plaît?**
*votr beeyay/voh beeyay seelvooplay*
Your ticket(s), please?

159

# SPORTS AND ACTIVITIES

● There are plenty of opportunities for outdoor activities such as tennis, golf, watersports, fishing (sea, river or lake), horse riding, walking and climbing, and winter sports. Contact tourist offices or travel agencies for information about locations.

You will need a permit for fishing or hunting

● At the beach, a red flag flying means it is dangerous to swim. An orange flag means swimming is not recommended, and a green flag means it is safe.

## You may see

| | |
|---|---|
| **Baignade interdite** | No swimming |
| **Centre sportif** | Sports centre |
| **Chasse gardée** | Hunting reserve |
| **Court de tennis** | Tennis court |
| **Danger d'avalanches** | Danger of avalanches |
| **École de ski** | Ski school |
| **Équitation** | Horse-riding |
| **Location de skis** | Ski hire |
| **Pêche interdite** | No fishing |
| **Pétanque** | French bowls |
| **Piscine** | Swimming pool |
| **Piste** | Course, track; ski-run |
| **Plage** | Beach |
| **Plage privée** | Private beach |
| **Planche à voile** | Windsurfing/sailboarding |
| **Plongeoir** | Diving board |
| **Randonnées** | Walks, rambles |
| **Remonte-pente** | Ski lift |
| **Ski de fond** | Cross-country skiing |

| | |
|---|---|
| **Ski de piste** | Downhill skiing |
| **Ski nautique** | Water-skiing |
| **Téléphérique** | Cable car |
| **Télésiège** | Chair lift |
| **Téléski** | Ski lift |
| **Terrain de football** | Football pitch |
| **Terrain de golf** | Golf course |

## You may want to say

### General phrases

Can I/we . . . ?
**Est-ce qu'on peut . . . ?**
*eskawñ puh . . .*

Can I/we go fishing?
**Est-ce qu'on peut pêcher?**
*eskawñ puh peshay*

Can I/we go riding?
**Est-ce qu'on peut monter à cheval?**
*eskawñ puh mawñtay a shuhval*

Is it possible (allowed) to . . . ?
**Est-ce qu'on a le droit de . . . ?**
*eskawn a luh drwa duh . . .*

Is it possible to fish here?
**Est-ce qu'on a le droit de pêcher ici?**
*eskawn a luh drwa duh peshay eesee*

Where can I/we . . . ?
**Où est-ce qu'on peut . . . ?**
*oo eskawñ puh . . .*

Where can I/we play tennis?
**Où est-ce qu'on peut jouer au tennis?**
*oo eskawñ puh jooay oh tenees*

Where can I/we go climbing?
**Où est-ce qu'on peut faire de l'alpinisme?**
*oo eskawñ puh fer duh lalpeeneezmuh*

I don't know how to . . .
**Je ne sais pas . . .**
*juh nuh say pa . . .*

I don't know how to ski
**Je ne sais pas skier**
*juh nuh say pa skee-ay*

Can I have lessons?
**Est-ce que je peux prendre des cours?**
*eskuh juh puh proñdr day koor*

I'm a beginner
**Je suis débutant** (*male*)/
**débutante** (*female*)
*juh swee daybewtoñ/daybewtoñt*

I'm quite experienced
**Je suis assez expert** (*male*)/
**experte** (*female*)
*juh sweez asay exper/expert*

How much is it per hour?
**C'est combien de l'heure?**
*say kawmbyañ duh luhr*

How much is it for the
whole day?
**C'est combien pour la journée?**
*say kawmbyañ poor la joornay*

How much is it per game?
**C'est combien la partie?**
*say kawmbyañ la partee*

Is there a reduction for
children?
**Est-ce qu'il y a une réduction
pour les enfants?**
*eskeelya ewn raydewksyawñ
poor layz oñfoñ*

Can I/we hire equipment?
**Est-ce qu'on peut louer
l'équipement?**
*eskawñ puh looay laykeepmoñ*

Can I/we hire bikes?
**Est-ce qu'on peut louer des
vélos?**
*eskawñ puh looay day vayloh*

Can I/we hire rackets?
**Est-ce qu'on peut louer des
raquettes?**
*eskawñ puh looay day raket*

Can I/we hire clubs?
**Est-ce qu'on peut louer des
clubs de golf?**
*eskawñ puh looay day klewb
duh golf*

Do I need a licence?
**Est-ce que j'ai besoin d'un
permis?**
*eskuh jay buhzwañ duñ permee*

Where can I get a permit?
**Où est-ce que je peux obtenir
un permis?**
*oo eskuh juh puh obtuhneer
uñ permee*

Is it necessary to be a member?
**Est-ce qu'il faut être membre?**
*eskeel foh etr mombr*

## Beach and pool

Can I/we swim here?
**Est-ce qu'on peut nager ici?**
*eskawñ puh najay eesee*

Can I/we swim in the river?
**Est-ce qu'on peut nager dans la rivière?**
*eskawñ puh najay doñ la reevyer*

Is it dangerous?
**Est-ce que c'est dangereux?**
*eskuh say doñjuhruh*

Is it safe for children?
**Est-ce que c'est sans danger pour les enfants?**
*eskuh say soñ doñjay poor layz oñfoñ*

When is high tide?
**À quelle heure est la marée haute?**
*a kel uhr e la maray oht*

## Skiing

What is the snow like?
**Comment est la neige?**
*komoñ e la nej*

Is there a ski-run for beginners?
**Est-ce qu'il y a une piste pour débutants?**
*eskeelya ewn peest poor daybewtoñ*

Is the ski-run wide?
**Est-ce que la piste est large?**
*eskuh la peest e larj*

Is it steep?
**Est-ce que c'est raide?**
*eskuh say red*

Where is the ski-lift?
**Où se trouve le téléski?**
*oo suh troov luh taylayskee*

How much is the lift pass?
**C'est combien le forfait?**
*say kawmbyañ luh forfay*

Per day
**Par jour**
*par joor*

Per week
**Par semaine**
*par suhmen*

What time is the last ascent?
**À quelle heure est la dernière montée?**
*a kel uhr e la dernyer mawñtay*

## You may hear

**Est-ce que vous êtes débutant/débutante?**
*eskuh vooz et daybewtoñ/ daybewtoñt*
Are you a beginner?

**Est-ce que vous savez skier?**
*eskuh voo savay skee-ay*
Do you know how to ski?

**Est-ce que vous savez faire de la planche à voile?**
*eskuh voo savay fer duh la ploñsh a vwal*
Do you know how to windsurf?

**C'est cent francs de l'heure**
*say soñ froñ duh luhr*
It's 100 francs per hour

**Il faut payer cinquante francs d'arrhes**
*eel foh payay sañkoñt froñ dar*
You have to pay a deposit of 50 francs

**Je regrette, c'est complet**
*juh ruhgret say kawmplay*
I'm sorry, we're booked up

**Quelle taille portez-vous?** (*clothing*)
*kel tiy portay voo*
What size are you?

**Quelle pointure portez-vous?** (*shoes*)
*kel pwañtewr portay voo*
What size are you?

**Il faut une photo**
*eel foh ewn fohtoh*
You need a photo

**La neige est dure/gelée**
*la nej e dewr/juhlay*
The snow is heavy/icy

**La neige est molle**
*la nej e mol*
The snow is soft

**Il n'y a pas beaucoup de neige**
*eelnya pa bohkoo duh nej*
There isn't much snow

164

# HEALTH

## Medical details - to show to a doctor

| (*Tick where appropriate, or fill in details*) | Self **Moi** | Other members of family/party | | |
|---|---|---|---|---|
| Blood group **Groupe sanguin** | | | | |
| Asthmatic **Asthmatique** | | | | |
| Blind **Aveugle** | | | | |
| Deaf **Sourd(e)** | | | | |
| Diabetic **Diabétique** | | | | |
| Epileptic **Épileptique** | | | | |
| Handicapped **Handicapé(e)** | | | | |
| Heart condition **Cardiaque** | | | | |
| High blood pressure **Tension** | | | | |
| Pregnant **Enceinte** | | | | |

| Allergic to: **Allergique à:** | | | | |
|---|---|---|---|---|
| Antibiotics **Antibiotiques** | | | | |
| Penicillin **Pénicilline** | | | | |
| Cortisone **Cortisone** | | | | |

Medicines **Médicaments**

Self **Moi** _____

Others **Autres** _____

_____

_____

● Your local Department of Health office can provide information about medical care abroad. Within the EC you can obtain the local equivalent of NHS treatment by producing the required form. You will probably have to pay first and reclaim the payment when you return to Britain. Switzerland is not part of the EC and medical treatment has to be paid for, so you would be well advised to arrange medical insurance.

● You can get first aid and advice from chemists, without charge.

● If you need to call an ambulance, the emergency numbers are:
France **18**
Belgium **100**
Switzerland **144**
Luxembourg **012**
(*see* Emergencies, *page 292*)

● To indicate where a pain is, you can simply point and say 'it hurts here' (**j'ai mal là**). Otherwise, look up the French for the appropriate part of the body (page 177).

## You may see

| | |
|---|---|
| **Agiter avant l'emploi** | Shake before use |
| **Cabinet (de consultation)** | Surgery |
| **Clinique** | Clinic, hospital |
| **Dentiste** | Dentist |
| **Docteur** | Doctor |
| **Hôpital** | Hospital |
| **Horaire des consultations** | Surgery hours |
| **Médecin** | Doctor |
| **Ne pas avaler** | Do not swallow |
| **Poison** | Poison |
| **Poste de secours** | First aid post |
| **Pour usage externe** | For external use |
| **Service de consultation externe** | Outpatients |
| **Service d'urgences** | Emergencies/Casualty department |

## You may want to say

### At the doctor's

I want to see a doctor
**Je voudrais voir un médecin**
*juh voodray vwar uñ maydsañ*

Please call a doctor
**Appelez-moi un médecin, s'il
vous plaît**
*apuhlay mwa uñ maydsañ
seelvooplay*

Quickly
**Vite**
*veet*

It's urgent
**C'est urgent**
*set ewrjoñ*

Is there someone who
speaks English?
**Est-ce qu'il y a quelqu'un qui
parle l'anglais?**
*eskeelya kelkuñ kee parl loñglay*

Can I make an appointment?
**Est-ce que je peux prendre
un rendez-vous?**
*eskuh juh puh proñdr uñ
roñdayvoo*

It's my husband
**C'est mon mari**
*say mawñ maree*

It's my wife
**C'est ma femme**
*say ma fam*

It's my friend
**C'est mon ami(e)**
*say mawn amee*

It's my son
**C'est mon fils**
*say mawñ fees*

It's my daughter
**C'est ma fille**
*say ma feey*

How much is it going to cost?
**Combien ça va coûter?**
*kawmbyañ sa va kootay*

## Your symptoms

I don't feel well
**Je ne me sens pas bien**
*juh nuh muh soñ pa byañ*

It hurts here
**J'ai mal là**
*jay mal la*

My . . . hurt(s)
**J'ai mal à la/au/aux . . .**
*jay mal a la/oh/oh . . .*

My head hurts
**J'ai mal à la tête**
*jay mal a la tet*

My stomach hurts
**J'ai mal à l'estomac**
*jay mal a lestoma*

My back hurts
**J'ai mal au dos**
*jay mal oh doh*

My eyes hurt
**J'ai mal aux yeux**
*jai mal ohz yuh*

I have a sore throat
**J'ai mal à la gorge**
*jay mal a la gorj*

I have a temperature
**J'ai de la fièvre**
*jay duh la fyevr*

## Someone else's symptoms

He/She doesn't feel well
**Il/Elle ne se sent pas bien**
*eel/el nuh suh soñ pa byañ*

He/She is unconscious
**Il/Elle s'est évanoui(e)**
*eel/el set ayvanwee*

It hurts here
**Il/Elle a mal là**
*eel/el a mal la*

His/Her . . . hurt(s)
**Il/Elle a mal à la/au/aux . . .**
*eel/el a mal a la/oh/oh . . .*

His/Her head hurts
**Il/Elle a mal à la tête**
*eel/el a mal a la tet*

His/Her stomach hurts
**Il/Elle a mal à l'estomac**
*eel/el a mal a lestoma*

His/Her back hurts
**Il/Elle a mal au dos**
*eel/el a mal oh doh*

His/Her eyes hurt
**Il/Elle a mal aux yeux**
*eel/el a mal ohz yuh*

He/She has a sore throat
**Il/Elle a mal à la gorge**
*eel/el a mal a la gorj*

He/She has a temperature
**Il/Elle a de la fièvre**
*eel/el a duh la fyevr*

I have diarrhoea
**J'ai la diarrhée**
*jay la dee-aray*

He/She has diarrhoea
**Il/Elle a la diarrhée**
*eel/el a la dee-aray*

I feel dizzy
**J'ai des vertiges**
*jay day verteej*

He/She feels dizzy
**Il/Elle a des vertiges**
*eel/el a day verteej*

I feel sick
**J'ai la nausée**
*jay la nohzay*

He/She feels sick
**Il/Elle a la nausée**
*eel/el a la nohzay*

I have been sick
**J'ai vomi**
*jay vomee*

He/She has been sick
**Il/Elle a vomi**
*eel/el a vomee*

I can't sleep
**Je ne peux pas dormir**
*juh nuh puh pa dormeer*

He/She can't sleep
**Il/Elle ne peut pas dormir**
*eel/el nuh puh pa dormir*

I can't breathe
**Je ne peux pas respirer**
*juh nuh puh pa respeeray*

He/She can't breathe
**Il/Elle ne peut pas respirer**
*eel/el nuh puh pa respeeray*

I can't move my . . .
**Je ne peux pas bouger
le/la . . .**
*juh nuh puh pa boojay
luh/la . . .*

He/She can't move his/her . . .
**Il/Elle ne peut pas bouger
le/la . . .**
*eel/el nuh puh pa boojay
luh/la . . .*

My . . . is bleeding
**Mon/Ma . . . saigne**
*mawñ/ma . . . senyuh*

His/Her . . . is bleeding
**Son/Sa . . . saigne**
*sawñ/sa . . . senyuh*

It's my . . .
**C'est mon/ma . . .**
*say mawñ/ma . . .*

It's his or her . . .
**C'est son/sa . . .**
*say sawñ/sa . . .*

It's my arm
**C'est mon bras**
*say mawñ bra*

It's his/her wrist
**C'est son poignet**
*say sawñ pwanyay*

It's my ankle
**C'est ma cheville**
*say ma shuhveey*

I think that . . .
**Je crois que . . .**
*juh krwa kuh . . .*

It's broken
**Il/Elle est cassé(e)**
*eel/el e kasay*

It's sprained
**Il/Elle est foulé(e)**
*eel/el e foolay*

I have cut myself
**Je me suis coupé(e)**
*juh muh swee koopay*

I have burnt myself
**Je me suis brûlé(e)**
*juh muh swee brewlay*

I have been stung by an insect
**J'ai été piqué(e) par un insecte**
*jay aytay peekay par un añsekt*

I have been bitten by a dog
**J'ai été mordu(e) par un chien**
*jay aytay mordew par uñ shyañ*

It's his/her leg
**C'est sa jambe**
*say sa jomb*

It's broken
**Il/Elle est cassé(e)**
*eel/el e kasay*

It's sprained
**Il/Elle est foulé(e)**
*eel/el e foolay*

He/She has cut himself/
herself
**Il/Elle s'est coupé(e)**
*eel/el se koopay*

He/She has burnt himself/
herself
**Il/Elle s'est brûlé(e)**
*eel/el se brewlay*

He/She has been stung by
an insect
**Il/Elle a été piqué(e) par un
insecte**
*eel/el a aytay peekay par un
añsekt*

He/She has been bitten by a
dog
**Il/Elle a été mordu(e) par un
chien**
*eel/el a aytay mordew par uñ
shyañ*

## At the dentist's

I want to see a dentist
**Je voudrais voir un dentiste**
*juh voodray vwar uñ doñteest*

I have toothache
**J'ai mal aux dents**
*jay mal oh doñ*

This tooth hurts
**J'ai mal à cette dent**
*jay mal a set doñ*

I have broken a tooth
**Je me suis cassé une dent**
*juh muh swee kasay ewn doñ*

I have lost a filling
**J'ai perdu un plombage**
*jay perdew uñ plawmbaj*

I have lost a crown/cap
**J'ai perdu une couronne**
*jay perdew ewn kooron*

He/She has toothache
**Il/Elle a mal aux dents**
*eel/el a mal oh doñ*

He/She has broken a tooth
**Il/Elle s'est cassé(e) une dent**
*eel/el se kasay ewn doñ*

He/She has lost a filling
**Il/Elle a perdu un plombage**
*eel/el a perdew uñ plawmbaj*

He/She has lost a crown/cap
**Il/Elle a perdu une couronne**
*eel/el a perdew ewn kooron*

Can you give me some
temporary treatment?
**Pourriez-vous me soigner
provisoirement?**
*pooree-ay voo muh swanyay
proveezwarmoñ*

Can you give me an injection?
**Pourriez-vous me faire une
piqûre?**
*pooree-ay voo muh fer ewn
peekewr*

Can you give him/her an
injection?
**Pourriez-vous lui faire une
piqûre?**
*pooree-ay voo lwee fer ewn
peekewr*

My denture is broken
**Mon dentier est cassé**
*mawñ doñtyay e kasay*

His/Her denture is broken
**Son dentier est cassé**
*sawñ doñtyay e kasay*

Can you repair it?
**Pourriez-vous le réparer?**
*pooree-ay voo luh rayparay*

How much is it going to cost?
**Combien ça va coûter?**
*kawmbyañ sa va kootay*

## You may hear

### At the doctor's

**Où avez-vous mal?**
*oo avay voo mal*
Where does it hurt?

**Avez-vous mal là?**
*avay voo mal la*
Does it hurt here?

**Beaucoup?/Pas beaucoup?**
*bohkoo/pa bohkoo*
A lot?/A little?

**Depuis combien de temps avez-vous ça?**
*duhpwee kawmbyañ duh toñ avay voo sa*
How long have you been like this?

**Depuis combien de temps il/elle a ça?**
*duhpwee kawmbyañ duh toñ eel/el a sa*
How long has he/she been like this?

**Quel âge avez-vous?**
*kel aj avay voo*
How old are you?

**Quel âge a-t-il/a-t-elle?**
*kel aj ateel/atel*
How old is he/she?

**Ouvrez la bouche, s'il vous plaît**
*oovray la boosh seelvooplay*
Open your mouth, please

**Déshabillez-vous, s'il vous plaît**
*dayzabeeyay voo seelvooplay*
Get undressed, please

**Étendez-vous là, s'il vous plaît**
*aytoñdayvoo la seelvooplay*
Lie down over there, please

**Prenez-vous des médicaments?**
*pruhnay voo day maydeekamoñ*
Are you taking any medicines?

**Êtes-vous allergique à un médicament quelconque?**
*et vooz alerjeek a uñ maydeekamoñ kelkawñk*
Are you allergic to any medicines?

**Êtes-vous vacciné(e) contre le tétanos?**
*et voo vakseenay kawñtr luh taytanos*
Have you been vaccinated against tetanus?

**Qu'est-ce que vous avez mangé aujourd'hui?**
*keskuh vooz avay moñjay ohjoordwee*
What have you eaten today?

**C'est infecté**
*set añfektay*
It is infected

**Vous avez une intoxication alimentaire**
*vooz avay ewn añtoxeekasyawñ aleemoñter*
You have food poisoning

**C'est une crise cardiaque**
*set ewn kreez cardyak*
It's a heart attack

**Je dois vous faire une piqûre**
*juh dwa voo fer ewn peekewr*
I have to give you an injection

**Je dois vous faire des points de suture**
*juh dwa voo fer day pwañ duh sewtewr*
I have to give you some stitches

**Il faut faire une radio**
*eel foh fer ewn radee-oh*
It is necessary to do an X-ray

**Je voudrais un prélèvement de sang/d'urine**
*juh voodray uñ praylevmoñ duh soñ/dewreen*
I want a blood/urine sample

**Je vais vous faire une ordonnance**
*juh vay voo fer ewn ordonoñs*
I am going to give you a prescription

**Prenez un comprimé trois fois par jour**
*pruhnay uñ kawmpreemay trwa fwa par joor*
Take a tablet three times a day

**Avant/Après les repas**
*avoñ/apray lay ruhpa*
Before/After meals

**Au coucher**
*oh kooshay*
At bedtime

**Il faut que vous vous reposiez**
*eel foh kuh voo voo ruhpozyay*
You must rest

**Il faut que vous restiez au lit pendant trois jours**
*eel foh kuh voo restyay oh lee poñdoñ trwa joor*
You must stay in bed for three days

**Il faut que vous reveniez dans cinq jours**
*eel foh kuh voo ruhvuhnyay doñ sañk joor*
You must come back in five days' time

**Il faut que vous buviez beaucoup de liquides**
*eel foh kuh voo bewvyay bohkoo duh leekeed*
You must drink plenty of liquids

**Il ne faut rien manger**
*eel nuh foh ryañ moñjay*
You must not eat anything

**Il faut que vous alliez à l'hôpital**
*eel foh kuh vooz alyay a lopeetal*
You will have to go to hospital

**Il faut qu'il/qu'elle aille à l'hôpital**
*eel foh keel/kel iy a lopeetal*
He/She will have to go to hospital

**Ce n'est pas grave**
*suh ne pa grav*
It is nothing serious

**Tout va bien**
*too va byañ*
There is nothing wrong with you

**Voulez-vous vous rhabiller, s'il vous plaît**
*voolayvoo voo rabeeyay seelvooplay*
Get dressed again, please

## At the dentist's

**Ouvrez la bouche, s'il vous plaît**
*oovray la boosh seelvooplay*
Open your mouth, please

**Vous avez besoin d'un plombage**
*vooz avay buhzwañ duñ plawmbaj*
You need a filling

**Il faut que je l'arrache**
*eel foh kuh juh larash*
I have to extract it

**Je vais vous faire une piqûre**
*juh vay voo fer ewn peekewr*
I am going to give you an injection

## Parts of the body

| | | |
|---|---|---|
| ankle | **la cheville** | *shuhveey* |
| appendix | **l'appendice** | *apoñdees* |
| arm | **le bras** | *bra* |
| back | **le dos** | *doh* |
| bladder | **la vessie** | *vesee* |
| blood | **le sang** | *soñ* |
| body | **le corps** | *kor* |
| bone | **l'os** | *os* |
| bottom | **le derrière** | *deree-er* |
| bowels | **les intestins** | *añtestañ* |
| breast | **le sein** | *sañ* |
| buttock | **la fesse** | *fes* |
| cartilage | **le cartilage** | *karteelaj* |
| chest | **la poitrine** | *pwatreen* |
| chin | **le menton** | *moñtawñ* |
| ear | **l'oreille** | *oray* |
| elbow | **le coude** | *kood* |
| eye, eyes | **l'œil, les yeux** | *uh-ee, layz yuh* |
| face | **le visage** | *veezaj* |
| finger | **le doigt** | *dwa* |
| foot | **le pied** | *pyay* |
| genitals | **les organes génitaux** | *organ jayneetoh* |
| gland | **la glande** | *gloñd* |
| hair | **les cheveux** | *shuhvuh* |
| hand | **la main** | *mañ* |
| head | **la tête** | *tet* |
| heart | **le cœur** | *kuhr* |
| heel | **le talon** | *talawñ* |
| hip | **la hanche** | *oñsh* |
| jaw | **la mâchoire** | *mashwar* |
| joint | **l'articulation** | *arteekewlasyawñ* |
| kidney | **le rein** | *rañ* |
| knee | **le genou** | *juhnoo* |
| leg | **la jambe** | *jomb* |

| | | |
|---|---|---|
| ligament | **le ligament** | *leegamoñ* |
| lip | **la lèvre** | *levr* |
| liver | **le foie** | *fwa* |
| lung | **le poumon** | *poomawñ* |
| mouth | **la bouche** | *boosh* |
| muscle | **le muscle** | *mewskl* |
| nail | **l'ongle** | *awñgl* |
| neck | **le cou** | *koo* |
| nerve | **le nerf** | *nerf* |
| nose | **le nez** | *nay* |
| penis | **le pénis** | *paynees* |
| private parts | **les parties génitales** | *partee jayneetal* |
| rectum | **le rectum** | *rektoom* |
| rib | **la côte** | *koht* |
| shoulder | **l'épaule** | *aypohl* |
| skin | **la peau** | *poh* |
| spine | **la colonne vertébrale** | *kolon vertaybral* |
| stomach | **l'estomac** | *estoma* |
| tendon | **le tendon** | *toñdawñ* |
| testicles | **les testicules** | *testeekewl* |
| thigh | **la cuisse** | *kwees* |
| throat | **la gorge** | *gorj* |
| thumb | **le pouce** | *poos* |
| toe | **l'orteil** | *ortay* |
| tongue | **la langue** | *loñg* |
| tonsils | **les amygdales** | *ameegdal* |
| tooth | **la dent** | *doñ* |
| vagina | **le vagin** | *vajañ* |
| wrist | **le poignet** | *pwanyay* |

# PROBLEMS AND COMPLAINTS

● You should report the loss or theft of personal belongings to
the police. If your passport is lost or stolen, you should also
contact the British Embassy or Consulate (addresses, page
216).

● **Gendarmes** is the name for the police in the French prov-
inces only. Otherwise they are **agents de police**.

## You may see

| | |
|---|---|
| **Commissariat de police** | Police station (national police) |
| **En panne** | Out of order |
| **Gendarmerie** | Police station (in French provinces) |
| **Hors service** | Out of order |
| **Objets trouvés** | Lost property |
| **Poste de police** | Police station |
| **Préfecture** | Administrative police headquarters |
| **SAMU** | Emergency medical service |

## You may want to say

(*For car breakdowns, see page 36;* Emergencies, *page 292*)

### General phrases

Can you help me?
**Pourriez-vous m'aider?**
*pooree-ay voo mayday*

Can you fix it
(immediately)?
**Pourriez-vous le réparer (tout de suite)?**
*pooree-ay voo luh rayparay (toot sweet)*

When can you fix it?
**Quand est-ce que vous pouvez le réparer?**
*koñt eskuh voo poovay luh rayparay*

Can I speak to the manager?
**Est-ce que je peux parler au directeur?**
*eskuh juh puh parlay oh deerektuhr*

There's a problem/
something wrong
**Il y a quelque chose qui ne va pas**
*eelya kelkuh shohz kee nuh va pa*

There isn't/aren't any . . .
**Il n'y a pas de . . .**
*eelnya pa duh . . .*

I need . . .
**J'ai besoin de . . .**
*jay buhzwañ duh . . .*

The . . . doesn't work
**Le/La . . . ne marche pas**
*luh/la . . . nuh marsh pa*

The . . . is broken
**Le/La . . . est cassé(e)**
*luh/la . . . e kasay*

I can't . . .
**Je ne peux pas . . .**
*juh nuh puh pa . . .*

It wasn't my fault
**Ce n'était pas ma faute**
*suh naytay pa ma foht*

I have forgotten my . . .
**J'ai oublié mon/ma . . .**
*jay ooblee-ay mawñ/ma . . .*

I have lost my . . .
**J'ai perdu mon/ma . . .**
*jay perdew mawñ/ma . . .*

Someone has stolen my . . .
**On m'a volé mon/ma . . .**
*awñ ma volay mawñ/ma . . .*

My . . . has disappeared
**Mon/Ma . . . a disparu**
*mawñ/ma . . . a deesparew*

My . . . isn't here
**Mon/Ma . . . n'est pas là**
*mawñ/ma . . . ne pa la*

The . . . is missing
**Il manque le/la . . .**
*eel mañk luh/la . . .*

Something is missing
**Il manque quelque chose**
*eel moñk kelkuh shohz*

This isn't mine
**Ce n'est pas à moi**
*suh ne paz a mwa*

## Where you're staying

There isn't any (hot) water
**Il n'y a pas d'eau (chaude)**
*eelnya pa doh (shohd)*

The light doesn't work
**Le lumière ne marche pas**
*la lewmyer nuh marsh pa*

There isn't any toilet paper
**Il n'y a pas de papier hygiénique**
*eelnya pa duh papyay eejayneek*

The shower doesn't work
**La douche ne marche pas**
*la doosh nuh marsh pa*

There isn't any electricity
**Il n'y a pas de courant**
*eelnya pa duh kooroñ*

The lock is broken
**La serrure est cassée**
*la serewr e kasay*

181

The switch on the lamp is broken
**L'interrupteur de la lampe est cassé**
*lañterewptuhr duh la lomp e kasay*

There aren't any towels
**Il n'y a pas de serviettes**
*eelnya pa duh servyet*

I need another pillow
**J'ai besoin d'encore un oreiller**
*jay buhzwañ doñkor un orayay*

I can't open the window
**Je ne peux pas ouvrir la fenêtre**
*juh nuh puh paz oovreer la fuhnetr*

I need another blanket
**J'ai besoin d'encore une couverture**
*jay buhzwañ doñkor ewn koovertewr*

I can't turn the tap off
**Je ne peux pas fermer le robinet**
*juh nuh puh pa fermay luh robeenay*

I need a light bulb
**J'ai besoin d'une ampoule**
*jay buhzwañ dewn ompool*

The toilet doesn't flush
**La chasse d'eau ne marche pas**
*la shas doh nuh marsh pa*

The wash-basin is blocked
**Le lavabo est bouché**
*luh lavaboh e booshay*

The wash-basin is dirty
**Le lavabo est sale**
*luh lavaboh e sal*

The room is . . .
**La chambre est . . .**
*la shombr e . . .*

The room is too dark
**La chambre est trop sombre**
*la shombr e troh sawmbr*

The room is too small
**La chambre est trop petite**
*la shombr e troh puhteet*

It's too hot in the room
**Il fait trop chaud dans la chambre**
*eel fay troh shoh doñ la shombr*

The bed is not very comfortable
**Le lit n'est pas très confortable**
*luh lee ne pa tre kawñfortabl*

There's a lot of noise
**Il y a beaucoup de bruit**
*eelya bohkoo duh brwee*

There's a smell of gas
**Il y a une odeur de gaz**
*eelya ewn ohduhr duh gaz*

# In bars and restaurants

This isn't cooked
**Ce n'est pas assez cuit**
*suh nay paz asay kwee*

This is overcooked
**C'est trop cuit**
*say troh kwee*

This is cold
**C'est froid**
*say frwa*

I didn't order this, I ordered . . .
**Je n'ai pas commandé ça, j'ai commandé un/une . . .**
*juh nay pa komoñday sa, jay komoñday uñ/ewn . . .*

This glass is cracked
**Ce verre est fêlé**
*suh ver e felay*

This is dirty
**C'est sale**
*say sal*

This smells bad
**Ça sent mauvais**
*sa soñ mohvay*

This tastes bad
**Ça a mauvais goût**
*sa a mohvay goo*

## In shops

I bought this here
(yesterday)
**J'ai acheté ça ici (hier)**
*jay ashtay sa eesee (ee-er)*

Can you change this for me?
**Pourriez-vous me changer ça?**
*pooree-ay voo muh shoñjay sa*

I want to return this
**Je voudrais rendre ça**
*juh voodray roñdr sa*

Can you give me a refund?
**Pourriez-vous me
rembourser?**
*pooree-ay voo muh
romboorsay*

Here is the receipt
**Voici le reçu**
*vwasee luh ruhsew*

There is a mistake on the
bill
**Il y a une erreur dans
l'addition**
*eelya ewn eruhr doñ
ladeesyawñ*

There is a flaw
**Il y a un défaut**
*eelya uñ dayfoh*

There is a hole
**Il y a un trou**
*eelya uñ troo*

There is a stain/mark
**Il y a une tache**
*eelya ewn tash*

This isn't fresh
**Ce n'est pas frais**
*suh ne pa fray*

The lid is missing
**Il manque le couvercle**
*eel moñk luh kooverkl*

# Forgetting and losing things and theft

I have forgotten my ticket
**J'ai oublié mon billet**
*jay ooblee-ay mawñ beeyay*

I have forgotten the key
**J'ai oublié la clé**
*jay ooblee-ay la klay*

I have lost my wallet
**J'ai perdu mon portefeuille**
*jay perdew mawñ portfuh-ee*

I have lost my driving licence
**J'ai perdu mon permis de conduire**
*jay perdew mawñ permee duh kawñdweer*

We have lost our rucksacks
**Nous avons perdu nos sacs à dos**
*nooz avawñ perdew noh sak a doh*

Where is the lost property office?
**Où se trouve le bureau des objets trouvés?**
*oo suh troov luh bewroh dayz objay troovay*

Where is the police station?
**Où se trouve le poste de police?**
*oo suh troov luh post duh polees*

Someone has stolen my handbag
**On m'a volé mon sac à main**
*awñ ma volay mawñ sak a mañ*

Someone has stolen my car
**On m'a volé ma voiture**
*awñ ma volay ma vwatewr*

Someone has stolen my money
**On m'a volé mon argent**
*awñ ma volay mawn arjoñ*

# If someone is bothering you

Leave me alone!
**Fichez-moi la paix!**
*feeshay mwa la pay*

Go away, or I'll call the police
**Allez-vous-en, sinon j'appelle un agent**
*alay vooz oñ, seenawñ japel un ajoñ*

There is someone bothering me
**Il y a un type qui m'embête**
*eelya uñ teep kee mombet*

There is someone following me
**Il y a un type qui me suit**
*eelya uñ teep kee muh swee*

# You may hear

## Helpful and unhelpful replies

**Un instant, s'il vous plaît**
*un añstoñ seelvooplay*
Just a moment, please

**D'accord**
*dakor*
Of course

**Voici**
*vwasee*
Here you are

**Je vous en apporterai un/une**
*juh vooz on aportuhray uñ/ewn*
I'll bring you one

**Je vous en apporterai un/une autre**
*juh vooz on aportuhray un/ewn ohtr*
I'll bring you another one

**Tout de suite**
*toot sweet*
Right away

**Je vous le réparerai demain**
*juh voo luh rayparuhray duhmañ*
I'll fix it for you tomorrow

**Je suis désolé(e), ce n'est pas possible**
*juh swee dayzolay suh ne pa poseebl*
I'm sorry, it's not possible

**Je suis désolé(e), je ne peux rien faire**
*juh swee dayzolay juh nuh puh ryañ fer*
I'm sorry, there's nothing I can do

**Je ne suis pas le responsable**
*juh nuh swee pa luh respawñsabl*
I am not the person responsible

**Nous ne sommes pas responsables**
*noo nuh som pa respawñsabl*
We are not responsible

**Vous devrez le signaler à la police**
*voo duhvray luh seenyalay a la polees*
You should report it to the police

**Le mieux serait . . .**
*luh myuh suhray . . .*
The best thing would be . . .

## Questions you may be asked

**Quand l'avez-vous acheté?**
*koñ lavay vooz ashtay*
When did you buy it?

**Vous avez le reçu?**
*vooz avay luh ruhsew*
Do you have the receipt?

**Quand cela s'est-il passé?**
*koñ suhla seetel pasay*
When did it happen?

**Où l'avez-vous perdu(e)?**
*oo lavay voo perdew*
Where did you lose it?

**Où vous l'a-t-on volé(e)?**
*oo voo latawñ volay*
Where was it stolen?

**Pourriez-vous décrire . . . ?**
*pooree-ay voo daykreer . . .*
Can you describe . . . ?

**Pourriez-vous décrire votre sac à main?**
*pooree-ay voo daykreer votr sak a mañ*
Can you describe your bag?

**Pourriez-vous décrire la voiture?**
*pooree-ay voo daykreer la vwatewr*
Can you describe the car?

**De quelle marque est-elle?**
*duh kel mark etel*
What make is it?

**Quel est le numéro d'immatriculation?**
*kel e luh newmayroh deematreekewlasyawñ*
What is the registration number?

**Où êtes-vous descendu(e)?**
*oo et voo desoñdew*
Where are you staying?

**Quel est votre adresse?**
*kel e votr adres*
What is your address?

**Quel est le numéro de votre chambre?**
*kel e luh newmayroh duh votr shombr*
What is your room number?

**Quel est le numéro de votre passeport?**
*kel e luh newmayroh duh votr paspor*
What is your passport number?

**Êtes-vous assuré(e)?**
*et vooz asewray*
Are you insured?

**Veuillez remplir ce formulaire/cette fiche**
*vuhyay rompleer suh formewler/set feesh*
Please fill in this form

# BASIC GRAMMAR

## Nouns

All French nouns have a gender – masculine or feminine.

Words for male people or animals are masculine; for females they are feminine.

Most nouns ending in **-age**, **-ment** or **-oir** are masculine.
Most nouns ending in **-ance**, **-ence**, **-té** and **-ion** are feminine.
Words with other endings can be either gender. The Dictionary indicates which.

Some nouns can be both masculine and feminine. Some nouns add an **e** to the masculine form to make the feminine, e.g. **ami** (*male friend*), **amie** (*female friend*).

A masculine plural noun can refer to a mixture of masculine and feminine.

e.g. **amis**  (male friends *or* male and female friends)
**les Français**  (French men *or* the French)

## Plurals

Nouns are generally made plural by adding **s**. The **s** is not pronounced, so there is no difference in the sound of the word between singular and plural.
e.g. **livre – livres** (both pronounced *leevr*)
**voiture – voitures** (both pronounced *vwatewr*)

The same applies to adjectives.
e.g. **blanc – blancs**    **bleu – bleus**

Some nouns add **x** in the plural, e.g. **bateau – bateaux**. The **x** is not pronounced.

Nouns ending in **-s**, **-x** or **-z** do not change.

Nouns ending in **-al** change to **-aux**, e.g. **animal – animaux**.

## Articles ('a'/'an', 'the')

The French indefinite article (the equivalent of 'a' or 'an') has different forms: **un** is used with masculine nouns, **une** with feminine ones.

e.g. **un livre    une voiture**

The definite article ('the') has different forms for masculine and feminine singular, but only one form for the plural:

|  | *masculine* | *feminine* |
|---|---|---|
| *singular* | **le** | **la** |
| *plural* | **les** | **les** |

e.g. **le livre             la voiture**
**les livres          les voitures**

**Le** and **la** are shortened to **l'** before a noun beginning with a vowel or **h**, e.g. **l'aspirine, l'hôtel**.

In the Dictionary, nouns are given with the definite article to show their gender (or with (*m*) or (*f*) if the article is **l'**).

## À and de

When **à** (at, to) and **de** (of) are followed by the articles **le** or **les**, they change:

**à + le = au          de + le = du**
**à + les = aux        de + les = des**

e.g. **au centre, le pont du Gard**

**De** becomes **d'** before a word beginning with a vowel or **h**.

# Adjectives

Adjectives 'agree' with the nouns they are describing – they have different endings for masculine and feminine, singular and plural. Plurals are formed as described above.

Most adjectives add **e** to the masculine singular to give the feminine form.

e.g. **bleu – bleue**          **grand – grande**     **petit – petite**

Some adjectives have only one ending for the singular, both masculine and feminine.

e.g. **un sac rouge**          **une voiture rouge**

Some adjectives double the final consonant and then add **e**.

e.g. **bon – bonne**          **gros – grosse**

Adjectives ending in **-f** change to **-ve** for the feminine; and **-x** changes to **-se**.

e.g. **vif – vive**          **heureux – heureuse**

In the Dictionary, feminine forms are indicated as well as masculine.

## Position of adjectives

Most adjectives come after the noun.

e.g. **vin blanc**          **le menu touristique**          **une chemise bleue**

**Autre** (other) and **chaque** (each, every) always come before the noun, as do **premier/première** (first) and other numerical adjectives.

e.g. **une autre personne**     **chaque année**     **la première fois**

# Comparatives and superlatives ('more', 'the most')

'More' is **plus** and comes before the adjective. It also gives the equivalent of 'bigger', 'smaller'.

e.g. **plus intéressant** (more interesting)
    **plus grand** (bigger)
    **plus jeune** (younger)

'Less' is **moins**:
**moins important** (less important)
**moins compliqué** (less complicated)

The comparatives of 'good' and 'bad' are **meilleur** (better) and **pire** (worse).

'Than', as in 'more than' and 'less than', is **que**.
e.g. **cette voiture est plus grande que l'autre** (this car is bigger than the other)

To say 'the most' or 'the least', put the definite article **le** or **la** before **plus** or **moins**.

e.g. **la région la plus intéressante** (the most interesting region)
    **le/la plus grand(e) du monde** (the biggest in the world)

## Possessives ('my', 'your', 'his', 'her', etc.)

Like other adjectives, possessive adjectives 'agree' with the nouns they are describing. The forms are:

|  | *singular* | | *plural* |
|  | *masculine* | *feminine* | *masculine and feminine* |
| my | **mon** | **ma** | **mes** |
| your | **ton** | **ta** | **tes** |
| his/her | **son** | **sa** | **ses** |
| our | | **notre** | **nos** |
| your | | **votre** | **vos** |
| their | | **leur** | **leurs** |

e.g. **mon frère** (my brother)
**notre maison** (our house)

To indicate possession, as in, for example, 'John's brother' or 'John and Susan's house', the word **de** (of) is used. There is no equivalent of the English apostrophe s.
e.g. **le frère de John, la maison de John et Susan**

## Demonstratives ('this', 'that')

The demonstrative pronoun 'this' or 'that' is **cela**, which is commonly shortened to **ça**.

Demonstrative adjectives used with a noun (as in 'this book') are:

|  | *masculine* | *feminine* |
| this, that | **ce** | **cette** |
| these, those | **ces** | **ces** |

To distinguish between 'this' and 'that', i.e. something close by and something further away, **-ci** or **-là** is added to the noun.
e.g. **ce livre-ci**      **cette livre-là**

## Subject pronouns ('I', 'you', 'he', 'she', etc.)

| | |
|---|---|
| I | **je** (**j'** before a verb beginning with a vowel or **h**) |
| you (informal) | **tu** |
| he/she | **il/elle** |
| we | **nous** |
| you (plural and formal) | **vous** |
| they | **ils** (*masculine*), **elles** (*feminine*) |

### 'You'

In English there is only one way of addressing people – using the word 'you'. In French there are two ways – one is more polite/formal, the other more casual/informal.

**Tu** is the informal way, and it is used between friends and relatives and people of the same age group, and to children. **Tu** is used with the second person singular of the verb.

**Vous** is both the formal way to address someone and the plural of 'you'. It is used with the second person plural of the verb. Most of the phrases in this book use the formal way of saying 'you'.

## Object pronouns

Direct object pronouns are the equivalent of 'me', 'him', 'it', 'us' etc.

e.g. **je le parle bien** (I speak it well)
**elle les aime** (she loves them)

Indirect object pronouns are the equivalent of 'to/for me', 'to/ for him', 'to/for us' etc.

e.g. **pourriez-vous lui donner un message?**
(could you give (to) him/her a message?)

The full list is:

| *direct object* | | *indirect object* | |
|---|---|---|---|
| me | nous | me | nous |
| te | vous | te | vous |
| le, la | les | lui | leur |

They generally come before the verb. When two object pronouns are used together, the direct object comes first.

e.g. **je le lui donnerai** (I will give it to him/her)

## Emphatic pronouns

These are used after prepositions

e.g. **à moi** (to me), **pour toi** (for you)

and after commands

e.g. **donnez-moi les clés** (give me the keys)

The pronouns are:

| | |
|---|---|
| moi | nous |
| toi | vous |
| lui, elle | eux, elles |

## Verbs

French verbs have different endings according to (i) the subject of the verb, (ii) the tense. There are three main groups of verbs, with different sets of endings for each group.

In dictionaries verbs are listed in the infinitive form, which ends in **-er**, **-ir** or **-re** (these are the three groups).

Below are the endings for the present tense of these three groups:

|          | -er     | -ir       | -re      |
|----------|---------|-----------|----------|
|          | parler  | finir     | vendre   |
| je       | parle   | finis     | vends    |
| tu       | parles  | finis     | vends    |
| il/elle  | parle   | finit     | vend     |
| nous     | parlons | finissons | vendons  |
| vous     | parlez  | finissez  | vendez   |
| ils/elles| parlent | finissent | vendent  |

The French present tense translates both the English 'I ...' and 'I am ...-ing' forms, e.g. **je parle** means both 'I speak' and 'I am speaking'.

## Reflexives

Reflexive verbs are listed in dictionaries with the reflexive pronoun **se**, e.g. **se laver** (to wash oneself), **s'appeler** (to be called).

The reflexive pronouns are:

|      |      |
|------|------|
| me   | nous |
| te   | vous |
| se   | se   |

e.g. **je me lave, tu te laves, il/elle se lave**, etc.

## Irregular verbs

Some common verbs are irregular. They include:

| **être** | **avoir** | **aller** | **faire** |
| (to be) | (to have) | (to go) | (to do, to make) |

| **être** | **avoir** | **aller** | **faire** |
|---|---|---|---|
| je suis | j'ai | je vais | je fais |
| tu es | tu as | tu vas | tu fais |
| il/elle est | il/elle a | il/elle va | il/elle fait |
| nous sommes | nous avons | nous allons | nous faisons |
| vous êtes | vous avez | vous allez | vous faites |
| ils/elles sont | ils/elles ont | ils/elles vont | ils/elles font |

| **venir** | **pouvoir** | **vouloir** |
| (to come) | (to be able) | (to want) |

| **venir** | **pouvoir** | **vouloir** |
|---|---|---|
| je viens | je peux | je veux |
| tu viens | tu peux | tu veux |
| il/elle vient | il/elle peut | il/elle veut |
| nous venons | nous pouvons | nous voulons |
| vous venez | vous pouvez | vous voulez |
| ils/elles viennent | ils/elles peuvent | ils/elles veulent |

## Other verb tenses

A few verbs in other tenses that you may find useful:

| | | |
|---|---|---|
| **être** | I was/have been | **j'ai été** |
| (to be) | we were/have been | **nous avons été** |
| | I was/used to be | **j'étais** |
| | we were/used to be | **nous étions** |
| **avoir** | I had/have had | **j'ai eu** |
| (to have) | we had/have had | **nous avons eu** |
| | I had/used to have | **j'avais** |
| | we had/used to have | **nous avions** |
| **aller** | I went | **je suis allé(e)** |
| (to go) | we went | **nous sommes allé(e)s** |
| | I used to go | **j'allais** |
| | we used to go | **nous allions** |
| **faire** | I did, I made | **j'ai fait** |
| (to do, | we did, we made | **nous avons fait** |
| to make) | I used to do/make | **je faisais** |
| | we used to do/make | **nous faisions** |
| **venir** | I came/have come | **je suis venu(e)** |
| (to come) | we came/have come | **nous sommes venu(e)s** |
| | I came/used to come | **je venais** |
| | we came/used to come | **nous venions** |

For talking about the future, in a similar way to English, you can say 'I am going to . . .', using the verb **aller**, followed by an infinitive.

e.g. **demain je vais jouer au tennis** (tomorrow I am going to play tennis)

**nous allons visiter Rouen** (we are going to visit Rouen)

(French also has a future tense with another set of verb endings.)

## Negatives

To make a verb negative, put **ne** before it and **pas** after it. Ne is shortened to **n'** before a verb beginning with a vowel or **h**.

e.g. **je n'ai pas d'enfants** (I don't have any children)

**je ne comprends pas** (I don't understand)

**Monsieur Dupont n'est pas là** (Mr Dupont isn't in)

Other words are used instead of **pas** to mean 'nothing', 'no one', 'never' etc.

e.g. **je ne connais personne** (I know no one *or* I don't know anyone)

**il ne va jamais à l'école** (he never goes to school)

## Questions

There are different ways of forming questions in French. Starting with a statement such as **vous avez une chambre** (you have a room), you can make a question (do you have a room?) as follows:

By adding **est-ce que** at the beginning,

e.g. **est-ce que vous avez une chambre?**

Or by changing the intonation of the voice – making it rise at the end of the sentence,

e.g. **vous avez une chambre?**

(These are the most usual ways.)

Also by changing the word order – that is, swopping the positions of the subject pronoun and the verb,

e.g. **avez-vous une chambre?**

# DAYS, MONTHS, DATES

Names of days and months are not written with capital letters.

## Days

| Monday | **lundi** | *luñdee* |
|---|---|---|
| Tuesday | **mardi** | *mardee* |
| Wednesday | **mercredi** | *merkruhdee* |
| Thursday | **jeudi** | *juhdee* |
| Friday | **vendredi** | *voñdruhdee* |
| Saturday | **samedi** | *samdee* |
| Sunday | **dimanche** | *deemoñsh* |

## Months

| January | **janvier** | *joñvyay* |
|---|---|---|
| February | **février** | *fayvree-ay* |
| March | **mars** | *mars* |
| April | **avril** | *avreel* |
| May | **mai** | *may* |
| June | **juin** | *jwañ* |
| July | **juillet** | *jweeyay* |
| August | **août** | *oot* |
| September | **septembre** | *septombr* |
| October | **octobre** | *oktobr* |
| November | **novembre** | *novombr* |
| December | **décembre** | *daysombr* |

## Seasons

| spring | **le printemps** | *luh prañtoñ* |
|---|---|---|
| summer | **l'été** | *laytay* |
| autumn | **l'automne** | *lohton* |
| winter | **l'hiver** | *leever* |

## General Phrases

| | | |
|---|---|---|
| day | **le jour** | *luh joor* |
| week | **la semaine** | *la suhmen* |
| fortnight | **quinze jours** | *kañz joor* |
| month | **le mois** | *luh mwa* |
| year | **l'an, l'année** | *loñ, lanay* |
| today | **aujourd'hui** | *ohjoordwee* |
| tomorrow | **demain** | *duhmañ* |
| yesterday | **hier** | *eeyer* |
| (in) the morning | **le matin** | *luh matañ* |
| (in) the afternoon | **l'après-midi** | *lapremeedee* |
| (in) the evening | **le soir** | *luh swar* |
| (at) night | **la nuit** | *la nwee* |
| this morning | **ce matin** | *suh matañ* |
| this afternoon | **cet après-midi** | *set apremeedee* |
| this evening | **ce soir** | *suh swar* |
| tonight | **cette nuit** | *set nwee* |
| tomorrow morning | **demain matin** | *duhmañ matañ* |
| yesterday evening | **hier soir** | *eeyer swar* |
| on Monday | **lundi** | *luñdee* |
| on Tuesdays | **le mardi** | *luh mardee* |
| every Wednesday | **tous les mercredis** | *too lay merkruhdee* |
| in August/spring | **en août/printemps** | *oñ...* |
| at the beginning of March | **au début de mars** | *oh daybew duh...* |
| in the middle of June | **au milieu de juin** | *oh meelyuh duh...* |
| at the end of September | **à la fin de septembre** | *a la fañ duh...* |
| in six months' time | **dans six mois** | *doñ...* |
| during the summer | **pendant l'été** | *poñdoñ...* |
| two years ago | **il y a deux ans** | *eelya...* |

199

| | | |
|---|---|---|
| (in) the sixties | **(dans) les années soixante** | *(doñ) layz anay…* |
| last… | **… dernier/dernière** | *… dernyay/dernyer* |
| last Monday | **lundi dernier** | *luñdee dernyay* |
| last week | **la semaine dernière** | *la suhmen dernyer* |
| last month | **le mois dernier** | *luh mwa dernyay* |
| last year | **l'année dernière** | *lanay dernyer* |
| next… | **… prochain/prochaine** | *… proshañ/proshen* |
| next Tuesday | **mardi prochain** | *mardee proshañ* |
| next week | **la semaine prochaine** | *la suhmen proshen* |
| next month | **le mois prochain** | *luh mwa proshañ* |
| next year | **l'année prochaine** | *lanay proshen* |

| | | |
|---|---|---|
| What day is it (today)? | **Quel jour sommes-nous (aujourd'hui)** | |
| | *kel joor som noo (ohjoordwee)* | |
| What is the date (today)? | **Quelle est la date (aujourd'hui)?** | |
| | *kel e la dat (ohjoordwee)* | |
| When is your birthday? | **Quand est votre anniversaire?** | |
| | *koñt e votr aneeverser* | |
| When is your saint's day?* | **Quand est votre fête (de saint)?** | |
| | *koñt e votr fet (duh sañ)* | |
| It's/Today is… | **Nous sommes…** | |
| | *noo som…* | |
| It's (on) the first of January | **C'est le premier janvier** | |
| | *say luh pruhmyay joñvyay* | |
| (on) Tuesday 10th May | **mardi le dix mai** | |
| | *mardee luh dees may* | |
| 1990 | **dix-neuf cent quatre-vingt-dix** | |
| | *deesnuhf soñ katr vañ dees* | |
| the 15th century | **le quinzième siècle** | |
| | *luh kañzyem syekl* | |

**200**

\* The French celebrate the saint's day corresponding to their
Christian name

# TIME

| | | |
|---|---|---|
| one o'clock | **une heure** | *ewn uhr* |
| two o'clock | **deux heures** | *duhz uhr* |
| twelve o'clock, etc. | **douze heures** | *dooz uhr* |
| quarter past... | **...et quart** | *...ay kar* |
| half past... | **...et demie** | *...ay duhmee* |
| five past... | **...cinq** | *...sañk* |
| twenty-five past... | **...vingt-cinq** | *...vañsañk* |
| quarter to... | **...moins le quart** | *...mwañ luh kar* |
| ten to... | **...moins dix** | *...mwañ dees* |
| twenty to... | **...moins vingt** | *...mwañ vañ* |
| in the morning (a.m.) | **du matin** | *dew matañ* |
| in the afternoon (p.m.) | **de l'après-midi** | *du lapremeedee* |
| in the evening | **du soir** | *dew swar* |
| noon/midday | **midi** | *meedee* |
| midnight | **minuit** | *meenwee* |
| a quarter of an hour | **un quart d'heure** | *uñ kar duhr* |
| half an hour | **une demi-heure** | *ewn duhmee uhr* |

## 24-hour clock

| | | |
|---|---|---|
| 0000 | **zéro heure** | *zayroh uhr* |
| 0900 | **neuf heures** | *nuhv uhr* |
| 1300 | **treize heures** | *trez uhr* |
| 1430 | **quatorze heures trente** | *katorz uhr troñt* |
| 2149 | **vingt et une heures** | *vañt ay ewn uhr* |
| |    **quarante-neuf** | *karoñt nuhf* |

| | | |
|---|---|---|
| at... | à... | *a...* |
| precisely...o'clock | ...heures précises | *...uhr prayseez* |
| just after... | un peu plus de... | *uñ puh plew duh...* |
| about/around... | vers... | *ver...* |
| nearly... | presque... | *preskuh...* |
| soon | bientôt | *byañtoh* |
| early | tôt | *toh* |
| late | tard | *tar* |
| on time | à l'heure | *a luhr* |
| earlier on | plus tôt | *plew toh* |
| later on | plus tard | *plew tar* |
| half an hour ago | il y a une demi-heure | *eelya...* |
| in ten minutes' time | dans dix minutes | *doñ...* |

What time is it?
**Quelle heure est-il?**
*kel uhr eteel*

It's...
**Il est...**
*eel e...*

It's one o'clock
**Il est une heure**
*eel e ewn uhr*

It's six o'clock
**Il est six heures**
*eel e seez uhr*

It's quarter past eight
**Il est huit heures et quart**
*eel e weet uhr ay kar*

(At) what time...?
**À quelle heure...?**
*a kel uhr...*

At...
**À...**
*a...*

At half past one
**À une heure et demie**
*a ewn uhr ay duhmee*

At quarter to seven
**À sept heures moins le quart**
*a set uhr mwañ luh kar*

At 2055
**À vingt heures cinquante-cinq**
*a vañt uhr sañkoñt sañk*

202

# COUNTRIES AND NATIONALITIES

Adjectives are written with a small letter, but nouns with a capital letter, e.g. **une voiture française** (a French car), **une Française** (a Frenchwoman).
Languages are the same as the masculine adjective.

| Country | Nationality (masculine, feminine) |
|---|---|
| Africa **l'Afrique** | **africain, africaine** |
| Algeria **l'Algérie** | **algérien, algérienne** |
| Asia **l'Asie** | **asiatique, asiatique** |
| Australia **l'Australie** | **australien, australienne** |
| Austria **l'Autriche** | **autrichien, autrichienne** |
| Basque Country **le Pays Basque** | **basque, basque** |
| Belgium **la Belgique** | **belge, belge** |
| Canada **le Canada** | **canadien, canadienne** |
| China **la Chine** | **chinois, chinoise** |
| Czechoslovakia **la Tchécoslovaquie** | **tchèque, tchèque** |
| Denmark **le Danemark** | **danois, danoise** |
| England **l'Angleterre** | **anglais, anglaise** |
| Europe **l'Europe** | **européen, européenne** |

| | |
|---|---|
| France **la France** | **français, française** |
| Germany **l'Allemagne** | **allemand, allemande** |
| Great Britain **la Grande-Bretagne** | **britannique, britannique** |
| Greece **la Grèce** | **grec, grecque** |
| Hungary **l'Hongrie** | **hongrois, hongroise** |
| India **l'Inde** | **indien, indienne** |
| Ireland **l'Irlande** | **irlandais, irlandaise** |
| Italy **l'Italie** | **italien, italienne** |
| Japan **le Japon** | **japonais, japonaise** |
| Luxembourg **le Luxembourg** | **luxembourgeois, luxembourgeoise** |
| Morocco **le Maroc** | **marocain, marocaine** |
| Netherlands **les Pays-Bas** | **hollandais, hollandaise** |
| New Zealand **la Nouvelle-Zélande** | **néo-zélandais, néo-zélandaise** |
| North America **l'Amérique du Nord** | **nord-américain, nord-américaine** |
| Northern Ireland **l'Irlande du Nord** | |
| Norway **la Norvège** | **norvégien, norvégienne** |
| Poland **la Pologne** | **polonais, polonaise** |
| Portugal **le Portugal** | **portugais, portugaise** |
| Russia **la Russie** | **russe, russe** |
| Scotland **l'Écosse** | **écossais, écossaise** |
| South America **l'Amérique du Sud** | **sud-américain, sud-américaine** |

| | |
|---|---|
| Soviet Union l'Union Soviétique | soviétique, soviétique |
| Spain   l'Espagne | espagnol, espagnole |
| Sweden   la Suède | suédois, suédoise |
| Switzerland   la Suisse | suisse, suisse |
| Tunisia   la Tunisie | tunisien, tunisienne |
| Turkey   la Turquie | turc, turque |
| United Kingdom le Royaume-Uni | |
| United States   les États-Unis | américain, américaine |
| Wales   le Pays de Galles | gallois, galloise |
| West Indies   les Antilles | antillais, antillaise |
| Yugoslavia   la Yougoslavie | yougoslave, yougoslave |

# GENERAL SIGNS AND NOTICES

| | |
|---|---|
| Accès interdit | No entry |
| À louer | To let, for rent |
| Appuyez | Press, push |
| Arrivées | Arrivals |
| Ascenseur | Lift |
| Attention | Beware |
| Attention au chien | Beware of the dog |
| À vendre | For sale |
| Bureau d'accueil | Information/Reception desk |
| Caisse | Cash desk |
| Chaud (C) | Hot |
| Chiens interdits | No dogs allowed |
| Chien méchant | Beware of the dog |
| Complet | Full, no vacancies |
| Conserver au frais | Keep in a cool place |
| Consommer avant le . . . | Eat by . . . |
| Dames | Ladies |
| Danger (de mort) | Danger (of death) |
| Date limite de vente | Sell-by date |
| Défense de . . . | . . . prohibited |
| Défense de cracher | No spitting |
| Défense d'entrer sous peine d'amende | Trespassers will be prosecuted |
| Défense de fumer | No smoking |
| Défense de marcher sur les pelouses | Keep off the grass |
| Dégustation | Tasting (wine etc.) |
| Départs | Departures |
| Douane | Customs |
| Droite | Right |
| Eau (non) potable | Water (not) for drinking |
| En panne | Out of order |

| | |
|---|---|
| **Entrée** | Entrance |
| **Entrée gratuite/libre** | Free admission |
| **Entrée interdite** | No entry |
| **Entrez sans frapper** | Enter without knocking |
| **Étage** | Floor |
| **Femmes** | Ladies |
| **Fermé** | Closed |
| **Fermeture annuelle** | Closed for annual holidays |
| **Fermeture automatique des portes** | Doors close automatically |
| **Frappez avant d'entrer** | Knock before entering |
| **Froid (F)** | Cold |
| **Fumeurs** | Smokers |
| **Grève** | Strike |
| **Haute tension** | High voltage |
| **Heures d'ouverture** | Opening hours |
| **Hommes** | Gentlemen |
| **Horaire** | Timetable |
| **Hors service** | Out of order |
| **Informations** | Information |
| **Interdiction de .../... interdit** | ... prohibited |
| **Introduire ...** | Insert ... |
| **Issue de secours** | Emergency exit |
| **Laver à main** | Hand wash |
| **Libre** | Free, vacant |
| **Libre-service** | Self-service |
| **Messieurs** | Gentlemen |
| **Mode d'emploi** | Instructions for use |
| **Ne pas ...** | Do not ... |
| **Ne pas toucher** | Do not touch |
| **Nettoyer à sec** | Dry-clean |
| **Non-fumeurs** | Non-smokers |
| **Objets trouvés** | Lost property |
| **Occupé** | Occupied, engaged |
| **Ouvert** | Open |
| **Papiers** | Litter |

|  |  |
|--------|---------|
| Passage interdit | No entry |
| Payez ici | Pay here |
| Peinture fraîche | Wet paint |
| Piste cyclable | Cycle path |
| Poussez | Push |
| Prenez un ticket | Take a ticket |
| Prière de . . . | Please . . . |
| Privé | Private |
| Renseignements | Information, enquiries |
| Réservé | Reserved |
| Retard | Delay |
| Rez-de-chaussée | Ground floor |
| Sonnez s.v.p. | Please ring |
| Sortie (de secours) | (Emergency) exit |
| Sous-sol | Basement |
| S.v.p. = s'il vous plaît | Please |
| Tirez | Pull |
| Toilettes | Toilets |
| Veuillez . . . | Please . . . |

# CONVERSION TABLES
## (approximate equivalents)

### Linear measurements

centimetres   **centimètres (cm)**
metres       **mètres (m)**
kilometres    **kilomètres (km)**

| | |
|---|---|
| 10 cm = 4 inches | 1 inch = 2.54 cm |
| 50 cm = 19.6 inches | 1 foot = 30 cm |
| 1 metre = 39.37 inches | 1 yard = 0.91 m |
| (just over 1 yard) | |
| 100 metres = 110 yards | |
| 1 km = 0.62 miles | 1 mile = 1.61 km |

To convert
km to miles: divide by 8 and multiply by 5
miles to km: divide by 5 and multiply by 8

| Miles | | Kilometres |
|---|---|---|
| 0.6 | 1 | 1.6 |
| 1.2 | 2 | 3.2 |
| 1.9 | 3 | 4.8 |
| 2.5 | 4 | 6.4 |
| 3 | 5 | 8 |
| 6 | 10 | 16 |
| 12 | 20 | 32 |
| 19 | 30 | 48 |
| 25 | 40 | 64 |
| 31 | 50 | 80 |
| 62 | 100 | 161 |
| 68 | 110 | 177 |
| 75 | 120 | 193 |
| 81 | 130 | 209 |

## Liquid measures

litre                                    **litre (l)**

1 litre = 1.8 pints          1 pint = 0.57 litre
5 litres = 1.1 gallons     1 gallon = 4.55 litres
'A litre of water's a pint and three quarters'

| Gallons | | Litres |
|---------|----|--------|
| 0.2 | 1 | 4.5 |
| 0.4 | 2 | 9 |
| 0.7 | 3 | 13.6 |
| 0.9 | 4 | 18 |
| 1.1 | 5 | 23 |
| 2.2 | 10 | 45.5 |

## Weights

gram                           **gramme (g)**
100 grams                   **cent grammes**
200 grams                   **deux cents grammes**
kilo                             **kilo(gramme) (kg)**

100 g = 3.5 oz          1 oz = 28 g
200 g = 7 oz             ¼ lb = 113 g
½ kilo = 1.1 lb          ½ lb = 227 g
1 kilo = 2.2 lb          1 lb = 454 g

| Pounds | | Kilos (Grams) |
|--------|----|---------------|
| 2.2 | 1 | 0.45 (450) |
| 4.4 | 2 | 0.9 (900) |
| 6.6 | 3 | 1.4 (1400) |
| 8.8 | 4 | 1.8 (1800) |
| 11 | 5 | 2.3 (2300) |
| 22 | 10 | 4.5 (4500) |

## Area

hectare                    **hectare (ha)**

1 hectare = 2.5 acres    1 acre = 0.4 hectares

To convert
hectares to acres: divide by 2 and multiply by 5
acres to hectares: divide by 5 and multiply by 2

| Hectares | | Acres |
|---|---|---|
| 0.4 | 1 | 2.5 |
| 2.0 | 5 | 12 |
| 4 | 10 | 25 |
| 10 | 50 | 124 |
| 40.5 | 100 | 247 |

## Clothing and shoe sizes

### Women's dresses and suits

| UK | 10 | 12 | 14 | 16 | 18 | 20 |
|---|---|---|---|---|---|---|
| Continent | 36 | 38 | 40 | 42 | 44 | 46 |

### Men's suits and coats

| UK | 36 | 38 | 40 | 42 | 44 | 46 |
|---|---|---|---|---|---|---|
| Continent | 46 | 48 | 50 | 52 | 54 | 56 |

### Men's shirts

| UK | 14 | 14½ | 15 | 15½ | 16 | 16½ | 17 |
|---|---|---|---|---|---|---|---|
| Continent | 36 | 37 | 38 | 39 | 41 | 42 | 43 |

### Shoes

| UK | 2 | 3 | 4 | 5 | 6 | 7 | 8 | 9 | 10 | 11 |
|---|---|---|---|---|---|---|---|---|---|---|
| Continent | 35 | 36 | 37 | 38 | 39 | 41 | 42 | 43 | 44 | 45 |

### Waist and chest measurements

| inches | 28 | 30 | 32 | 34 | 36 | 38 | 40 | 42 | 44 | 46 | 48 | 50 |
|---|---|---|---|---|---|---|---|---|---|---|---|---|
| centimetres | 71 | 76 | 81 | 87 | 91 | 97 | 102 | 107 | 112 | 117 | 122 | 127 |

### Tyre pressures

| lb/sq in | 15 | 18 | 20 | 22 | 24 | 26 | 28 | 30 | 33 | 35 |
|---|---|---|---|---|---|---|---|---|---|---|
| kg/sq cm | 1.1 | 1.3 | 1.4 | 1.5 | 1.7 | 1.8 | 2.0 | 2.1 | 2.3 | 2.5 |

# NATIONAL HOLIDAYS

*F = France, B = Belgium, S= Switzerland, L = Luxembourg*

| | | |
|---|---|---|
| **Nouvel An** | New Year | 1 January *(FBSL)* |
| | | 2 January *(S)* |
| **Lundi du Carnaval** | Monday before Shrove Tuesday | *(L)* |
| **Vendredi-Saint** | Good Friday | *(S)* |
| **Lundi de Pâques** | Easter Monday | *(FBSL)* |
| **Fête du Travail** | Labour Day | 1 May *(FBSL)* |
| **Fête de la Libération** | VE Day | 8 May *(F)* |
| **Ascension** | Ascension | *(FBSL)* |
| **Lundi de Pentecôte** | Whit Monday | *(FBSL)* |
| **Fête Nationale** | National Day | 23 June *(L)* |
| **Fête Nationale** | Bastille Day | 14 July *(F)* |
| **Fête Nationale** | National Day | 21 July *(B)* |
| **Fête Nationale** | National Day | 1 August *(S)* |
| **Assomption** | Assumption | 15 August *(FBL)* |
| **Toussaint** | All Saints Day | 1 November *(FBL)* |
| **Fête des Morts** | All Souls' Day | 2 November *(L)* |
| **Armistice** | Armistice Day | 11 November *(FB)* |
| **Noël** | Christmas Day | 25 December *(FBSL)* |
| **Saint-Etienne** | St Stephen's Day | 26 December *(S)* |

# USEFUL ADDRESSES

## Tourist Offices

**French Government
Tourist Office**
178 Piccadilly
London W1V 0AL
Tel: 071-499 6911

**Belgian National
Tourist Office**
Premier House
2 Gayton Road
Harrow
Middlesex HA1 2XU
Tel: 081-861 3300

**Luxembourg National Trade
and Tourist Office**
36–37 Piccadilly
London W1V 9PA
Tel: 071-434 2800

**Swiss National Tourist Office**
Swiss Centre
New Coventry Street
London W1V 8EE
Tel: 071-734 1921

## Embassies in the UK

**French Embassy**
58 Knightsbridge
London SW1X 7JT
Tel: 071-235 8080

**Belgian Embassy**
103–105 Eaton Square
London SW1W 9AB
Tel: 071-235 5422

**Embassy of Luxembourg**
27 Wilton Crescent
London SW1X 8SD
Tel: 071-235 6961

**Embassy of Switzerland**
16–18 Montagu Place
London W1H 2BQ
Tel: 071-723 0701

## Embassies in Ireland

**French Embassy**
36 Ailesbury Road
Dublin 4
Tel: Dublin 69 47 77

**Belgian Embassy**
2 Shrewsbury Road
Dublin 4
Tel: Dublin 69 20 82

**Embassy of Switzerland**
6 Ailesbury Road
Ballsbridge
Dublin 4
Tel: Dublin 69 25 15

## Other organisations

**French Chamber of Commerce**
2nd Floor,
Knightsbridge House
197 Knightsbridge
London SW7 1RB
Tel: 071-225 5250

**French Institute**
(for cultural information)
17 Queensberry Place
London SW7 2DT
Tel: 071-589 6211

**French Railways**
179 Piccadilly
London W1V 0BA
Tel: 071-409 1224

**Belgian National Railways**
Premier House
10 Greycoat Place
London SW1P 1SB
Tel: 071-233 0360

**Belgo-Luxembourg Chamber of Commerce**
6 John Street
London WC1N 2ES
Tel: 071-831 3508

**Swiss Federal Railways**
Swiss Centre
New Coventry Street
London W1V 8EE
Tel: 071-734 1921

# British embassies and consulates abroad

### France
Embassy:
35 rue du Faubourg St-Honoré
75383 Paris Cedex 08
Tel: 42 66 91 42

Consulate:
16 rue d'Anjou
75008 Paris
Tel: 42 66 91 42

There are also consulates in:
Bordeaux, Boulogne, Calais, Cherbourg, Dunkerque, Le Havre, Lille, Lyon, Marseille, Nantes, Nice, Perpignan, St Malo-Dinard, Toulouse and Ajaccio (Corsica).

### Belgium
Britannia House
28 rue Joseph II
1040 Brussels
Tel: 217 90 00

There are also consulates in Antwerp and Liège.

### Luxembourg
14 Boulevard Roosevelt
PO Box 874
L-2018 Luxembourg Ville
Tel: 2 98 64/66

### Switzerland
Thunstrasse 50
3005 Berne
Tel: 44 50 21/6

There are also consulates in Geneva, Lugano, Montreux and Zurich.

# Irish embassies abroad

**France**
4 rue Rude
75116 Paris
Tel: 45 00 20 87

**Belgium**
19 rue du Luxembourg
1040 Brussels
Tel: 513 66 33

**Luxembourg**
28 route d'Arlon
1140 Luxembourg Ville
Tel: 4 20 47

**Switzerland**
Eigerstrasse 71
3007 Berne
Tel: 46 23 53

# NUMBERS

| | | |
|---|---|---|
| 0 | **zéro** | *zayro* |
| 1 | **un** | *uñ* |
| 2 | **deux** | *duh* |
| 3 | **trois** | *trwa* |
| 4 | **quatre** | *katr* |
| 5 | **cinq** | *sañk* |
| 6 | **six** | *sees* |
| 7 | **sept** | *set* |
| 8 | **huit** | *weet* |
| 9 | **neuf** | *nuhf* |
| 10 | **dix** | *dees* |
| 11 | **onze** | *awñz* |
| 12 | **douze** | *dooz* |
| 13 | **treize** | *trez* |
| 14 | **quatorze** | *katorz* |
| 15 | **quinze** | *kañz* |
| 16 | **seize** | *sez* |
| 17 | **dix-sept** | *deeset* |
| 18 | **dix-huit** | *deezweet* |
| 19 | **dix-neuf** | *deeznuhf* |
| 20 | **vingt** | *vañ* |
| 21 | **vingt et un** | *vañtay uñ* |
| 22 | **vingt-deux** | *vañ duh* |
| 23 etc. | **vingt-trois** | *vañ trwa* |
| 30 | **trente** | *troñt* |
| 31 | **trente et un** | *troñt ay uñ* |
| 32 etc. | **trente-deux** | *troñt duh* |
| 40 | **quarante** | *karoñt* |
| 50 | **cinquante** | *sañkoñt* |
| 60 | **soixante** | *swasoñt* |
| 70 | **soixante-dix** | *swasoñt dees* |

| | | |
|---|---|---|
| 71 | **soixante et onze** | *swasoñt ay awñz* |
| 72 etc. | **soixante-douze** | *swasoñt dooz* |
| 80 | **quatre-vingts** | *katr vañ* |
| 81 | **quatre-vingt-un** | *katr vañtuñ* |
| 82 etc. | **quatre-vingt-deux** | *katr vañ duh* |
| 90 | **quatre-vingt-dix** | *katr vañ dees* |
| 91 | **quatre-vingt-onze** | *katr vañ awñz* |
| 92 etc. | **quatre-vingt-douze** | *katr vañ dooz* |
| 100 | **cent** | *soñ* |
| 110 etc. | **cent dix** | *soñ dees* |
| 200 | **deux cents\*** | *duh soñ* |
| 300 etc. | **trois cents** | *trwa soñ* |
| 1,000 | **mille** | *meel* |
| 2,000 etc. | **deux mille** | *duh meel* |
| 1,000,000 | **un million** | *uñ meelyawñ* |
| 1,000,000,000 | **un milliard** | *uñ meelyar* |

● Years:

| | |
|---|---|
| **1990** | **dix-neuf cent quatre-vingt-dix** |
| **1789** | **dix-sept cent quatre-vingt-neuf** |

\* When **cents** is followed by another number, it is written without the **s**, e.g. **deux cent dix** (210).

# DICTIONARY

French nouns are given with the definite article ('the') to show their gender: **le** for masculine, **la** for feminine (**les** in the plural). Where the gender is not clear, the abbreviations (*m*) or (*f*) are added.

Where adjectives have different endings or forms for masculine and feminine, the masculine is given first, e.g. **bleu(e)** (i.e. **bleu** for masculine, **bleue** for feminine); **courageux/euse** (i.e. **courageux**, **courageuse**); **fou**, **folle**.

Other abbreviations: (*pl*) – plural.

Words for food and drink are given in the Menu reader, page 110.

See also General signs and notices, page 206, and the You may see lists in the individual sections.

## A

**à** to; at
  **à . . . kilomètres/minutes** . . . kilomètres/minutes away
  **à . . . heures** at . . . o'clock
l'**abonnement** (*m*) season ticket
**absolument** absolutely
**accepter** to accept
l'**accident** (*m*) accident
**accord: être d'accord** to agree
l'**accueil** (*m*) welcome; reception
l'**achat** (*m*) purchase
les **achats** (*mpl*) shopping
**acheter** to buy
l'**acier** (*m*) steel
l'**activité** (*f*) activity
**actuel(le)** present, current
**actuellement** at present
l'**addition** (*f*) bill
l'**adresse** (*f*) address
l'**adulte** (*m/f*) adult
l'**aéroglisseur** (*m*) hovercraft
l'**aéroport** (*m*) airport
les **affaires** (*fpl*) business; things, belongings
**affreux/euse** awful, dreadful

l'**âge** (*m*) age
  **quel âge avez-vous?** how old are you?
l'**agence** (*f*) agency
l'**agenda** (*m*) diary
**agité(e)** rough (*sea*)
l'**agneau** (*m*) lamb
**agréable** pleasant
**aider** to help
**aigre** sour
l'**aiguille** (*f*) needle
l'**ail** (*m*) garlic
**aimer** to like
**ainsi** thus, like this, in this way
l'**air** (*m*) air
  **en plein air** in the open air
les **alentours** (*mpl*) surrounding area, outskirts
l'**aliment** (*m*) food
**aller** to go
l'**aller-retour** (*m*) return (*ticket*)
l'**aller simple** single, one way (*ticket*)
**allumer** to light; to switch/turn on
les **allumettes** (*fpl*) matches
**alors** then
l'**ambassade** (*f*) embassy
l'**amende** (*f*) fine
**amer, amère** bitter
l'**ami(e)** (*m/f*) friend

221

l'ampoule (f) (light)bulb
l'amuse-gueule (m) appetiser
l'an (m) year
ancien(ne) old
l'âne (m) donkey
anglais(e) English
animé(e) busy, lively
l'année (f) year
l'anniversaire (m) anniversary; birthday
l'annonce (f) advertisement
l'annuaire (m) (telephone) directory
l'antenne (f) aerial
l'antigel (m) anti-freeze
les antiquités (fpl) antiques
l'appareil (m) appliance, machine
l'appareil-photo (m) camera
l'appartement (m) apartment, flat

l'appel (m) call
appeler to call
s'appeler to be called
    comment vous appelez-vous? what is your name?
apprendre to learn
approprié(e) suitable
approximativement approximately
appuyer (sur) to push, press
après after(wards); later on
apr. J-C = après Jésus-Christ AD
l'après-midi (m) afternoon
l'après-shampooing (m) (hair) conditioner
l'araignée (f) spider
l'arbitre (m) referee
l'arbre (m) tree

l'argent (m) money; silver
l'armoire (m) cupboard
arracher to pull/take out, extract
l'arrêt (m) stop; (taxi) rank
arrêter to stop
les arrhes (fpl) deposit
arrière rear
    en arrière backwards
l'arrivée (f) arrival
arriver (à) to arrive (at), reach
l'art (m) art
l'articulation (f) joint (body)
l'artisanat (m) craft goods
l'ascenseur (m) lift
assez enough; quite, fairly; quite a lot
l'assiette (f) plate
assis(e) sitting (down)
l'associé(e) (m/f) member; partner
l'assurance (f) insurance
l'atelier (m) workshop
attaquer to attack
attendre to wait (for)
attention beware, take care, look out!
au = à + le, aux = à + les at/to the
l'auberge (m) hotel, hostel
au-delà (de) beyond
au-dessous (de) under, below
au-dessus (de) above
augmenter to increase
aujourd'hui today
au revoir goodbye
aussi also, as well, too
autant que as much/many as

l'**autobus** (*m*) bus
l'**autocar** (*m*) coach
l'**automne** (*m*) autumn
l'**autoroute** (*f*) motorway
l'**auto-stop** (*m*) hitch-hiking
**autour** (**de**) around
**autre** another, other
    **autre chose?** anything
      else?
**autrefois** in the past, once
**autrement** otherwise
**avance: à l'avance** in
    advance
**avant** before; front
    **en avant** forward(s)
**av. J-C = avant Jésus-**
    **Christ** BC
l'**avantage** (*m*) advantage
**avec** with
l'**avenir** (*m*) future
**avertir** to tell, inform; to
    warn
**aveugle** blind
l'**avion** (*m*) aeroplane
l'**avis** (*m*) opinion; notice;
    warning
l'**avocat** (*m*) lawyer
**avoir** to have

# B

les **bagages** (*mpl*) luggage,
    baggage
la **bague** ring
la **baguette** loaf of bread
    (French stick)
la **baie** bay; berry
la **baignoire** bath(tub)
le **bain** bath
le **baiser** kiss

**baisser** to lower; to turn
    down (*volume*)
la **balade** walk, stroll
le **baladeur** personal stereo
le **balai** broom
le **balcon** balcony; (*theatre*)
    circle
la **balle** ball
le **ballon** ball; balloon
la **bande dessinée** comic strip
la **bande magnétique**
    (recording) tape
la **banque** bank
la **barbe** beard
    **bas, basse** low; short
    **en bas** down, downstairs,
      below
les **bas** (*mpl*) stockings
le **bateau** boat
le **bâtiment** building
le **bâton** stick, pole
la **batterie** car battery
    **beau, belle** beautiful;
      handsome; lovely; fine
**beaucoup** very (much), a lot
**beaucoup de** a lot of, many
le **beau-fils** son-in-law;
    stepson
le **beau-frère** brother-in-law;
    stepbrother
le **beau-père** father-in-law;
    stepfather
la **beauté** beauty
les **beaux-parents** (*mpl*) in-laws
le **bébé** baby
    **belge** Belgian
    **belle** (see **beau**)
la **belle-fille** daughter-in-law;
    stepdaughter
la **belle-mère** mother-in-law;
    stepmother

**la belle-soeur** sister-in-law; stepsister

**besoin: avoir besoin de** to need

**bête** stupid, silly

**le biberon** baby's bottle

**la bibliothèque** library

**la bicyclette** bicycle

**bien** well; fine

**bien entendu** of course

**bien que** although

**bien sûr** of course

**bientôt** soon

**à bientôt** see you later

**bienvenu(e)** welcome

**le billet** ticket; banknote

**bizarre** strange, odd

**blanc, blanche** white

**en blanc** blank

**la blanchisserie** laundry

**blessé(e)** injured, wounded

**le bleu** bruise

**bleu(e)** blue; very rare (*steak*)

**bleu marine** navy blue

**le bloc(-notes)** notepad, writing pad

**bloqué(e)** blocked, jammed

**la blouse** overall; white coat

**boire** to drink

**le bois** wood

**la boisson** drink

**la boîte** box; tin, can

**la boîte aux lettres** letterbox, postbox

**la boîte de nuit** nightclub

**le bol** bowl, basin

**la bombe** bomb; aerosol, spray can

**bon, bonne** good

**bon appétit!** enjoy your meal!

**les bonbons** (*mpl*) sweets

**la bonde** plug (*bath*)

**bondé(e)** crowded

**bonjour** good day, good morning, good afternoon

**bonne** (see **bon**)

**bonsoir** good evening

**le bord** edge; border

**à bord** aboard

**la botte** boot

**la bouche** mouth

**bouclé(e)** curly

**bouger** to move

**la bougie** candle; sparking plug

**bouilli(e)** boiled

**la bourse** stock exchange

**le bout** end

**la bouteille** bottle

**le bouton** button; switch, knob

**la branche** branch

**le bras** arm

**bref, brève** brief, short

**le bricolage** do-it-yourself

**brillant(e)** shiny; bright

**le brillant** lip gloss

**briller** to shine

**le briquet** (cigarette) lighter

**bronzé(e)** (sun-)tanned

**la brosse** brush

**le brouillard** fog

**le bruit** noise

**brûler** to burn

**brun(e)** brown; dark (*hair/skin*)

**le bureau** office

**le bureau de poste** post office

**le bureau de tabac** tobacconist's

**le but** goal; aim, purpose

## C

**ça** this, that

**la cabine** cabin; cubicle

**cacher** to hide

**le cadeau** gift, present

**le cadre** frame, setting; scope; executive, manager

**le café** café; coffee

**la cafetière** coffee pot

**le cahier** exercise book

**la caisse** box; cash desk

**la caisse d'épargne** savings bank

**le camion** lorry

**la camionnette** van

**la campagne** country(side)

**camper** to camp

**la canne** walking stick

**le canoë** canoe

**le canot** boat

**le caoutchouc** rubber

**car** because

**le carnet** (note)book

**le carré** square

**carreaux: à carreaux** check(ed) (*material*)

**le carrefour** crossroads; junction

**la carrière** career

**la carte** map; card; menu

**la carte postale** postcard

**le carton** cardboard; carton

**le cas** case

**en cas de** in case of

**en tout cas** in any case

**le casse-croûte** snack

**casser** to break

**la casserole** saucepan

**cause: à cause de** because of

**la cave** cellar

**la caverne** cave

**ce/cet, cette** this, that

**ceci** this

**la CE** EC, European Community

**la ceinture** belt

**cela** this, that

**célibataire** single, unmarried

**celle** (see **celui**)

**celles** (see **ceux**)

**celle-ci, celle-là** (see **celui-ci, celui-là**)

**celles-ci, celles-là** (see **ceux-ci, ceux-là**)

**celui, celle** the one

**celui-ci, celle-ci** this one

**celui-là, celle-là** that one

**le cendrier** ashtray

**le centre** centre; middle

**cependant** however

**certainement** certainly

**ces** these, those

**c'est** it/that/he/she is

**c'est-à-dire** that's to say, in other words

**c'est ça!** that's right!

**cette** (see **ce**)

**ceux, celles** the ones

**ceux-ci, celles-ci** these ones

**ceux-là, celles-là** those ones

**chacun(e)** each (one); every (one)

**la chaîne** chain

**la chaise** chair

**la chaleur** heat

la **chambre** room
la **chambre à coucher** bedroom
le **champ** field
la **chance** luck
    **bonne chance!** good luck!
**changer** to change
la **chanson** song
**chanter** to sing
le **chapeau** hat
**chaque** each; every
le **charbon** coal
la **charcuterie** cooked pork meats
le **chariot** trolley
**charmant(e)** charming; lovely
le **chat** cat
le **château** castle
    **chaud(e)** hot
    **il fait chaud** it's hot (weather)
    **avoir chaud** to be hot
le **chauffage** heating
le **chauffeur** driver
la **chaussée** carriageway, road surface
la **chaussette** sock
la **chaussure** shoe
le **chef** chef; boss, head, chief
le **chemin de fer** railway
le **chemin** path; lane; way, route
la **chemise** shirt
le **chemisier** blouse
    **cher, chère** expensive; dear
    **chercher** to look for, to search
le **cheval** horse
les **cheveux** (*mpl*) hair
la **chèvre** goat

**chez . . .** at . . . 's house
le **chien** dog
le **chiffon** cloth, rag
le **chiffre** figure, number
le **choix** choice; range
le **chômage** unemployment
la **chose** thing
la **chute d'eau** waterfall
la **cicatrice** scar
    **Cie.** = **compagnie** company
le **ciel** sky; heaven
la **cigarette** cigarette
le **cinéma** cinema
le **cirage** shoe polish
la **circulation** traffic
les **ciseaux** (*mpl*) scissors
la **cité** city
    **clair(e)** clear; light (coloured), pale
la **clé/clef** key; spanner
le **client, la cliente** customer; client
le **climat** climate
la **climatisation** air conditioning
la **cloche** bell
le **clou** nail
le **cœur** heart
le **coiffeur, la coiffeuse** hairdresser
le **coin** corner
le **col** collar; (mountain) pass
la **colère** anger
le **colis** parcel
le **collant** tights
la **colle** glue
le **collier** necklace; dog collar
la **colline** hill
    **combien?** how much?; how many?

**combien den temps?** how long?, how much time?

**la combinaison** combination; wetsuit; flying suit; petticoat, slip

**comme** as, like

**comme ça** thus, like this/that

**comme d'habitude** as usual

**commencer** to begin

**comment?** how?; pardon?

**le commissariat (de police)** police station

**commun(e)** common

**la compagnie** company

**complet, complète** full (up)

**complètement** completely

**comprendre** to understand

**compris(e)** included

**le compte** account

**le compteur** meter

**le concours** competition

**le conducteur, la conductrice** driver

**conduire** to drive

**la confiture** jam

**confortable** comfortable

**le congé** holiday, day off; leave

**le congrès** conference, congress

**connaître** to know, be acquainted with

**conseiller** to advise

**la conserve** tinned food

**conserver** to keep

**le conte** story

**le contenu** contents

**content(e)** content(ed), pleased

**le contraceptif** contraceptive

**contre** against

**la coquille** shell

**la corde** rope; string

**le corps** body

**la correspondance** connection; correspondence

**le costume** suit; costume

**la côte** rib; chop; hill; coast

**le côté** side

**à côté de** beside, next to

**le coton** cotton

**le coton hydrophile** cotton wool

**les couches** (*fpl*) nappies

**la couleur** colour

**le couloir** corridor

**le coup** blow, hit; shot

**le coup de soleil** sunburn

**couper** to cut, to cut off

**la cour** courtyard; court

**courageux/euse** brave

**couramment** fluently

**le courant** (electrical) power, current

**le courant d'air** draught

**courir** to run

**la couronne** crown

**le cours** course; lesson

**la course** race

**faire des courses** (*fpl*) to go shopping

**court(e)** short

**le cousin, la cousine** cousin

**le couteau** knife

**coûter** to cost

**la couture** sewing

**le couvercle** top, lid

**couvert(e)** covered

**les couverts** (*mpl*) cutlery

**la couverture** blanket

**couvrir** to cover

**cracher** to spit
**la cravate** tie
**le crayon** pencil
**la crème** cream; lotion
**le cri** shout, cry
**le crime** crime
**croire** to think, believe
**la croisière** cruise
**la croix** cross
**cru(e)** raw
**la cuiller** spoon
**le cuir** leather
**cuire** to cook
**la cuisine** cooking; kitchen

## D

**d'abord** (at) first
**d'accord** agreed, fine, very well
**le daim** suede
**la dame** lady
**le danger** danger
**dans** in, inside
**danser** to dance
**davantage** (any) more; (any) longer
**de** of; from; about
**debout** standing (up)
**le début** beginning
**le débutant, la débutante** beginner
**déchiré(e)** torn
**décider** to decide
**découvrir** to discover
**décrire** to describe
**dedans** inside
**le degré** degree (*temperature*)
**la dégustation** tasting, sampling
**dehors** outside

**déjà** already; now
**le déjeuner** lunch
**demain** tomorrow
**demander** to ask (for)
**demi(e)** half
**le demi-frère** stepbrother
**la demi-sœur** stepsister
**la dent** tooth
**le départ** departure
**dépêchez-vous!, dépêche-toi!** hurry up!
**dépenser** to spend
**le dépliant** brochure
**depuis** since
**dernier, dernière** last; latest
**derrière** behind
**des = de + les** of the
**dès** from; since
**désagréable** unpleasant
**le désavantage** disadvantage
**descendre** to come/go down; to get off (*bus etc.*); to stay (at a hotel); to take down
**désirer** to want, desire
**le dessin** drawing; design, pattern
**le dessin animé** cartoon film
**dessous** underneath
**dessus** on top; above
**deux** two
**les deux** both
**deuxième** second
**devant** in front (of)
**dévisser** to unscrew
**devoir** to have to
**d'habitude** usually
**la diapositive** slide (*photo*)
**différent(e)** different
**difficile** difficult
**le dîner** dinner

**dire** to say, to tell
**la discussion** discussion, argument
**disons** let's say
**le disque** disc; record
**divers(e)** varied; various
**le doigt** finger
**le doigt de pied** toe
**dois: je dois** I must, have to
**le domaine** estate, property
**le dommage** damage
**quel dommage!** what a pity!
**donc** so
**donner** to give
**dont** whose; of which
**dormir** to sleep
**le dossier** file
**la douane** customs
**douce** (see **doux**)
**la douche** shower
**la douleur** pain, ache
**le doute** doubt
**sans doute** no doubt, doubtless
**doux, douce** sweet; soft; mild; gentle
**le drap** sheet
**la droite** right
**à droite** on/to the right
**les droits (de douane)** (customs) duty
**drôle** funny, amusing
**du = de + le** of/from the
**dur(e)** hard; tough
**durant** during
**durer** to last

# E

**l'eau** (f) water
**l'échantillon** (m) sample
**l'école** (f) school
**écouter** to listen (to)
**l'écran** (m) screen
**écrire** to write
**E.U. = États-Unis** United States
**efficace** effective
**effectivement** really, in fact; exactly
**effrayé(e)** frightened
**égal(e)** equal; the same; even
**ça m'est égal** it's all the same to me, I don't care
**l'église** (f) church
**l'égratignure** (f) scratch
**l'élastique** (m) rubber band; elastic
**l'électrophone** (m) record player
**l'élève** (m/f) pupil
**élevé(e)** high
**elle** she; her; it
**elle-même** herself
**elles** they; them
**l'émail** (m) enamel
**l'embarquement** (m) boarding, embarcation
**embêter** to bother, annoy
**l'embouteillage** (m) traffic jam
**embrasser** to kiss
**l'emploi** (m) use
**employer** to use, employ
**emporter** to take away
**en** in; to; some, any
**encaisser** to cash (cheque)

229

**enceinte** pregnant
**enchanté(e)** delighted; pleased to meet you
**encore** still; yet
  **encore une fois** again, once more
l' **endroit** (*m*) place; right side
l' **énergie** (*f*) energy, power
l' **enfant** (*m*) child
l' **enfer** (*m*) hell
**enfin** at last
**ennuyé(e)** bored
**énorme** enormous
**enregistrer** to record; to register; to check in
**enrhumé: être enrhumé(e)** to have a cold
**enseigner** to teach
**ensemble** together
**ensuite** then
**entendre** to hear
**entier, entière** whole
**entouré(e) (de)** surrounded (by)
l' **entracte** (*m*) interval
**entre** among; between
l' **entrée** (*f*) entrance, way in; admission; ticket; starter (*food*)
**entrer** to enter, go in
l' **entrevue** (*f*) interview
l' **enveloppe** (*f*) envelope
l' **envers: à l'envers** upside down, inside out, back to front
**environ** about; around
l' **environnement** (*m*) environment
**envoyer** to send
**épais(se)** thick

l' **épice** (*f*) spice
l' **épingle** (*f*) pin
**épuisé(e)** exhausted; sold out, out of stock
l' **équipage** (*m*) crew
l' **équipe** (*f*) team
l' **équipement** (*m*) equipment
l' **escalier** (*m*) stairs, staircase
l' **espace** (*m*) space; area
l' **espèce** (*f*) sort, kind
**espérer** to hope (for); to expect
**essayer** to try
l' **essence** (*f*) petrol
**est: il/elle est** he/she/it is
l' **est** (*m*) east
l' **estomac** (*m*) stomach
**et** and
l' **étage** (*m*) floor, storey
l' **étagère** (*f*) shelf
l' **état** (*m*) state
l' **été** (*m*) summer
**éteindre** to switch/turn off
l' **étoile** (*f*) star
**étonnant(e)** surprising, amazing
**étrange** strange, odd
l' **étranger** (*m*), l'**étrangère** (*f*) foreigner
à l'**étranger** abroad
**être** to be
**étroit(e)** narrow; tight
l' **étude** (*f*) study
l' **étudiant(e)** (*m/f*) student
**eux** them
  **eux-mêmes** themselves
**excusez-moi** excuse me, pardon me
l' **exemple** (*m*) example
**expliquer** to explain

**l'exposition** (*f*) exhibition
**exprès** deliberately, on
purpose

## F

**face: en face (de)** facing;
opposite
**fâché(e)** annoyed
**facile** easy
la **façon** way, manner
**de toute façon** anyway
**faible** weak
**faim: avoir faim** to be
hungry
**faire** to do; to make
le **fait** fact
la **famille** family
**fatigué(e)** tired
les **faubourgs** (*mpl*) outskirts
**fausse** (see **faux**)
**faut: il faut** you have to,
you must, it is necessary
to
la **faute** fault
le **fauteuil** armchair
le **fauteuil roulant** wheelchair
**faux, fausse** false; fake
**félicitations!**
congratulations!
la **femme** woman; wife
la **fenêtre** window
le **fer** iron
la **ferme** farm
**fermer** to close
la **fermeture** closing, closure;
catch, fastener
la **fermeture éclair** zip
la **fête** festival, holiday
le **feu** fire
la **feuille** leaf; sheet of paper

les **feux** (*mpl*) traffic lights
la **ficelle** string; stick of
French bread
le **fichier** file (*computer*)
la **fièvre** fever; (high)
temperature
le **fil** thread
le **filet** net
la **fille** girl; daughter
le **fils** son
la **fin** end
**finalement** finally, in the
end
**finir** to end
la **fleur** flower
le **fleuve** river
la **foire** fair
la **fois** time
**à la fois** at the same time
**folle** (see **fou**)
le **fond** back; end; bottom
la **fontaine** fountain
la **forêt** forest
la **forme** form, shape; figure
le **formulaire** form
**fort(e)** strong; loud; great
**fou, folle** crazy, mad
le **four** oven
le **four à micro-ondes**
microwave oven
la **fourchette** fork
**frais, fraîche** fresh; cool
**français(e)** French
**frapper** to hit; to strike; to
knock
**fréquemment** frequently,
often
**fréquent(e)** frequent
le **frère** brother
le **frigidaire** refrigerator
le **frigo** fridge

**frit(e)** fried
**froid(e)** cold
    **il fait froid** it's cold
    (weather)
    **avoir froid** to be cold
**le fromage** cheese
**la frontière** border, frontier
**le fruit** fruit
**les fruits de mer** (*mpl*) seafood,
    shellfish
**la fumée** smoke
    **fumer** to smoke

## G

**gagner** to earn; to win; to
    gain
**la galerie** gallery; roof rack
**le gant** glove
**le garçon** boy; waiter
    **garde: de garde** on duty
    **garder** to keep; to look after
**la gare** station
**la gauche** left
    **à gauche** on/to the left
**le gazon** lawn, grass
**les gens** (*mpl*) people
    **gentil(le)** kind
**le gérant** manager
**la gérante** manageress
**la gestion** management
**le gilet** waistcoat
**le gitan, la gitane** gypsy
**la glace** ice; ice cream; mirror
**le glaçon** ice cube
    **glissant(e)** slippery
**la gomme** rubber (*eraser*)
    **gonfler** to inflate
**la gorge** throat
    **gourmand(e)** greedy
**le goût** taste

**le goûter** (afternoon) tea
**la goutte** drop; drip
**le gouvernement** government
    **grand(e)** big, large; great
**la Grande-Bretagne** Great
    Britain
**le grand magasin** department
    store
**la grand-mère** grandmother
**le grand-père** grandfather
    **gras, grasse** fat; fatty; greasy
    **gratuit(e)** free
    **grave** serious
**la grève** strike
**la grippe** flu
    **gris(e)** grey; dull
**le groom** bellboy
    **gros, grosse** fat; big, large
**la grosseur** size, bulk; lump
    **grossier, grossière** rude
**la grotte** cave
**la guerre** war
**le guichet** ticket office
**le guide** guide-book
**le/la guide** guide

## H

**l'habitude** (*f*) custom, habit
    **haut(e)** high; tall
    **en haut** up, upstairs,
    above
    **hebdomadaire** weekly
**l'herbe** (*f*) grass; herb
    **hésiter** to hesitate
**l'heure** (*f*) hour
**les heures d'affluence/de pointe**
    rush hour
    **heureux/euse** happy;
    fortunate
    **hier** yesterday

**l'histoire** (f) history; story
**l'hiver** (m) winter
**l'homme** (m) man
**l'horaire** (m) timetable
**l'horloge** (f) clock
**hors (de)** out (of)
**l'hôte** (m) host; landlord; guest
**l'hôtel** (m) hotel
**l'hôtel de ville** (m) town hall
**l'hôtesse** (f) hostess; air stewardess
**l'huile** (m) oil
**humide** damp; wet

## I

**ici** here
**ignorer** to ignore; not to know
**il** he; it
**il n'y en a pas** there isn't/aren't any
**il y a** there is/are
  **il y a . . . (ans)** . . . (years) ago
**l'île** (f) island
**ils** they
**l'imperméable** (m) raincoat
**impoli(e)** rude
**importer** to import; to matter
  **n'importe qui/où** no matter who/where, anyone/where
**l'impôt** (m) tax
**impressionnant(e)** impressive
**imprévu(e)** unexpected
**l'incendie** (m) fire

**inconnu(e)** unknown, strange
**l'inconvénient** (m) disadvantage, drawback
**inférieur(e)** lower, bottom
**l'informatique** (f) computer science/studies, information technology
**inquiet, inquiète** worried
**l'insolation** (f) sunstroke
**insolite** unusual
**instantané(e)** instant
**l'instituteur** (m), **l'institutrice** (f) (primary school) teacher
**interdit(e)** prohibited, forbidden
**intérieur(e)** interior
  **à l'intérieur** inside, indoors
**introduire** to introduce; to insert
**inutile** useless; unnecessary
**l'issue** (f) exit
**ivre** drunk

## J

**j'** = **je** I
**j'ai** I have
**jamais** never; ever
**la jambe** leg
**le jambon** ham
**le jardin** garden
**jaune** yellow
**je** I
**le jean** jeans
**jeter** to throw (away)
  **à jeter** disposable
**le jeu** game; gambling; set, collection

233

**jeune** young
la **jeunesse** youth
**joli(e)** pretty, nice, lovely
**jouer** to play; to gamble
le **jouet** toy
le **jour** day
le **jour férié** (public) holiday
le **journal** newspaper
le/la **journaliste** journalist
la **journée** day
la **jupe** skirt
le **jus** juice
**jusqu'à** until; as far as
**juste** fair; just; correct; tight

## L

**l' = le** or **la** the
**la** the; her; it
**là** there
**là-bas** (over) there, down there
le **lac** lake
**là-haut** up there
**laid(e)** ugly
la **laine** wool
**laisser** to leave; to let, allow
le **lait** milk
la **lame** blade
la **lampe** lamp, light
**lancer** to throw
la **langue** tongue; language
**laquelle** (see **lequel**)
**large** broad, wide
le **lavabo** wash-basin
les **lavabos** (*mpl*) toilets
**laver** to wash
le **the**; him; it
la **lecture** reading
**léger, légère** light
le **lendemain** day after

**lent(e)** slow
**lentement** slowly
la **lentille** lens
**lequel, laquelle** which (one)
**les** the; them
**lesquels, lesquelles** which (ones)
la **lessive** washing powder, detergent; washing
**leur** (to/for) them
**leur(s)** their
le/la **leur** theirs
**lever** to lift, raise
la **librairie** bookshop
**libre** free, unoccupied, vacant; for hire
le **lieu** place
**au lieu de** instead of
**avoir lieu** to take place
la **ligne** line; route
la **lime** file (*tool*)
**lire** to read
**lisse** smooth
le **lit** bed
la **livre** pound
le **livre** book
le/la **locataire** tenant
la **location** rental, hire
le **logement** accommodation
la **loi** law
**loin** far (away)
**Londres** London
**long, longue** long
le **long de** along
**longtemps** (for) a long time, (for) long
**lorsque** when
la **lotion** lotion
**louer** to rent, hire
**lourd(e)** heavy

234

**lui** him; her; it
**lui-même** himself
la **lumière** light
la **lune** moon
les **lunettes** (*fpl*) glasses, spectacles
**luxe: grand luxe** luxury

# M

**M = Monsieur** Mr
**m' = me** me
**ma** (see **mon**)
la **machine** machine
la **machine à écrire** typewriter
**Madame** Mrs; madam
**Mademoiselle** Miss
le **magasin** shop
le **magnétophone** tape recorder
le **magnétoscope** video recorder
le **maillot de bain** bathing costume, swimsuit
la **main** hand
**maintenant** now
le **maire** mayor
la **mairie** town hall
**mais** but
la **maison** house; home
le **maître** teacher
la **maîtresse** teacher
la **majorité** majority
**mal** badly
    **avoir mal à . . .** to have a pain in . . .
    **pas mal (de)** quite a lot (of)
**malade** ill
**malgré** despite, in spite of
le **malheur** misfortune

**malheureusement** unfortunately
la **malle** trunk
la **manche** sleeve
la **Manche** English Channel
**manger** to eat
la **manière** way, manner
la **manifestation** demonstration (*protest*)
**manquer** to miss; to be lacking
le **manteau** coat
le **maquillage** make-up
le **marchand** dealer, merchant
la **marche** step; stair
    **en marche** moving, working
le **marché** market
    **bon marché** cheap
**marcher** to walk; to work, function
le **mari** husband
le **mariage** wedding
**marié(e)** married
la **marque** make, brand
**marron** brown
le **marteau** hammer
le **matelas** mattress
le **matériel** equipment; materials
la **matière** subject; material; matter
le **matin** morning
**mauvais(e)** bad
**me** (to) me
**méchant(e)** naughty
le **médecin** doctor
la **médecine** medicine
le **médicament** medicine, drug
**meilleur(e)** better; best
le **mélange** mixture

le **membre** member; limb
**même** same; even
le **ménage** housework; household; couple
la **ménagère** housewife
**mensuel(le)** monthly
la **mer** sea
**merci (beaucoup/bien)** thank you (very much)
la **mère** mother
**merveilleux/euse** marvellous, wonderful
**mes** my
**Mesdames** Ladies
la **messe** mass
**Messieurs** Gentlemen
la **mesure** measurement; size
le **métier** occupation, trade, job
**mettre** to put (on)
**meublé(e)** furnished
les **meubles** (*mpl*) furniture
**midi** (*m*) midday, noon
le **Midi** South of France
le **mien, la mienne** mine
**mieux** better; best
le **milieu** middle; environment
**mince** slim
**minuit** (*m*) midnight
le **miroir** mirror
la **mi-temps** half-time
**mixte** mixed
**Mlle = Mademoiselle** Miss
**Mme = Madame** Mrs
la **mode** fashion
**moi** me
**moi-même** myself
**moins** less; minus
   **au moins** at least
le **mois** month
la **moitié** half

**mon, ma** my
le **monde** world
la **monnaie** currency; coin; change
le **monsieur** gentleman
**Monsieur** Mr; sir
la **montagne** mountain(s)
le **montant** amount
**monter** to go up; to take up; to climb; to ride
la **montre** watch
**montrer** to show
le **morceau** piece, bit
**mort(e)** dead
le **mot** word; note
la **moto(cyclette)** motorbike
la **mouche** fly
le **mouchoir** handkerchief
**mouillé(e)** wet
le **moulin** mill
le **mouton** sheep
**moyen(ne)** medium; average
les **moyens** (*mpl*) means
le **mur** wall
**mûr(e)** mature; ripe

# N

**n' = ne** not
**nager** to swim
la **natation** swimming
le **navire** ship
**né(e)** born
la **neige** snow
**ne . . . jamais** never
**ne . . . pas** not
**ne . . . rien** nothing
**n'est-ce pas?** isn't that so?, isn't it?

**nettoyer** to clean
  **nettoyer à sec** to dry clean
**neuf, neuve** new
le **neveu** nephew
le **nez** nose
**ni . . . ni** neither . . . nor
la **nièce** niece
la **noce** wedding
  **Noël** Christmas
**noir(e)** black
le **nom** name
le **nom de famille** surname
  **non** no; not
le **nord** north
  **nos** our
  **notre** our
le/la **nôtre** ours
  **nouer** to tie
la **nourriture** food
  **nous** we; us
  **nous-mêmes** ourselves
  **nouveau, nouvelle** new
  **de nouveau** again
les **nouvelles** (*fpl*) news
  **nu(e)** naked, nude
le **nuage** cloud
la **nuit** night
  **nul(le)** void
    **nulle part** nowhere
le **numéro** number
le **numéro d'immatriculation** registration number

## O

l' **objet** (*m*) object
  **obtenir** to obtain, get
l' **occasion** (*f*) occasion; bargain
  **d'occasion** second-hand

**occupé(e)** occupied, taken; engaged; busy
l' **odeur** (*f*) smell
l' **œil** (*m*) eye
l' **œuf** (*m*) egg
l' **œuvre** (*m*) work (*art etc.*)
  **offrir** to offer; to give (as a gift)
l' **oiseau** (*m*) bird
l' **ombre** (*f*) shade; shadow
  **on** one, people, you
l' **oncle** (*m*) uncle
l' **onde** (*f*) wave
l' **ongle** (*m*) nail (*finger/toe*)
l' **or** (*m*) gold
l' **orchestre** (*m*) orchestra; stalls (*theatre*)
l' **ordinateur** (*m*) computer
l' **ordonnance** (*f*) prescription
les **ordures** (*fpl*) rubbish
l' **oreille** (*f*) ear
l' **oreiller** (*m*) pillow
l' **orteil** (*m*) toe
l' **os** (*m*) bone
  **ou** or
    **ou (bien) . . . ou (bien)** either . . . or
  **où?** where?
  **oublier** to forget
l' **ouest** (*m*) west
  **oui** yes
  **outre: en outre** besides, as well
  **ouvert(e)** open
l' **ouverture** (*f*) opening
l' **ouvre-boîtes** (*m*) tin/can opener
l' **ouvre-bouteilles** (*m*) bottle opener
l' **ouvrier** (*m*) workman
  **ouvrir** to open

# P

la **paix** peace
**pâle** pale
le **pain** bread
le **panaché** shandy
**panaché(e)** mixed
la **pancarte** notice; sign
le **panier** basket
**panne: en panne** broken down, out of order
le **panneau** sign
le **pantalon** trousers
le **papier** paper
**Pâques** (*m*) Easter
**par** by; for; per; through; via
**par exemple (p.ex.)** for example
**paraître** to appear; to seem
  **il paraît (que)** . . . it seems (that) . . .
le **parapluie** umbrella
le **parc** park
**parce que** because
**pardon** sorry; pardon; excuse me
**pareil(le)** same; similar
le **parent, la parente** relation, relative
**paresseux/euse** lazy
**parfois** sometimes
**par hasard** by chance
**parler** to speak, to talk
**parmi** among
**part: à part** apart (from); extra
le **parti** (political) party
**particulier, particulière** private; particular, specific

la **partie** part
**partir** to leave, depart
  **à partir de** (starting) from
**partout** everywhere
le **passage à niveau** level crossing
le **passage clouté** pedestrian crossing
le **passager** passenger
**passé(e)** past
**passer** to pass; to spend (*time*); to happen
**passionnant(e)** exciting
les **patins** (*mpl*) skates
la **pâtisserie** (small) cake, pastry; cake shop
le **patron** owner, boss; pattern (*dressmaking etc.*)
la **patronne** owner, boss
**pauvre** poor
**payer** to pay (for)
le **pays** country
le **paysage** scenery, countryside
le **PDG = le président-directeur général** managing director, president
le **péage** toll
la **peau** skin; hide, leather; rind, peel
la **pêche** peach; fishing
le **peigne** comb
**peine: à peine** hardly, scarcely
  **ce n'est pas la peine** it's not worth it
le **peintre** painter
la **peinture** paint, painting
la **pellicule** film (*photo*)
la **pelouse** lawn

**pendant** during
**pendant ce temps** meanwhile
**pendant que** while
**penser** to think
la **pension** pension; boarding house
la **pente** slope
**perdre** to lose; to miss
**perdu(e)** lost
le **père** father
le **permis** licence, permit
le **permis de conduire** driving licence
**permis(e)** allowed
**personne** no one, nobody; anyone
la **personne** person
**peser** to weigh
**petit(e)** small, little
le **petit déjeuner** breakfast
la **petite-fille** granddaughter
le **petit-fils** grandson
le **petit pain** roll
les **petits-enfants** (*mpl*) grandchildren
**peu** little, not much
**peu de** few; little
un **peu** a bit, a little
le **peuple** people, populace
**peur: avoir peur** to be afraid
**peut-être** perhaps, maybe
**peux: je peux** I can
le **pichet** pitcher, jug
la **pièce** piece; component; room; coin; play (*theatre*)
la **pièce de rechange** spare part
le **pied** foot
la **pierre** stone
le **piéton** pedestrian
la **pile** pile; battery

la **pilule** pill
la **piqûre** prick; sting, bite (*insect*); injection
**pire** worse; worst
la **piscine** swimming pool
la **piste** runway; track, course; (ski-)run
le **placard** cupboard
la **place** square; place; seat
le **plafond** ceiling
la **plage** beach
la **plaisanterie** joke
la **planche** plank; board
la **planche à voile** sailboard; windsurfing
le **plancher** floor
la **plante** plant
le **plat** dish; course
**plat(e)** flat; level
le **plateau** tray
**plein(e)** full (up)
**pleurer** to cry
**pleut: il pleut** it's raining
**plier** to fold; to bend
le **plomb** lead
le **plombier** plumber
le **plongeoir** diving board
**plonger** to dive
la **pluie** rain
la **plupart** most, majority
**plus** more; plus
**plusieurs** several
**plutôt** rather
la **poche** pocket
la **poêle** frying pan
le **poêle** stove
le **poids** weight
la **poignée** handle; handful
le **poignet** wrist
le **poing** fist

le **point** point; stitch
    **à point** medium (*steak*)
la **pointe** point, tip
la **pointure** size (*shoe*)
le **poisson** fish
le **poivre** pepper
**poli(e)** polite
la **police** police
la **politique** politics
**pollué(e)** polluted
les **pompiers** (*mpl*) fire brigade
le **pont** bridge; ramp; deck
le **porc** pig; pork
le **port** port, harbour, docks
la **porte** door; gate
le **portefeuille** wallet
le **porte-monnaie** purse
**porter** to carry; to wear
**poser** to put (down)
la **poste** post, mail
le **poste** post, job; set (*radio/TV*); extension (*telephone*)
le **poste de police** police station
le **pot** pot, jar; jug; (child's) potty
la **poubelle** dustbin
le **pouce** thumb
la **poudre** dust; powder
le **poulet** chicken
la **poupée** doll
**pour** for
le **pourboire** tip
**pourquoi?** why?
**pourri(e)** rotten
**pourtant** however
**pousser** to push
la **poussette** push-chair
**pouvoir** to be able
**précieux/euse** precious
**préférer** to prefer

**premier, première** first
**prendre** to take, catch, get; to have
le **prénom** first name, Christian name
**préparer** to prepare, get ready
**près (de)** close (to), near
**présenter** to present, to introduce
**presque** almost, nearly
**pressé(e)** in a hurry; (freshly-)squeezed
**prêt(e)** ready
le **prêtre** priest
**prière de . . .** please . . .
le **printemps** spring
la **prise** plug; socket
**privé(e)** private
le **prix** price; prize
le **problème** problem
**prochain(e)** next
**proche** close
le **professeur** professor; teacher
**profond(e)** deep
la **promenade** walk; ride
**propos: à propos de** about, on the subject of
**propre** clean; (one's) own
le/la **propriétaire** owner
**public, publique** public
**puis** then
**puisque** since
**puissant(e)** powerful

## Q

le **quai** platform; quay
la **qualité** quality
**quand** when

**quand même** still, even so, all the same

**quant à** as for

le **quart** quarter

le **quartier** district, quarter

**que** that, which; whom; what; than

**quel(le)?** what?; which?

**quelque** some

**quelque chose** something; anything

**quelquefois** sometimes

**quelque part** somewhere

**quelques** some, a few

**quelques-uns/unes** some, a few

**quelqu'un** someone; anyone

la **queue** tail; queue

**qui** who; which

**quitter** to leave; to take off

**quoi** what

## R

le **rabais** discount

**raccrocher** to hang up (*telephone*)

**raconter** to tell

**raide** steep

la **raison** reason

**avoir raison** to be right

**raisonnable** sensible

la **randonnée** hike, ramble

le **rang** row, tier

le **rappel** reminder

le **rapport** relationship, connection; report

**raser: se raser** to shave

le **rasoir (électrique)** (electric) razor/shaver

**ravi(e)** delighted

**rayé(e)** striped

le **rayon** shelf; department, section (*in store*)

la **réalité** reality

**réaliser** to carry out, bring about

**récemment** recently; lately

**récent(e)** recent

la **recette** recipe

la **recharge** refill

la **réclamation** complaint

**reconnaissant(e)** grateful

le **reçu** receipt

**regarder** to look (at), to watch

le **régime** diet

la **région** region, area

la **règle** ruler

les **règles** (*fpl*) (menstrual) period

**regretter** to regret, be sorry for

la **reine** queen

le **remboursement** refund

le **remède** remedy, cure

la **remise** delivery; reduction; postponement

**remorquer** to tow

**remplir** to fill (in)

**rencontrer** to meet

le **rendez-vous** appointment, date

**rendre** to give back, return

les **renseignements** (*mpl*) information

**rentrer** to go/come back (in)

**réparer** to repair

le **repas** meal

**répéter** to repeat

**répondre** to answer

la **réponse** reply
le **reportage** report
le **repos** rest
la **représentation** performance
le **réseau** network
la **réservation** reservation, booking
**réserver** to reserve, book
**rester** to remain, stay
le **résultat** result
le **retard** delay
le **retour** return
**retourner** to return
**retraité(e)** retired
**réveiller** to wake
le **réverbère** street lamp
la **revue** review; revue; magazine
le **rez-de-chaussée** ground floor
**riche** rich
le **rideau** curtain
**rien** nothing; anything
**rire** laugh
la **rivière** river
la **robe** dress
le **robinet** tap
le **roi** king
**rond(e)** round
**rose** pink
**rôti(e)** roast
la **roue** wheel
**rouge** red
le **rouge à lèvres** lipstick
**rouillé(e)** rusty
**rouler** to roll; to go, drive
la **route** (main) road; route
le **routier** lorry driver
le **ruban** ribbon; tape
la **rue** street
**rugueux/euse** rough

**242**

la **ruine** ruin
le **ruisseau** stream

# S

**S = Saint** Saint
**SA = Société Anonyme** Limited, PLC
**sa** (see **son**)
le **sable** sand
le **sac** bag
le **sac à dos** rucksack
le **sac à main** handbag
**saignant(e)** rare (*steak*)
**saigner** to bleed
**saint(e)** holy; saint
**sais: je sais** I know
la **saison** season
le **salaire** wage
**sale** dirty
**salé(e)** salty; savoury
la **salle** room, lounge; (concert) hall
la **salle à manger** dining-room
le **salon** lounge, living-room
**salut** hello
le **sang** blood
**sans** without
**sans doute** no doubt
la **santé** health
**sauf** except
**sauter** to jump
**sauvage** wild
**sauver** to rescue, save
**savoir** to know (how to)
le **savon** soap
la **scie** saw
**se** oneself; him/her/itself; themselves
la **séance** (cinema) performance, screening
le **seau** bucket

sec, sèche dry
sécher to dry
la seconde second
le secours help
le séjour stay
le sel salt
selon according to, depending on
la semaine week
le sens sense; meaning; direction
la sensation sensation; feeling
sensible sensitive
le sentier path
sentir to feel; to smell; to taste
sérieux/euse serious; dependable, reliable
serré(e) tight
la serrure lock
la serveuse waitress
le service service; service charge
la serviette towel; serviette, napkin; briefcase
les serviettes hygiéniques (*fpl*) sanitary towels
servir to serve; to be of use
seul(e) only; alone
seulement only
ses his; her; its
si if; whether; so; yes (*emphatic*)
le SIDA AIDS
le siècle century
le sien, la sienne his/hers/its
signaler to report
signer to sign
signifier to mean
silencieux/euse silent
s'il vous plaît please

simple simple
sinon otherwise; if not
le sirop syrup
skier to ski
le slip panties; underpants
la société society; company
la sœur sister
la soie silk
soif: avoir soif to be thirsty
soi-même oneself
le soir evening
la soirée evening; party
soit . . . soit either . . . or
le sol ground; soil
le soleil sun; sunshine
son, sa his; her; its
la sortie exit, way out; departure
sortir to come/go out
la soucoupe saucer
soudain suddenly
soudain(e) sudden
le soulier shoe
la soupe soup
sourd(e) deaf
le sourire smile
sous under(neath)
le sous-sol basement
les sous-vêtements (*mpl*) underwear
souterrain(e) underground
le soutien-gorge bra
souvent often
le sparadrap sticking plaster
spécial(e) special; particular
le spectacle show, spectacle
St, Ste = Saint, Sainte Saint
le stade stadium
la station (underground) station; resort

**la station-service** petrol station
**le stationnement** parking
**stationner** to park
**le store** (Venetian) blind
**le stylo** pen
**le stylo à bille** ballpoint pen
**le succès** success
**la succursale** branch (*office, shop*)
**la sucette** lollipop; dummy
**le sucre** sugar
**le sud** south
**suffit: ça suffit** that's enough
**suis: je suis** I am
**suisse** Swiss
**suivant(e)** following, next
**le sujet** matter, subject, topic
**supérieur(e)** higher; upper, top; advanced
**le suppositoire** suppository
**sur** on; upon; about
**sûr(e)** sure, certain
**surgelé(e)** (deep) frozen
**la surprise** surprise
**surtout** above all, especially
**le survêtement** tracksuit
**sus: en sus** extra, in addition
**suspendre** to hang up
**s.v.p. = s'il vous plaît** please
**sympa, sympathique** nice, charming, pleasant

244

## T

**t' = te** you
**ta** (see **ton**)
**le tabac** tobacco
**le tableau** picture, painting
**la tache** spot; stain

**la taie d'oreiller** pillowcase
**la taille** waist; size
**taisez-vous!, tais-toi!** be quiet!, shut up!
**tant (de)** so much (of), so many
**tant de** so much of, so many
**la tante** aunt
**le tapis** carpet
**tard** late
**le tas** heap
**la tasse** cup
**te** you
**tel, telle** such
**le téléphérique** cable car
**tellement** so (much)
**le témoin** witness
**la tempête** storm
**le temps** time; weather
**de temps en temps** from time to time, occasionally
**tenir** to hold; to keep
**la tente** tent
**le terrain** ground; (playing) field, pitch
**la terrasse** terrace
**la terre** earth; land; ground
**tes** your
**la tête** head
**le théâtre** theatre
**le tien, la tienne** yours
**le timbre** stamp; bell
**le tire-bouchon** corkscrew
**tirer** to pull; to shoot
**le tiroir** drawer
**le tissu** fabric
**toi** you
**les toilettes** (*fpl*) (public) toilets
**toi-même** yourself

**le toit** roof
**tomber** to fall (down/over)
**ton, ta** your
**la tonne** ton
**tordu(e)** twisted, sprained
**tort: avoir tort** to be wrong
**tôt** early
**la touche** key (*piano,
typewriter*)
**toucher** to touch
**toujours** yet; still; always
**la tour** tower
**le tour** tour, trip; ride; turn
**le tourne-disque** record player
**tourner** to turn
**le tournevis** screwdriver
**tous, toutes** all
**tout** everything
**tout(e)** all, every
**tout à fait** completely, quite
**tout de même** all the same
**tout de suite** immediately,
right away
**tout droit** straight on
**tout le monde** everyone
**la toux** cough
**la traduction** translation
**traduire** to translate
**le train** train
**en train de** in the process
of
**traiter** to treat
**tranchant(e)** sharp
**la tranche** slice
**tranquille** calm, quiet
**le travail** work, job
**travailler** to work
**travers: à travers** through
**traverser** to cross
**très** very
**triste** sad, unhappy

**troisième** third
**trompé(e)** mistaken, wrong
**trop** too (much)
**le trottoir** pavement
**le trou** hole
**trouver** to find
**tu** you
**tuer** to kill
**le tuyau** pipe; hose
**la TVA** VAT
**le type** type, sort, kind; bloke,
guy

# U

**un, une** a/an; one
**unique** unique; only
**l'université** (*f*) university
**l'usine** (*f*) factory
**utile** useful
**utiliser** to use

# V

**va: il/elle va** he/she/it goes/
is going
**les vacances** (*fpl*) holiday(s)
**la vache** cow
**la vague** wave
**vaincre** to defeat, beat
**vais: je vais** I go/am going
**la vaisselle** crockery; washing-
up
**la valise** suitcase
**la vallée** valley
**valoir** to be worth
**la vapeur** steam
**le vapeur** steamship
**vaut** is worth
**le vélo** bike
**la vendange** (wine) harvest,
vintage

le **vendeur, la vendeuse** salesman, saleswoman
**vendre** to sell
**venir** to come
le **vent** wind
la **vente** sale
la **verdure** greenery
**vérifier** to check
le **verre** glass; lens
**vers** towards; about
**verser** to pour; to pay (in)
**vert(e)** green
la **veste** jacket
le **vestiaire** cloakroom
le **vêtement** garment
les **vêtements** (*mpl*) clothes, clothing
le **veuf** widower
**veut: ça veut dire** it means
la **veuve** widow
**veux: je veux** I want
la **viande** meat
la **vie** life
**vide** empty
**vieux, vieille** old
**vif, vive** live, alive; vivid, bright; sharp, acute (*pain*)
le **vignoble** vineyard
la **ville** town
le **vin** wine
**violer** to rape
**violet(te)** purple
le **virage** bend, curve
la **vis** screw
le **visage** face
**visiter** to visit
**visser** to screw
**vite** fast; quickly
la **vitesse** speed
la **vitre** pane; window (*car etc.*)
la **vitrine** shop window

**vive** (see **vif**)
**vivre** to live
**voici** here is/are
la **voie** lane (*on road*); (railway) track
**voilà** there is/are; there you are
la **voile** sail, sailing
**voir** to see
le **voisin, la voisine** neighbour
la **voiture** car; coach, carriage (*train*)
la **voiture d'enfant** pram
la **voix** voice
le **vol** flight; theft, robbery
**voler** to fly; to rob, steal
**vos** your
**votre** your
le/la **vôtre** yours
**voudrais: je voudrais** I would like
**vouloir** to want
**vous** you; to you
**vous-même, vous-mêmes** yourself, yourselves
le **voyage** journey, trip
**voyager** to travel
**vrai(e)** true; real, genuine
**vraiment** really; very
la **vue** (eye)sight; look; view; sight

# W

le **wagon** carriage (*train*)

# Y

**y** there; it
les **yeux** (*mpl*) eyes

# English-French

There is a list of car parts on page 40, and parts of the body on page 177. Numbers are on page 218.

## A

a/an **un, une**
abbey **l'abbaye** (f)
about (on the subject of) **de, au sujet de**
  (approximately) **environ**
above **au-dessus (de)**
abroad **à l'étranger**
abscess **l'abcès** (m)
to accept **accepter**
accident **l'accident** (m)
accommodation **le logement**
according to **selon**
account (bank) **le compte**
accountant **le comptable**
ache **la douleur**
acid **l'acide** (m)
across (on the other side of) **de l'autre côté de**
acrylic **acrylique**
to act **agir**
  (theatre) **jouer**
activity **l'activité** (f)
actor **l'acteur** (m)
actress **l'actrice** (f)
adaptor (voltage) **l'adaptateur** (m)
  (plug) **la prise multiple**
address **la direction**
adhesive tape **le ruban adhésif**
admission **l'entrée** (f)
adopted **adopté(e)**
adult **l'adulte** (m/f)

advance: in advance **à l'avance**
advanced (level) **supérieur(e)**
advertisement (newspaper) **l'annonce** (f)
advertising **la publicité**
aerial **l'antenne** (f)
aeroplane **l'avion** (m)
afraid: to be afraid **avoir peur** (avoir, see page 195)
after(wards) **après**
afternoon **l'après-midi** (m)
aftershave **la lotion après-rasage**
again **de nouveau**
against **contre**
age **l'âge** (m)
agency **l'agence** (f)
ago: . . . ago **il y a . . .**
to agree **être d'accord** (être, see page 195)
AIDS **le SIDA**
air **l'air** (m)
  by air **par avion**
air conditioning **la climatisation**
air force **l'armée** (f) **de l'air**
airline **la compagnie d'aviation**
air mattress **le matelas pneumatique**
airport **l'aéroport** (m)

aisle l'allée (f)
  (church) l'allée centrale
alarm l'alarme (f)
alarm clock le réveil
alcohol l'alcool (m)
alcoholic alcoolique
alive vivant(e)
all tout(e); tous, toutes
allergic to allergique à
to allow permettre
  allowed permis(e)
all right (agreed) d'accord
almond l'amande (f)
alone seul(e)
along par
  along (e.g. the river) le long
  de
already déjà
also aussi
although bien que
always toujours
am (see to be)
ambition l'ambition (f)
ambulance l'ambulance (f)
among entre
amount (total) le montant
amusement park le parc
  d'attractions
anaesthetic l'anesthésique (m)
and et
angry en colère
animal l'animal (m)
anniversary l'anniversaire (m)
annoyed fâché(e)
anorak l'anorak (m)
another (one) un(e) autre
answer la réponse
to answer répondre
antibiotic l'antibiotique (m)
anti-freeze l'antigel (m)

**248**

antique l'objet (m) d'art ancien
antiseptic l'antiseptique (m)
any (some) quelque(s)
  I don't have any je n'en ai
  pas
anyone (someone) quelqu'un
anything (something) quelque
  chose
  anything else? autre chose?,
  et avec ça?
anyway de toute façon
anywhere (nowhere) nulle part
apart (from) à part
apartment l'appartement (m)
aperitif l'apéritif (m)
appendicitis l'appendicite (f)
apple la pomme
appointment le rendez-vous
approximately
  approximativement, environ
apricot l'abricot (m)
arch l'arc (m)
archaeology l'archéologie (f)
architect l'architecte (m)
architecture l'architecture (f)
are (see to be)
area (surface) la surface, la
  superficie
  (region) la région
argument la discussion
arm le bras
armband (swimming) le
  flottant
army l'armée (f)
around autour (de)
  around the corner après le
  coin
to arrange organiser
arrest: under arrest en état
  d'arrestation

arrival l'arrivée (f)
to arrive arriver
art l'art (m)
    fine arts les beaux-arts
    art gallery la galerie d'art, le musée d'art
arthritis l'arthrite (f)
artichoke l'artichaut (m)
article l'article (m)
artificial artificiel(le)
artist l'artiste (m/f)
as comme
as far as jusqu'à
ash la cendre
ashtray le cendrier
to ask (for) demander
asparagus les asperges (fpl)
aspirin l'aspirine (f)
assistant l'aide (m/f)
    (shop) le vendeur, la vendeuse
asthma l'asthme (m)
at à
athletics l'athlétisme (m)
atmosphere l'atmosphère (f)
to attack attaquer
attractive attirant(e)
aubergine l'aubergine (f)
auction la vente aux enchères
aunt la tante
author l'auteur
automatic automatique
autumn l'automne (m)
avalanche l'avalanche (f)
avocado l'avocat (m)
to avoid éviter
away: . . . (kilometres) away à . . . (kilomètres)
awful affreux/euse

# B

baby le bébé
baby food les petits pots pour bébés
baby's bottle le biberon
baby wipes les serviettes (fpl) rafraîchissantes
babysitter la babysitter
back: at the back à l'arrière
    (reverse side) le verso
backwards en arrière
bacon le bacon, le lard
bad mauvais(e)
badly mal
bag le sac
baggage les bagages (mpl)
baker le boulanger
baker's la boulangerie
balcony le balcon
bald chauve
ball (small) la balle
    (large) le ballon
ballet le ballet
ballpoint pen le stylo à bille
banana la banane
band (music) la bande, le groupe
bandage le pansement
bank la banque
bar le bar
barber's le coiffeur
basement le sous-sol
basket le panier
basketball le basket
bath le bain
    to have a bath prendre un bain
bathing costume le maillot de bain
bathroom la salle de bains

battery **la pile**
(*car*) **la batterie**
bay **la baie**
to be **être** (*see page 195*)
I am **je suis**
we are **nous sommes**
he/she is **il/elle est**
you are **vous êtes**
beach **la plage**
bean **le haricot**
French/green **le haricot vert**
beard **la barbe**
beautiful **beau, belle**
because **parce que**
bed **le lit**
bedroom **la chambre à coucher**
bee **l'abeille** (*f*)
beef **le bœuf**
beer **la bière**
before **avant (de)**
to begin **commencer**
beginner **le débutant, la débutante**
beginning **le début**
behind **derrière**
beige **beige**
to believe **croire**
I believe so/not **je crois que oui/non**
Belgian **belge**
Belgium **la Belgique**
bell **la cloche**
(*doorbell*) **la sonnette**
to belong to **appartenir à**
(*to be a member of*) **être membre de** (**être**, *see page 195*)
below **en bas**
(*beneath*) **sous**
belt **la ceinture**
bend **le virage**
bent **tordu(e)**

berry **la baie**
berth **la couchette**
beside (*next to*) **à côté de**
besides **d'ailleurs**
best **(le/la) mieux**
better **mieux**
between **entre**
beyond **au-delà (de)**
bib **le bavoir**
Bible **la Bible**
bicycle **la bicyclette, le vélo**
big **grand(e)**
bigger **plus grand(e)**
bill **l'addition** (*f*)
bin **la poubelle**
bindings (*ski*) **les fixations** (*fpl*)
bin liner **le sac poubelle**
binoculars **les jumelles** (*fpl*)
biology **la biologie**
bird **l'oiseau** (*m*)
birthday **l'anniversaire** (*m*)
biscuit **le biscuit**
bishop **l'évêque** (*m*)
a bit **un peu**
to bite **mordre**
bitter **amer, amère**
black **noir(e)**
black and white (*film*) **en noir et blanc**
blackberry **la mûre**
black coffee **le café noir**
blackcurrant **le cassis**
blanket **la couverture**
bleach **l'eau** (*f*) **de Javel**
to bleed **saigner**
blind **aveugle**
blind (*Venetian*) **le store**
blister **l'ampoule** (*f*)
blocked **bloqué(e)**
(*pipe etc.*) **bouché(e)**

blond(e) **blond(e)**
blood **le sang**
blouse **le chemisier**
to blow **souffler**
blow-dry **le brushing**
blue **bleu(e)**
blusher **le fard à joues**
boarding **l'embarquement** (m)
boarding card **la carte
  d'embarquement**
boat **le bateau**
  by boat **en bateau**
body **le corps**
boiled **bouilli(e)**
boiled egg **l'œuf à la coque**
boiler **la chaudière**
bomb **la bombe**
bone **l'os** (m)
book **le livre**
to book **réserver**
booking **la réservation**
booking office (railway etc.)
  **le bureau de réservations**
  (theatre) **le bureau de
  location, le guichet**
bookshop **la librairie**
boot **la botte**
border (edge) **le bord**
  (frontier) **la frontière**
boring **ennuyeux/euse**
both **(tous/toutes) les deux**
bottle **la bouteille**
bottle-opener **l'ouvre-
  bouteilles** (m)
bottom **le fond**
  (body) **le derrière**
bow (ship) **l'avant** (m)
bow (knot) **le nœud**
bowl **le bol**
bowls (game) **les boules** (fpl)

box **la boîte**
  (theatre) **la loge**
box office **le guichet**
boy **le garçon**
boyfriend **le petit ami**
bra **le soutien-gorge**
bracelet **le bracelet**
braces **les bretelles** (fpl)
brain **le cerveau**
branch **la branche**
  (bank etc.) **la succursale**
brand **la marque**
brandy **le cognac**
brass **le cuivre jaune**
brave **courageux/euse**
bread **le pain**
to break **casser**
  I have broken **j'ai cassé**
breakdown truck **la
  dépanneuse**
breakfast **le petit déjeuner**
to breathe **respirer**
bricklayer **l'ouvrier maçon** (m)
bride **la mariée**
bridegroom **le marié**
bridge **le pont**
briefcase **la serviette**
bright **vif, vive**
to bring **apporter**
British **britannique**
broad **large**
broad bean **la fève**
brochure **la brochure**
broken **cassé(e)**
broken down **en panne**
bronchitis **la bronchite**
bronze **le bronze**
brooch **la broche**
broom **le balai**
brother **le frère**

brother-in-law **le beau-frère**
brown **brun(e), marron**
brown sugar **le sucre brun**
bruise **le bleu**
brush **la brosse**
bucket **le seau**
budgerigar **la perruche**
buffet **le buffet**
to build **construire**
building **le bâtiment**
bulb *(light)* **l'ampoule** *(f)*
bull **le taureau**
bumper **le pare-chocs**
burn **la brûlure**
to burn **brûler**
   burnt **brûlé(e)**
bus **l'autobus** *(m)*, **le bus**
   by bus **en autobus**
bush **le buisson**
business **les affaires** *(fpl)*
business studies **les études commerciales** *(fpl)*
business trip **le voyage d'affaires**
businessman **l'homme** *(m)* **d'affaires**
businesswoman **la femme d'affaires**
bus station **la gare routière**
bus stop **l'arrêt** *(m)* **d'autobus**
busy **occupé(e)**
but **mais**
butane gas **le butane**
butcher's **la boucherie**
butter **le beurre**
butterfly **le papillon**
button **le bouton**
to buy **acheter**
by **par**

## C

cabbage **le chou**
cabin **la cabine**
cable car **le téléphérique**
café **le café**
cake **le gâteau**; *(small)* **la pâtisserie**
cake shop **la pâtisserie**
calculator **la calculatrice**
call *(phone)* **l'appel** *(m)*
to call **appeler**
   to be called: I am called . . .
   **je m'appelle** . . .
   he/she is called . . . **il/elle s'appelle** . . .
   what is he/she called?
   **comment s'appelle-t-il/elle?**
calm **calme**
camera **l'appareil-photo** *(m)*
camomile tea **la camomille**
to camp **camper**
campbed **le lit de camp**
camping **le camping**
campsite **le camping**
can *(to be able)* **pouvoir** *(see page 00)*
   I can **je peux**
   can you . . .? **pourriez-vous . . .?**
   *(to know how to)* **savoir**
   I (don't) know how to . . .
   **je (ne) sais (pas)** . . .
can *(tin)* **la boîte**
to cancel **annuler**
cancer **le cancer**
candle **la bougie**
canoe **le canoë**
can opener **l'ouvre-boîtes** *(m)*
capital *(city)* **la capitale**
captain **le capitaine**

car la voiture
  by car en voiture
carafe la carafe
caravan la caravane
caravan site le camping pour
  caravanes
cardigan le gilet
care: to take care faire
  attention (faire, see page 195)
  I don't care ça m'est égal
careful prudent(e)
careless négligent(e)
car park le parking
carpenter le charpentier
carpet le tapis
carriage le wagon (train)
carrier bag le sac (en
  plastique)
carrot la carotte
to carry porter
to carry on continuer
car wash le lave-autos
cash: to pay cash payer
  comptant
to cash (cheque) encaisser
cash desk la caisse
cassette la cassette
cassette player le
  magnétophone à cassette
castle le château
cat le chat
catalogue le catalogue
to catch (train/bus) prendre
cathedral la cathédrale
Catholic catholique
cauliflower le chou-fleur
to cause causer
cave la caverne
ceiling le plafond
celery le céléri

cellar (food) le cellier
  (wine) la cave
cemetery le cimetière
centimetre le centimètre
central central(e)
central heating le chauffage
  central
centre le centre
  town centre le centre-ville
century le siècle
cereal les céréales (fpl)
  (for babies) la bouillie
certain certain(e)
certainly certainement
certificate l'attestation (f)
chain la chaîne
chair la chaise
chair lift le télésiège
chalet le chalet
champagne le champagne
change (small coins) la
  monnaie
to change changer
changing room le salon
  d'essayage
chapel la chapelle
charcoal le charbon de bois
charge le prix
charter flight le vol en charter
cheap bon marché
to check vérifier
  checked (pattern) à carreaux
check-in (desk)
  l'enregistrement (m) des
  bagages
to check in enregistrer
cheek la joue
cheeky insolent(e)
cheers! santé!, à la vôtre!
cheese le fromage

cheesecake **le flan au fromage**
chef **le chef**
chemist's **la pharmacie**
chemistry **la chimie**
cheque **le chèque**
cherry **la cerise**
chess **les échecs** (*mpl*)
chestnut **la châtaigne, le marron**
chewing gum **le chewing-gum**
chicken **le poulet**
chickenpox **la varicelle**
child **l'enfant** (*m/f*)
children **les enfants** (*mpl*)
chimney **la cheminée**
china **la porcelaine**
chips **les frites** (*fpl*)
chocolate **le chocolat**
to choose **choisir**
chop (*meat*) **la côte, la côtelette**
Christian **chrétien(ne)**
Christian name **le prénom**
Christmas **Noël** (*m*)
Christmas Eve **la veille de Noël**
church **l'église** (*f*)
cigar **le cigare**
cigarette **la cigarette**
cigarette lighter **le briquet**
cinema **le cinéma**
cinnamon **la cannelle**
circle **le cercle**
(*theatre*) **le balcon**
circus **le cirque**
city **la ville**
civil servant **le/la fonctionnaire**
class **la classe**
classical music **la musique classique**

clean **propre**
to clean **nettoyer**
cleansing cream **la crème démaquillante**
clear **clair(e)**
(*transparent*) **transparent(e)**
(*obvious*) **évident(e)**
clerk **l'employé(e)** (*m/f*)
clever **intelligent(e)**
cliff **la falaise**
climate **le climat**
to climb (up) **monter**
climber (*mountain*) **l'alpiniste** (*m/f*)
climbing **l'alpinisme** (*m*)
clinic **la clinique**
cloakroom **le vestiaire**
clock **l'horloge** (*f*)
close (by) **proche**
close to **près de**
to close **fermer**
closed **fermé(e)**
cloth (*rag*) **le chiffon**
clothes **les vêtements** (*mpl*)
clothes peg **la pince à linge**
cloud **le nuage**
cloudy **nuageux/euse**
club **le club**
coach **le car**
(*train*) **le wagon**
coal **le charbon**
coarse (*texture*) **grossier, grossière**
(*skin etc.*) **rude**
coast **la côte**
coat **le manteau**
coat-hanger **le cintre**
cocktail **le cocktail**
coffee **le café**
coin **la pièce**

cold **froid(e)**
　I'm cold **j'ai froid**
　it's cold (weather) **il fait froid**
cold: to have a cold **être enrhumé(e) (être,** *see page 195*)
collar **le col**
　(dog's etc.) **le collier**
colleague **le/la collègue**
to collect **collectionner**
collection (*stamps etc.*) **la collection**
　(*rubbish*) **l'enlèvement** (*m*)
college **le collège**
colour **la couleur**
colour-blind **daltonien(ne)**
comb **le peigne**
to come **venir** (*see page 195*)
　are you coming? **vous venez?**
to come back **revenir**
to come down **descendre**
comedy **la comédie**
to come in **entrer**
　come in! **entrez!**
to come out **sortir**
comfortable **confortable**
comic (*magazine*) **le comic**
commercial **commercial(e)**
common **commun(e)**
communion **la communion**
communism **le communisme**
communist **communiste**
compact disc **le disque compact**
company **la compagnie**
compared with **en comparaison de**
compartment **le compartiment**
compass **la boussole**
complaint **la réclamation**

completely **complètement**
complicated **compliqué(e)**
composer **le compositeur**
compulsory **obligatoire**
computer **l'ordinateur** (*m*)
computer science/studies **l'informatique** (*f*)
concert **le concert**
concert hall **la salle de concert**
concussion **la commotion cérébrale**
condition **la condition**
conditioner (*hair*) **l'après-shampooing** (*m*)
condom **le préservatif**
conference **le congrès**
to confirm **confirmer**
connection (*travel*) **la correspondance**
conscious **conscient(e)**
conservation **la conservation**
conservative (*politics*) **conservateur, conservatrice**
constipation **le constipation**
consulate **le consulat**
to contact **contacter**
contact lens **le verre de contact**
contact lens cleaner **le produit de nettoyage pour les verres de contact**
continent **le continent**
contraceptive **le contraceptif**
contract **le contrat**
convent **le couvent**
convenient **commode**
　it's not convenient for me **ça ne me convient pas**
cook **le cuisinier, la cuisinière**
to cook **faire cuire**
cooked **cuit(e)**
cooker **la cuisinière**

cool frais, fraîche
copper le cuivre
copy la copie
  (book) l'exemplaire (m)
cork le bouchon
corkscrew le tire-bouchon
corner le coin
correct correct(e)
corridor le couloir
cosmetics les cosmétiques
  (mpl)
cost (price) le prix
to cost coûter
  how much does it cost?
  ça coûte combien?
cot le lit d'enfant
cottage la petite maison
  (thatched) la chaumière
cotton (material) le coton
  (thread) le fil
cotton wool le coton
  hydrophile
couchette la couchette
cough la toux
cough medicine le sirop pour
  la toux
to count compter
counter (shop) le comptoir
country (nation) le pays
country(side) la campagne
couple le couple
courgette la courgette
course (lessons) le cours
  (food) le plat
  of course bien sûr
court (law) le tribunal
  (sport) le court
cousin le cousin, la cousine
cover le couvercle
cover charge le couvert
cow la vache

cramp (medical) la crampe
crash (car) la collision
crayon le crayon de couleur
crazy fou, folle
cream la crème
credit card la carte de crédit
crispbread le pain suédois
crisps les chips (mpl)
cross la croix
to cross (road etc.) traverser
cross-country skiing le ski de
  fond
crossing (sea) la traversée
crossroads le carrefour
crowded bondé(e)
crown la couronne
cruise la croisière
crutch la béquille
to cry pleurer
crystal le cristal
cucumber le concombre
cuff la manchette
cup la tasse
cupboard le placard
cure (remedy) le remède
to cure guérir
curling tongs le fer à friser
curly bouclé(e)
current (electrical, water etc.)
  le courant
curtain le rideau
curve la courbe
cushion le coussin
custard la crème anglaise
customs la douane
cut la coupure
to cut, to cut off couper
cutlery les couverts (mpl)
cycling le cyclisme
cyclist le/la cycliste
cystitis la cystite

# D

daily **quotidien(ne)**
damaged **endommagé(e)**
damp **humide**
dance **le bal**
to dance **danser**
danger **le danger**
dangerous **dangereux/euse**
dark **sombre**
  (*hair/skin*) **brun(e)**
  (*colour*) **foncé(e)**
darts **les fléchettes** (*fpl*)
data (*information*) **l'information**
  (*f*)
date (*day*) **la date**
  (*fruit*) **la datte**
daughter **la fille**
daughter-in-law **la belle-fille**
day **le jour, la journée**
day after **le lendemain**
day after tomorrow **après-demain**
day before yesterday **avant-hier**
dead **mort(e)**
deaf **sourd(e)**
dealer **le marchand**
dear **cher, chère**
death **la mort**
debt **la dette**
decaffeinated **décaféiné(e)**
deck **le pont**
deckchair **la chaise longue**
to decide **décider**
to declare **déclarer**
deep **profond(e)**
deep freeze **le congélateur**
deer **le cerf**
defect **le défaut**
definitely! **bien sûr!**

to defrost **dégeler**
degree (*temperature*) **le degré**
  (*university*) **la licence**
delay **le retard**
delicate **délicat(e)**
delicious **délicieux/euse**
demonstration **la démonstration**
  (*protest*) **la manifestation**
dentist **le dentiste**
dentures **le dentier**
deodorant **le déodorant**
to depart **partir**
department **le département**
department store **le grand magasin**
departure **le départ**
departure lounge **la salle de départ**
deposit **les arrhes** (*fpl*)
to describe **décrire**
description **la description**
desert **le désert**
design **le dessin**
  (*plan, intention*) **le dessein**
to design **dessiner**
dessert **le dessert**
destination **la destination**
detail **le détail**
detergent **le détergent**
developing (*film*) **le développement**
diabetes **le diabète**
to dial **composer**
dialling code **l'indicatif** (*m*)
dialling tone **la tonalité**
diamond **le diamant**
diarrhoea **la diarrhée**
diary **l'agenda** (*m*); **le journal**
dice **le dé**, (*pl*) **les dés**
dictionary **le dictionnaire**

257

to die **mourir**
   . . . died . . . **est mort(e)**
diesel **le gas-oil**
diet **le régime**
   to be on a diet **suivre un régime**
different **différent(e)**
difficult **difficile**
dining room **la salle à manger**
dinner **le dîner**
dinner jacket **le smoking**
diplomat **le diplomate**
direct **direct(e)**
direction **la direction**
director **la directeur**
directory **l'annuaire** (*m*)
dirty **sale**
disabled **handicapé(e)**
disappointed **déçu(e)**
disc **le disque**
disco(thèque) **la discothèque**
discount **la remise**
dish **le plat**
dishwasher **le lave-vaisselle**
disinfectant **le désinfectant**
dislocated **disloqué(e)**
disposable nappies **les couches** (*fpl*) **à jeter**
distance **la distance**
distilled water **l'eau** (*f*) **distillée**
district **le quartier**
to dive **plonger**
diversion (*road*) **la déviation**
diving-board **le plongeoir**
divorced **divorcé(e)**
dizzy **pris(e) de vertige**
to do **faire** (*see page 195*)
docks **le dock**
doctor **le médecin**
document **le document**
dog **le chien**
doll **la poupée**

dollar **le dollar**
dome **le dôme**
dominoes **les dominos** (*mpl*)
donkey **l'âne** (*m*)
door **la porte**
double **double**
double bed **le grand lit**
double room **la chambre pour deux personnes**
dough **la pâte**
down(stairs) **en bas**
drain(pipe) **le tuyau d'écoulement**
drama **le drame**
draught (*air*) **le courant d'air**
draught beer **la bière à la pression**
to draw **dessiner**
drawer **le tiroir**
drawing **le dessin**
drawing-pin **la punaise**
dreadful **affreux/euse**
dress **la robe**
dressing (*medical*) **le pansement**
   (*salad*) **la vinaigrette**
drink **la boisson**
   to have a drink **prendre un verre**
to drink **boire**
to drip **goutter**
to drive **conduire**
driver **le conducteur, la conductrice**
   (*bus, taxi etc.*) **le chauffeur**
driving licence **le permis de conduire**
drowned **noyé(e)**
drug **la drogue**
drug addict **le/la drogué(e)**

drum **le tambour**
drunk **ivre**
dry **sec, sèche**
dry-cleaner's **la tinturerie,
le pressing**
dubbed **doublé(e)**
duck **le canard**
dull (*weather*) **couvert(e),
gris(e)**
dumb **muet, muette**
dummy (*baby's*) **la sucette**
during **pendant**
dust **la poussière**
dustbin **la poubelle**
dusty **poussiéreux/euse**
duty (*customs*) **le droit**
duty-free **hors taxe**
duvet **la couette**

# E

each **chaque**
each one **chacun(e)**
ear **l'oreille** (*f*)
earache **le mal d'oreille**
earlier (*before*) **avant**
early **tôt**
to earn **gagner**
earring **la boucle d'oreille** (*f*)
earth **la terre**
earthquake **le tremblement de
terre**
east **l'est** (*m*)
eastern **oriental(e)**
Easter **Pâques**
easy **facile**
to eat **manger**
economical **économique**
economy, economics
**l'économie** (*f*)
egg **l'œuf** (*m*)

either . . . or **ou (bien) . . . ou
(bien)**
elastic band **l'élastique** (*m*)
election **l'élection** (*f*)
electric **électrique**
electrician **l'électricien** (*m*)
electricity **l'électricité** (*f*)
electronic **électronique**
embarrassing **gênant(e)**
embassy **l'ambassade** (*f*)
emergency: it's an emergency
**c'est très urgent**
empty **vide**
to empty **vider**
enamel **l'émail** (*m*)
end **la fin**
to end **terminer**
energetic **énergique**
energy **l'énergie** (*f*)
engaged (*to be married*)
**fiancé(e)**
(*occupied*) **occupé(e)**

259

engine **le moteur**
engineer **l'ingénieur** (*m*)
engineering **la génie, la
technique**
England **l'Angleterre** (*f*)
English **anglais(e)**
English Channel **la Manche**
enough **assez**
to enter **entrer (dans)**
entertainment **le
divertissement**
enthusiastic **enthousiaste**
entrance **l'entrée** (*f*)
envelope **l'enveloppe** (*f*)
environment **l'environnement**
(*m*)
equal **égal(e)**
equipment **l'équipement** (*m*)

-er (e.g. bigger, cheaper)
plus . . .
escalator l'escalier roulant (m)
especially surtout
essential indispensable
estate (*property*) le domaine
estate agent l'agent immobilier
(m)
even (*including*) même
(*not odd*) pair
evening le soir, la soirée
evening dress (*for man*) la
tenue de soirée
(*woman's*) la robe du soir
every (*each*) chaque
(*all*) tous, toutes
everyone tout le monde
everything tout
everywhere partout
exactly exactement

examination (*school etc.*)
l'examen (m)
example l'exemple (m)
for example par exemple
excellent excellent(e)
except sauf
excess luggage l'excès (m) de
bagages
to exchange changer
exchange rate le cours du
change
excited excité(e)
exciting passionnant(e)
excursion l'excursion (f)
excuse me excusez-moi,
pardon
executive le cadre
exercise l'exercice (m)
exhibition l'exposition (f)
exit la sortie
to expect espérer
expensive cher, chère

experience l'expérience (f)
expert l'expert (m)
to explain expliquer
explosion l'explosion (f)
export l'exportation (f)
to export exporter
extension (*telephone*) le
poste
external extérieur(e)
extra (*in addition*) en
supplément
eye l'œil (m), (*pl*) les yeux
eyebrow le sourcil
eyelash le cil
eyelid la paupière
eyeliner l'eye-liner (m)
eyeshadow l'ombre (f) de
paupières

## F

fabric le tissu
face le visage
face cream la crème pour
le visage
face powder la poudre
(de riz)
facilities les installations
(*fpl*)
fact le fait
in fact en fait
factory l'usine (f)
to fail (*exam/test*) échouer
failure l'échec (m)
faint: fainted, in a faint
évanoui(e)
fair (*hair*) blond(e)
(*just*) juste
fair la foire
fairly (*quite*) assez
faith la foi
faithful fidèle
fake faux, fausse

to fall **tomber**
false **faux, fausse**
family **la famille**
famous **célèbre**
fan **l'éventail** (*m*)
   (*electric*) **le ventilateur**
   (*supporter*) **le fan**
fantastic **fantastique**
far (away) **loin**
   is it far? **est-ce que c'est**
   **loin?**
fare **le prix du billet**
farm **la ferme**
farmer **le fermier, la fermière**
fashion **la mode**
fashionable/in fashion **à la**
   **mode**
fast **rapide**
fat **la graisse**
fat (*large*) **gros, grosse**
fatal **fatal(e)**
father **le père**
father-in-law **le beau-père**
fault (*defect*) **le défaut**
faulty **défectueux/euse**
favourite **préféré(e)**
feather **la plume**
fed up: I'm fed up **j'en ai eu**
   **assez**
to feed **donner à manger à**
   (*baby*) **allaiter**
to feel **sentir**
   I feel **je me sens**
   he/she feels **il/elle se sent**
felt-tip pen **le stylo-feutre**
female **femelle**
feminine **féminin(e)**
feminist **féministe**
fence **la barrière**
ferry **le ferry**

festival (*village etc.*) **la fête**
   (*film etc.*) **le festival**
fever **la fièvre**
a few (*not many/much*) **(un) peu**
   **de**
   (*some*) **quelques**
fiancé(e) **le fiancé, la fiancée**
fibre **la fibre**
field **le champ**
fig **la figue**
fight **la bagarre**
file **le dossier**
   (*computer*) **le fichier**
   (*nail, DIY*) **la lime**
to fill (in/up) **remplir**
filling (*dental*) **le plombage**
film (*cinema*) **le film**
   (*for camera*) **la pellicule**
film star **la vedette**
filter **le filtre**
finance **la finance**
to find **trouver**
fine (*weather*) **beau, belle**
   (*OK*) **bien**
fine (*penalty*) **l'amende** (*f*)
to finish **finir**
fire **le feu**
fire brigade **les pompiers** (*mpl*)
fire extinguisher **l'extincteur**
   (*m*)
firewood **le bois de chauffage**
fireworks **les feux** (*mpl*)
   **d'artifice**
firm (*company*) **la compagnie,**
   **la firme**
first **premier, première**
first aid **les premiers soins**
   (*mpl*)
first aid box/kit **la trousse de**
   **pharmacie**

fish le poisson
to fish/go fishing pêcher
fishing la pêche
fishing rod la canne à pêche
fishmonger's la poissonnerie
fit (healthy) en forme
to fit aller bien (aller, see page 195)
    it doesn't fit me ça ne me va pas
fitting room le salon d'essayage
to fix fixer
fizzy gazeux/euse
flag le drapeau
flashbulb l'ampoule (f) de flash
flat (apartment) l'appartement (m)
flat (level) plat(e)
    (battery, tyre) à plat
flavour le goût
    (ice-cream) le parfum
flaw le défaut
flea la puce
flea market le marché aux puces
flight le vol
flight bag le sac avion
flippers les palmes (fpl)
flood l'inondation (f)
floor le plancher
    (storey) l'étage (m)
    ground floor le rez-de-chaussée
flour la farine
flower la fleur
flu la grippe
fluid le liquide
fly la mouche
fly sheet le double toit
fog le brouillard
foggy: it's foggy il fait du brouillard

foil le papier aluminium
folding (chair etc.) pliant(e)
following (next) suivant(e)
food la nourriture
food poisoning l'intoxication (f) alimentaire
foot le pied
    on foot à pied
football le football
footpath le sentier
for pour
forbidden interdit(e)
foreign étranger, étrangère
forest la forêt
to forget oublier
to forgive pardonner
fork la fourchette
form (document) le formulaire
fortnight la quinzaine
forward en avant
foundation (make-up) le fond de teint
fountain la fontaine
foyer le foyer
fracture la fracture
fragile fragile
France la France
frankly franchement
freckle la tache de rousseur
free gratuit(e) (available, unoccupied) libre
freedom la liberté
to freeze geler
    (food) congeler
freezer le congélateur
French français(e)
frequent fréquent(e)
fresh frais, fraîche

fridge **le frigo**
fried **frit(e)**
friend **l'ami(e)** (*m/f*)
frightened **effrayé(e)**
fringe **la frange**
frog **la grenouille**
from **de**
front: in front (of) **devant**
front door **la porte d'entrée**
frontier **la frontière**
frost **le gel**
frozen (*water etc.*) **gelé(e)**
    (*food*) **congelé(e)**
fruit **le fruit**
fruit shop **la fruiterie**
frying pan **la poêle**
fuel **le combustible**
full **plein, pleine**
full board **la pension complète**
full up **complet, complète**
funeral **l'enterrement** (*m*)
funfair **la fête foraine**
funny (*amusing*) **drôle**
    (*peculiar*) **bizarre**
fur **la fourrure**
furniture **les meubles** (*mpl*)
further on **plus loin**
fuse **le fusible**

# G

gallery **la galerie**
gambling **le jeu**
game **le jeu**
    (*match*) **le match**
    (*hunting*) **la chasse**
garage **le garage**
garden **le jardin**
gardener **le jardinier, la jardinière**
garlic **l'ail** (*m*)

gas **le gaz**
gas bottle/cylinder **la bouteille de gaz**
gas refill **la recharge de gaz**
gastritis **la gastrite**
gate **la porte**
general **général(e)**
generous **généreux/euse**
gentle **doux, douce**
gentleman **le monsieur** (*pl les messieurs*)
genuine **authentique**
geography **la géographie** (*f*)
German measles **la rubéole**
to get (*obtain*) **obtenir**
to get off (*bus etc.*) **descendre**
to get on (*bus etc.*) **monter (dans)**
gift **le cadeau**
gin **le gin**
gin and tonic **le gin-tonic**
girl **la fille**
girlfriend **la petite amie**
to give **donner**
glass **le verre**
glasses **les lunettes** (*fpl*)
glove **le gant**
glue **la colle**
to go **aller** (*see page 195*)
    I am going (to) **je vais**
to go down **descendre**
to go in **entrer (dans)**
to go out **sortir**
to go up **monter**
goal (*sport*) **le but**
goat **la chèvre**
God **Dieu**
goggles (*diving*) **les lunettes de plongée**
gold **l'or** (*m*)
    (made of) gold **en or**
golf **le golf**

golf clubs **les clubs de golf**
golf course **le terrain de golf**
good **bon, bonne**
goodbye **au revoir**
good day, good morning **bonjour**
good evening **bonsoir**
goodnight **bonne nuit**
government **le gouvernement**
gram **le gramme**
grammar **la grammaire**
grandchildren **les petits-enfants** (*mpl*)
granddaughter **la petite-fille**
grandfather **le grand-père**
grandmother **la grand-mère**
grandparents **les grands-parents** (*mpl*)
grandson **le petit-fils**
grandstand **la tribune**
grape **le raisin**
grapefruit **le pamplemousse**
grass **l'herbe** (*f*)
grateful **reconnaissant(e)**
greasy **gras, grasse**
great **grand(e)**
great! **formidable!, super!**
Great Britain **la Grande-Bretagne**
green (*inc. environmentally aware*) **vert(e)**
green card **la carte verte**
greengrocer's **le marchand de légumes**
grey **gris(e)**
grilled **grillé(e)**
grocer's **l'épicier** (*m*)
ground **la terre**
ground floor **le rez-de-chaussée**
groundsheet **le tapis de sol**

group **le groupe**
to grow (*cultivate*) **cultiver**
guarantee **la garantie**
guest **l'invité(e)** (*m/f*)
  (*hotel*) **le client, la cliente**
guest house **la pension**
guide **le/la guide**
guide-book **le guide**
guided tour **la visite guidée**
guilty **coupable**
guitar **la guitare**
gun (*rifle*) **le fusil**
guy rope **la corde de tente**
gymnastics **la gymnastique**

## H

habit (*custom*) **l'habitude** (*f*)
hail **la grêle**
hair **les cheveux** (*mpl*)
hairbrush **la brosse à cheveux**
hair curlers **les bigoudis** (*mpl*)
haircut **la coupe de cheveux**
hairdresser **le coiffeur, la coiffeuse**
hairdryer **le séchoir**
hairgrip **la pince à cheveux**
hairspray **la laque**
half **la moitié**
half **demi(e)**
  half an hour **une demi-heure**
  half past (*see* Time, *page 201*)
half board **la demi-pension**
half price/fare **le demi-tarif**
hall (*in house*) **le vestibule**
  (*concert*) **la salle**
ham **le jambon**
hamburger **le hamburger**
hammer **le marteau**
hand **la main**
handbag **le sac à main**

hand cream **la crème pour les mains**
handicapped **handicapé(e)**
handkerchief **le mouchoir**
handle (door, suitcase etc.) **la poignée**
(basket, bucket etc.) **l'anse** (f)
(broom, knife etc.) **la manche**
hand luggage **les bagages à main**
hand-made **fait(e) à la main**
hangover **la gueule de bois**
to hang (up) **suspendre**
(phone) **raccrocher**
to happen **passer**
what has happened? **qu'est-ce qui s'est passé?**
happy **heureux/euse**
harbour **le port**
hard **dur(e)**
(difficult) **difficile**
hard shoulder **la bande d'arrêt d'urgence**
hat **le chapeau**
to hate **détester**
to have **avoir** (see page 195)
do you have . . .? **est-ce que vous avez . . .?**
hay fever **le rhume des foins**
hazelnut **la noisette**
he **il**
head **la tête**
(boss) **le chef**
headache **le mal de tête**
headphones **le casque à écouteurs**
to heal **guérir**
health **la santé**
healthy **en bonne santé**
health foods **les aliments naturels** (mpl)

to hear **entendre**
hearing aid **l'appareil** (m) **acoustique**
heart **le cœur**
heart attack **la crise cardiaque**
heat **la chaleur**
heater **l'appareil** (m) **de chauffage**
heating **le chauffage**
heaven **le ciel**
heavy **lourd(e)**
hedge **la haie**
heel **le talon**
height **la grandeur**
helicopter **l'hélicoptère** (m)
hell **l'enfer** (m)
hello **bonjour, salut**
help **l'aide** (f)
help! **au secours!**
to help **aider**
her **la; elle**
(of her) **son, sa;** (pl) **ses** (see page 191)
herb **l'herbe** (f)
herbal tea **la tisane**
here **ici, là**
hers: it's hers **c'est à elle**
hiccups: to have hiccups **avoir le hoquet** (avoir, see page 195)
high **haut(e)**
high chair **la chaise haute**
to hijack **détourner**
hill **la colline**
him **le; lui**
to hire **louer**
his **son, sa;** (pl) **ses** (see page 191)
it's his **c'est à lui**
history **l'histoire** (f)
to hit **frapper**
to hitch-hike **faire de l'auto-stop**

hobby le hobby
hole le trou
holiday(s) les vacances (*fpl*)
  on holiday en vacances
  public holiday la fête
holy saint(e)
Holy Week la Semaine Sainte
home la maison
  at (my) home chez moi
  at (your) home chez vous
  to go home rentrer
home address le lieu de
  domicile
homosexual homosexuel(le)
honest honnête
honeymoon la lune de miel
to hope espérer
  I hope so/not j'espère que
  oui/non
horrible horrible, affreux/euse

horse le cheval (*pl* les chevaux)
horse-riding l'équitation (*f*)
hose le tuyau
hospital l'hôpital (*m*)
hot chaud(e)
  I'm hot j'ai chaud
  it's hot (weather) il fait
  chaud
  (*spicy*) fort(e)
hotel l'hôtel (*m*)
hour l'heure (*f*)
house la maison
housewife la ménagère
housework le ménage
hovercraft l'aéroglisseur (*m*)
how? comment?
  how are you? comment
  allez-vous?
how long? combien de temps?
how many/much? combien?
how much is it? c'est combien?

human humain(e)
hungry: to be hungry avoir
  faim (avoir, *see page 195*)
to hunt chasser
hunting la chasse
hurry: to be in a hurry être
  pressé(e) (être, *see page 195*)
hurt: my . . . hurts j'ai mal à
  la/au . . .
husband le mari
hut la cabane
hydrofoil l'hydroptère (*m*),
  l'hydrofoil (*m*)
hypermarket l'hypermarché
  (*m*)

## I

I je
ice la glace
  (*piece of ice, ice-cube*) le
  glaçon
ice cream la glace
ice rink la patinoire
icy gelé(e)
  (*road*) verglacé(e)
idea l'idée (*f*)
if si
ill malade
illness la maladie
to imagine imaginer
imagination l'imagination (*f*)
immediately tout de suite
immersion heater le chauffe-
  eau électrique
impatient impatient(e)
important important(e)
impossible impossible
impressive impressionnant(e)
in dans
included compris(e)

income le revenu
independent indépendant(e)
indigestion l'indigestion (f)
indoors à l'intérieur
industrial industriel(le)
industry l'industrie (f)
infected infecté(e)
infection l'infection (f)
infectious (illness) infectieux/
  euse
  (person) contagieux/euse
inflamed enflammé(e)
inflammation l'inflammation
  (f)
influenza la grippe
informal familier, familière
information les informations
  (fpl), les renseignements
  (mpl)
information office le bureau
  de renseignements
injection la piqûre
injured blessé(e)
injury la blessure
ink l'encre (f)
inner intérieur(e)
innocent innocent(e)
insect l'insecte (m)
insect bite la piqûre d'insecte
insect repellent la crème anti-
  insecte
inside à l'intérieur (de)
to insist insister
instant coffee le café
  instantané
instead of au lieu de
instructor le moniteur
insulin l'insuline (f)
insult l'insulte (f)
insurance l'assurance (f)
insurance certificate le
  certificat d'assurance

intelligent intelligent(e)
interested: I'm interested in
  . . . je m'intéresse à . . .
interesting intéressant(e)
interior intérieur(e)
international international(e)
interpreter l'interprète (m)
interval (theatre etc.) l'entracte
  (m)
interview l'entrevue (f)
into dans
to introduce présenter
invitation l'invitation (f)
to invite inviter
iodine l'iode (f)
Ireland l'Irlande (f)
Irish irlandais(e)
iron le fer
to iron repasser
ironmonger's la quincaillerie
is (see to be)
  is there . . .? est-ce qu'il
  y a . . .?
island l'île (f)
it il/elle; le/la
itch la démangeaison

J

jacket la veste
jam la confiture
jar le pot
jazz le jazz
jeans le jean
Jesus, Jesus Christ Jésus,
  Jésus-Christ
jelly la gelée
jellyfish la méduse
jeweller's la bijouterie
Jewish juif, juive
job le travail

jogging: to go jogging **faire du jogging**
joke **la plaisanterie**
journalist **le/la journaliste**
journey **le voyage**
judge **le juge**
jug **le pot, le pichet**
juice **le jus**
to jump **sauter**
jump leads **les câbles de raccordement de batterie**
jumper **le pull**
junction **la bifurcation**
just (*only*) **seulement**

## K

to keep **garder**
kettle **la bouilloire**
key **la clé/clef**
key ring **le porte-clés**
kidney (*food*) **le rognon**
  (*body*) **le rein**
to kill **tuer**
kilo(gram) **le kilo**
kilometre **le kilomètre**
kind (*sort*) **le genre**
kind (*generous*) **gentil, gentille**
king **le roi**
kiss **le baiser**
to kiss **embrasser**
kitchen **la cuisine**
knickers **le slip**
knife **le couteau**
to knit **tricoter**
to knock **frapper**
knot **le nœud**
to know (*someone*) **connaître**
  I don't know him/her **je ne le/la connais pas**
  (*something*) **savoir**
  I (don't) know **je (ne) sais (pas)**

to know how to **savoir**
  I (don't) know how to . . . **je (ne) sais (pas) . . .**

## L

label **l'étiquette** (*f*)
lace **la dentelle**
  (*shoe*) **le lacet**
ladder **l'échelle** (*f*)
ladies and gentlemen **mesdames et messieurs**
lady **la dame**
lager **la bière blonde**
lake **le lac**
lamb **l'agneau** (*m*)
lamp **la lampe**
lamp post **le réverbère**
land **la terre**
to land **atterrir**
landlady **la propriétaire**
landlord **le propriétaire**
lane (*country road*) **le chemin**
language **la langue**
large **grand(e)**
last **dernier, dernière**
to last **durer**
late **tard**
later **plus tard**
laugh **le rire**
to laugh **rire**
launderette **la laverie automatique**
laundry **la blanchisserie**
law **la loi**
  (*study subject*) **le droit**

lawyer l'avocat (m)
laxative le laxatif
lazy paresseux/euse
lead le plomb
lead-free sans plomb
leaf la feuille
leaflet le dépliant
to learn apprendre
learner le débutant, la débutante
least: at least au moins
leather le cuir
to leave (message etc.) laisser
(to go) partir
left la gauche
on/to the left à gauche
left-hand de gauche
left-handed gaucher, gauchère
left luggage (office) la consigne
leg la jambe
legal légal(e)
lemon le citron
lemonade la limonade
to lend prêter
length la longueur
(duration) la durée
lens (camera) l'objectif (m)
(spectacles) le verre
less moins
lesson la leçon
to let (allow) permettre
(rent) louer
letter la lettre
letterbox la boîte aux lettres
lettuce la laitue
level (height, standard) le niveau
level (flat) plat(e)
level crossing le passage à niveau
library la bibliothèque

licence le permis
lid le couvercle
life la vie
lifebelt la ceinture de sauvetage
lifeboat le canot de sauvetage
lifeguard le surveillant de plage
lifejacket le gilet de sauvetage
lift l'ascenseur (m)
light la lumière
light (coloured) clair(e)
(weight) léger, légère
to light (fire etc.) allumer
light bulb l'ampoule (f)
lighter (cigarette) le briquet
lighter fuel le gaz à briquet
lightning la foudre
like (similar to) comme
like this/that comme ça
to like aimer
likely probable
limited limité(e)
line la ligne
lion le lion
lip salve le baume pour les lèvres
lipstick le rouge à lèvres
liqueur la liqueur
liquid le liquide
list la liste
to listen (to) écouter
litre le litre
litter les ordures (fpl)
little (small) petit(e)
a little un peu (de)
to live vivre
liver le foie
living-room le salon
loaf (of bread) le pain
(French stick) la baguette
local local(e)
lock la serrure

to lock **fermer à clé**
London **Londres**
lonely **seul(e)**
long **long, longue**
to look (at) **regarder**
to look after **garder**
to look for **chercher**
to look like **ressembler à**
loose (*clothes*) **ample**
lorry **le camion**
lorry-driver **le camionneur**
to lose **perdre**
lost **perdu(e)**
lost property office **le bureau des objets trouvés**
a lot (of) **beaucoup (de)**
lotion **la lotion**
lottery **la loterie**
loud **fort(e)**
lounge **le salon**
love **l'amour** (*m*)
to love **aimer**
lovely **charmant(e)**
low **bas, basse**
lower **inférieur(e)**
lozenge **la pastille**
LP **le microsillon**
lucky: to be lucky **avoir de la chance** (avoir, *see page 195*)
luggage **les bagages** (*mpl*)
lump **la grosseur**
lump of sugar **le morceau de sucre**
lunch **le déjeuner**
Luxembourg **le Luxembourg**
of Luxembourg **luxembourgeois(e)**

# M

machine **la machine**
machinist **le/la machiniste**
mad **fou, folle**
madam **madame**
magazine **la revue**
main **principal(e)**
make (*brand*) **la marque**
to make **faire** (*see page 195*)
make-up **le maquillage**
male **mâle**
man **l'homme** (*m*)
manager **le directeur**
managing director **le président-directeur général**
many **beaucoup (de)**
not many **pas beaucoup (de)**
map **la carte**
marble **le marbre**
margarine **la margarine**
market **le marché**
married **marié(e)**
mascara **le mascara**
masculine **masculin(e)**
mask **le masque**
mass (*church*) **la messe**
match (*game*) **le match**
matches **les allumettes** (*fpl*)
material **le tissu**
mathematics **la mathématique**
matter: it doesn't matter **ça ne fait rien**
what's the matter? **qu'est-ce qui se passe?**
mattress **le matelas**
mature **mûr(e)**
mayonnaise **la mayonnaise**
me **me; moi**
meadow **le pré**
meal **le repas**

mean: what does this mean? **qu'est-ce que ça veut dire?**
meanwhile **pendant ce temps**
measles **la rougeole**
to measure **mesurer**
measurement **la mesure**
meat **la viande**
mechanic **le mécanicien**
medical **médical(e)**
medicine (*subject*) **la médecine** (*drug*) **le médicament**
Mediterranean **la Méditerranée**
medium (*size*) **moyen, moyenne** (*steak*) **à point**
medium dry (*wine*) **demi-sec**
meeting **la réunion**
melon **le melon**
member **le membre**
to mend **réparer**
menu **la carte** set menu **le menu**
message **le message**
metal **le métal**
meter **le compteur**
metre **le mètre**
microwave (oven) **le four à micro-ondes**
midday **midi** (*m*)
middle **le centre**
middle-aged **d'un certain âge**
midnight **minuit** (*m*)
migraine **la migraine**
mild **doux, douce**
mile **le mille**
milk **le lait**
milkshake **le milk-shake**
mill **le moulin**
mince **le bifteck haché**
mind: I don't mind **ça m'est égal**

mine: it's mine **c'est à moi**
minister **le ministre**
minute (*time*) **la minute**
mirror **le miroir**
Miss **Mademoiselle**
to miss (*bus etc.*) **manquer**
mist **la brume**
mistake **l'erreur** (*f*)
mixed **mixte;** (*salad*) **composé(e)** (*assorted*) **assorti(e)s** (*pl*)
mixture **le mélange**
model **le modèle**
modern **moderne**
moisturiser **le lait hydratant**
monastery **le monastère**
money **l'argent** (*m*)
month **le mois**
monument **le monument**
moon **la lune**
moped **la mobylette**
more **plus**
morning **le matin**
mortgage **l'emprunt-logement** (*m*)
mosque **la mosquée**
mosquito **le moustique**
mosquito net **la moustiquaire**
most (of) **la plupart (de)**
mother **la mère**
mother-in-law **la belle-mère**
motor **le moteur**
motorboat **le bateau à moteur**
motorcycle **la moto**
motor racing **la course automobile**
motorway **l'autoroute** (*f*)
mountain **la montagne**
mountaineering **l'alpinisme** (*m*)
moustache **la moustache**
mouth **la bouche**

271

to move **bouger**
Mr **Monsieur**
Mrs **Madame**
much **beaucoup**
  not much **pas beaucoup**
mug **la grande tasse**
to murder **assassiner**
museum **le musée**
mushroom **le champignon**
music **la musique**
musical **musical(e)**
musician **le musicien,
  la musicienne**
must: you must . . . **il faut
  (que)** . . .
mustard **la moutarde**
my **mon, ma;** (*pl*) **mes** (*see page
  191*)

# N

nail **le clou**
  (*finger/toe*) **l'ongle** (*m*)
nail file **la lime à ongles**
nail polish **le vernis à ongles**
nail polish remover **le
  dissolvant**
naked **nu(e)**
name **le nom**
  my name is . . .
  **je m'appelle** . . .
  what is your name?
  **comment vous appelez-
  vous?, quel est votre nom?**
napkin **la serviette**
  paper napkin **la serviette en
  papier**
nappy **la couche**
  disposable nappies **les
  couches à jeter**
nappy liner **le protège-couche**

narrow **étroit(e)**
national **national(e)**
nationality **la nationalité**
natural **naturel(e)**
naturally **naturellement**
naughty **méchant(e)**
navy **la marine**
navy blue **bleu marine**
near (to) **près (de)**
nearly **presque**
necessary **nécessaire**
necklace **le collier**
to need **avoir besoin de (avoir,** *see
  page 195*)
needle **l'aiguille** (*f*)
negative (*photo*) **le négatif**
neighbour **le voisin, la voisine**
neither . . . nor **ni . . . ni**
nephew **le neveu**
nervous **nerveux/euse**
net **le filet**
never **jamais**
new **nouveau, nouvelle**
  New Year **le Nouvel An**
news **les informations** (*fpl*)
newsagent's **le tabac-journaux**
newspaper **le journal**
next **prochain(e)**
  week/month/year (*see page
  199*)
nice (*person*) **sympathique**
  (*place etc.*) **joli(e)**
niece **la nièce**
night **la nuit**
nightclub **la boîte de nuit**
nightdress **la chemise de nuit**
no **non**
nobody **personne**
noise **le bruit**
noisy **bruyant(e)**

non-alcoholic **non alcoolisé(e)**
none **aucun(e)**
non-smoking **non-fumeur**
normal **normal(e)**
north **le nord**
northern **du nord**
nose **le nez**
nose-bleed **le saignement du nez**
not **ne . . . pas**
note (*bank*) **le billet**
notepad **le bloc-notes**
nothing **rien**
nothing else **rien d'autre**
nothing much **pas grand-chose**
now **maintenant**
nowhere **nulle part**
nuclear **nucléaire**
nuclear energy **l'energie (f) nucléaire**
number (*quantity*) **le nombre** (*telephone*) **le numéro**
nurse **l'infirmier (m), l'infirmière (f)**
nut **la noix** (*for bolt*) **l'écrou (m)**
nylon **le nylon**

# O

oar **la rame**
object **l'objet (m)**
obvious **évident(e)**
occasionally **de temps en temps**
occupied (*seat*) **occupé(e)**
odd **bizarre** (*not even*) **impair**
of **de**
of course **bien sûr**

off (*switched off*) **éteint(e)** (*engine*) **coupé(e)**
offended **offensé(e)**
office **le bureau**
official **officiel(le)**
often **souvent**
how often? **combien de fois?**
oil **l'huile (f)**
OK **bien**
old **vieux, vieille**
how old are you? **quel âge avez-vous?**
how old is he/she? **quel âge a-t-il/elle?**
I am . . . years old **j'ai . . . ans**
old-fashioned **démodé(e)**
olive **l'olive (f)**
olive oil **l'huile (f) d'olive**
on **sur** (*switched on*) **allumé(e)** (*engine*) **en marche**
once **une fois**
one-way **à sens unique**
onion **l'oignon (m)**
only **seulement**
open **ouvert(e)**
to open **ouvrir**
opera **l'opéra (m)**
operation **l'opération (f)**
opinion **l'opinion (f)**
in my opinion **à mon avis**
opposite (*contrary*) **opposé(e)**
opposite (to) **en face (de)**
optician **l'opticien (m)**
or **ou**
orange (*fruit*) **l'orange (f)** (*colour*) **orange**
order **l'ordre (m)**
to order (*in restaurant*) **commander**

ordinary **ordinaire**
to organise **organiser**
original **original(e)**
other **autre**
our **notre**; (pl) **nos**
ours: it's ours **c'est à nous**
out: he/she is out **il/elle est sorti(e)**
outdoors **en plein air**
outside **dehors**
outside (of) **à l'extérieur (de)**
over (above) **au-dessus de**
overcast (sky) **couvert(e)**
overcoat **le manteau**
to overtake **doubler**
owner **le/la propriétaire**

# P

package tour **le voyage organisé**
packet **le paquet**
padlock **le cadenas**
page (book) **la page**
pain **la douleur**
painful **douloureux/euse**
painkiller **le calmant**
paint, painting **la peinture**
to paint **peindre**
painter **le peintre**
painting (picture) **le tableau**
pair **la paire**
palace **le palais**
pale **pâle**
(colour) **clair(e)**
panties, pants (women's) **le slip**
paper **le papier**
paper clip **le trombone**
paraffin **le pétrole**
parcel **le paquet**
pardon? **pardon?**

parent **le parent**
park **le parc**
to park **stationner**
parking **le stationnement**
parking disc **le disque de stationnement**
parking meter **le parc-mètre**
parliament **le parlement**
part **la partie**
parting (hair) **la raie**
partly **en partie**
partner (business) **l'associé(e) (m/f)**
party (celebration) **la fête**
to pass (salt etc.) **passer**
(exam/test) **réussir (à)**
passenger **le passager**
passport **le passeport**
passport control **le contrôle des passeports**
past **le passé**
past (Time, see page 201)
pasta **les pâtes (fpl)**
pastille **la pastille**
pastry **la pâte**
path **le chemin**
patient (hospital) **le/la malade**
pattern **le motif**
pavement **le trottoir**
to pay **payer**
to pay cash **payer comptant**
peace **la paix**
peach **la pêche**
peanut **la cacahuète**
pear **la poire**
peas **les petits pois (mpl)**
pedal **la pédale**
pedestrian **le piéton**
pedestrian crossing **le passage clouté**

to peel **peler**
peg **la cheville**
　(*clothes*) **la pince**
pen **le stylo**
pencil **le crayon**
pencil sharpener **la taille-crayon**
penfriend **le correspondant, la correspondante**
penknife **le canif**
pension **la pension**
pensioner **le/la retraité(e)**
people **les gens** (*mpl*)
　(*populace*) **le peuple**
pepper **le poivre**
　green/red **le poivron vert/rouge**
peppermint **la menthe poivrée**
　(*sweet*) **la pastille de menthe**
per **par**
perfect **parfait(e)**
performance **la représentation**
　(*cinema*) **la séance**
perfume **le parfum**
perhaps **peut-être**
period (*menstrual*) **les règles** (*fpl*)
period pains **les douleurs** (*fpl*) **des règles**
perm **la permanente**
permit **le permis**
to permit **permettre**
person **la personne**
personal **personel(le)**
personal stereo **le baladeur**
petrol **l'essence** (*f*)
petrol can **le bidon à essence**
petrol station **la station-service**
petticoat **le jupon**
philosophy **la philosophie**
photocopy **la photocopie**

to photocopy **photocopier**
photo(graph) **la photo**
photographer **le/la photographe**
photography **la photographie**
phrase book **le recueil d'expressions**
physics **la physique**
piano **le piano**
to pick (*choose*) **choisir**
　(*flowers etc.*) **cueillir**
to pick up **ramasser**
picnic **le pique-nique**
picture **le tableau**
piece **le morceau**
pier **la jetée**
pierced (*ear*) **percé(e)**
pig **le cochon**
pill **la pilule**
　(*contraceptive*) **la pilule**
pillow **l'oreiller** (*m*)
pillowcase **la taie d'oreiller**
pilot **le pilote**
pilot light **la veilleuse**
pin **l'épingle** (*f*)
pineapple **l'ananas** (*m*)
pink **rose**
pipe (*smoking*) **la pipe**
　(*drain etc.*) **le tuyau**
place **l'endroit** (*m*), **le lieu**
　(*seat*) **la place**
plan (*of town*) **le plan**
plant **la plante**
plaster (*sticking*) **le sparadrap**
plastic **le plastique**
plastic bag **le sac en plastique**
plate **l'assiette** (*f*)
platform (*station*) **le quai**
play (*theatre*) **la pièce**
to play **jouer**
pleasant **agréable**

please s'il vous plaît
pleased content(e)
plenty (of) beaucoup (de)
pliers la pince
plimsolls les tennis (fpl)
plug (bath) la bonde
  (electrical) la prise
plumber le plombier
pneumonia la pneumonie
pocket la poche
point le point
poison le poison
poisonous (gas) toxique
  (plants) vénéneux/euse
  (animals) vénimeux/euse
pole la perche
police la police
police car la voiture de police
police station le commissariat,
  le poste de police
polish (shoe etc.) le cirage
polite poli(e)
political politique
politician l'homme politique
  (m), la femme politique
politics la politique
polluted pollué(e)
pollution la pollution
pool (swimming) la piscine
poor pauvre
pop (music) la musique pop
Pope le pape
popular populaire
pork le porc
port (harbour) le port
  (wine) le porto
portable portatif, portative
porter le porteur
porthole le hublot
portrait le portrait

possible possible
  if possible si possible
possibly peut-être
post (mail) la poste
to post mettre à la poste
postbox la boîte aux lettres
postcard la carte postale
postcode le code postal
poster le poster, l'affiche (f)
postman le facteur
post office la poste, le bureau
  de poste
to postpone renvoyer
pot le pot
potato la pomme de terre
pottery la poterie
potty (child's) le pot
pound (sterling) la livre
  (sterling)
  (weight) la livre
to pour verser
powder la poudre
powdery (snow etc.)
  poudreux/euse
power la puissance
  (electrical) le courant
power cut la coupure de
  courant
pram la voiture d'enfant
to prefer préférer
pregnant enceinte
to prepare préparer
prescription l'ordonnance (f)
present (gift) le cadeau
pretty joli(e)
price le prix
priest le prêtre
prime minister le premier
  ministre
prince le prince
princess la princesse

print (*photo*) **l'épreuve** (*f*)
  (*picture*) **la gravure**
prison **la prison**
private **privé(e)**
prize **le prix**
probably **probablement**
problem **le problème**
producer (*radio, TV*)
  **le réalisateur, la réalisatrice**
profession **la profession**
professor **le professeur**
profit **le profit**
program (*computer*)
  **le programme**
programme (*radio, TV*)
  **l'émission** (*f*)
  (*theatre*) **le programme**
prohibited **interdit(e)**
promise **la promesse**
to pronounce **prononcer**
pronunciation **la**
  **prononciation**
properly **correctement**
property **la propriété**
protestant **protestant(e)**
public **le public**
public **public, publique**
public holiday **le jour férié**
to pull **tirer**
to pump up **gonfler**
puncture **la crevaison**
pure **pur(e)**
purple **violet, violette**
purse **le porte-monnaie**
to push **pousser**
push-chair **la poussette**
to put **mettre**
to put (down) **poser**
pyjamas **le pyjama**

## Q

quality **la qualité**
quarter **le quart**
  (*of a town*) **le quartier**
quay **le quai**
queen **la reine**
question **la question**
queue **la queue**
quick **rapide**
quickly **vite**
quiet **tranquille**
quite (*fairly*) **assez**
  (*completely*) **complètement**

## R

rabbi **le rabbin**
rabbit **le lapin**
rabies **la rage**
race **la course**
racecourse/track **la piste**
  (*horse*) **le champs de courses**
racing **les courses** (*fpl*)
racket (*tennis*) **la raquette**
radio **la radio**
radioactive **radioactif,**
  **radioactive**
radio station **la station de**
  **radio**
raft **le radeau**
railway **le chemin de fer**
railway station **la gare**
rain **la pluie**
to rain **pleuvoir**
  it's raining **il pleut**
raincoat **l'imperméable** (*m*)
rainy **pluvieux/euse**
to rape **violer**
rare **rare**
  (*steak*) **saignant(e)**

rash **les rougeurs** (*fpl*),
**l'éruption** (*f*)
raspberry **la framboise**
rate (*speed*) **la vitesse**
(*tariff*) **le tarif**
rather (*quite*) **assez**
raw **cru(e)**
razor **le rasoir**
razor blade **la lame de rasoir**
to reach (*arrive at*) **arriver à**
to read **lire**
reading **la lecture**
ready **prêt(e)**
real (*authentic*) **authentique,
vrai(e)**
really (*very*) **vraiment**
really? **vraiment?**
rear **arrière**
reason **la raison**
the reason why **le pourquoi**
receipt **le reçu**
receiver (*telephone*) **le
récepteur**
reception **la réception**
receptionist **le/la
réceptionniste**
recipe **la recette**
to recognise **reconnaître**
to recommend **recommander**
record **le disque**
to record **enregistrer**
record-player **l'électrophone**
(*m*)
red **rouge**
reduction **la réduction**
refill **la recharge**
refrigerator **le frigo, le frigidaire**
to refund **rembourser**
region **la région**
to register (*letter*) **recommander**
(*luggage etc.*) **enregistrer**

registration number **le
numéro d'immatriculation**
relation (*relative*) **le parent,
la parente**
religion **la religion**
to remain **rester**
to remember **se rappeler**
I remember . . . **je me
rappelle . . .**
do you remember . . .?
**est-ce que vous vous
rappelez . . .?**
to remove **enlever**
to rent **louer**
rent **le loyer**
rental **la location**
to repair **réparer**
to repeat **répéter**
reply **la réponse**
to reply **répondre**
report (*business*) **le rapport**
(*newspaper*) **le reportage**
to report (*crime etc.*) **signaler**
to rescue **sauver**
reservation **la réservation**
to reserve **réserver**
reserved **réservé(e)**
responsible **responsable**
to rest **se reposer**
restaurant **le restaurant**
restaurant-car **le wagon-
restaurant**
result **le résultat**
retired **retraité(e)**
return **le retour**
(*ticket*) **aller-retour**
to return (*give back*) **rendre**
reversed charge call
**l'appel en PCV**
rheumatism **le rhumatisme**

ribbon le ruban
rice le riz
rich riche
ride: to go for a car ride faire un tour en voiture
to ride a bike/horse monter à bicyclette/cheval
right la droite
    on/to the right à droite
right: to be right avoir raison (avoir, *see page 195*)
    that's right c'est ça
right-hand de droite
right-handed droitier, droitière
ring (*jewellery*) la bague
ripe mûr(e)
river la rivière
road (*main*) la route
roadworks les travaux (*mpl*)
roast rôti(e)
to rob voler
    I've been robbed j'ai été volé
robbery le vol
roll (*bread*) le petit pain
roof le toit
roof rack la galerie
room (*house*) la pièce
    (*hotel*) la chambre
    (*space*) la place
rope la corde
rose la rose
rosé rosé(e)
rotten pourri(e)
rough (*surface*) rugueux/euse
    (*sea*) gros, grosse
round rond(e)
roundabout (*traffic*) le rond-point
    (*funfair*) le manège
row (*theatre etc.*) le rang
to row ramer

rowing boat le canot à rames
royal royal(e)
rubber (*material*) le caoutchouc
    (*eraser*) la gomme
rubber band l'élastique (*m*)
rubbish les ordures (*fpl*)
rucksack le sac à dos
rude impoli(e)
ruins les ruines (*fpl*)
ruler (*for measuring*) la règle
rum le rhum
to run courir
rush hour les heures (*fpl*) d'affluence/de point
rusty rouillé(e)

# S

sad triste
safe (*strongbox*) le coffre-fort
safe sans danger
safety pin l'épingle (*f*) de nourrice
sail la voile
sailboard la planche à voile
sailing la voile
sailing boat le bateau à voiles
sailor le marin
saint le saint, la sainte
salad la salade
salami le saucisson
sale la vente
    (*reduced prices*) la liquidation
sales representative le/la représentant(e) de commerce
salesman le vendeur
saleswoman la vendeuse
salmon le saumon
salt le sel
salty salé(e)

same **même**
sample **l'échantillon** (*m*)
sand **le sable**
sandal **la sandale**
sandwich **le sandwich**
sanitary towel **la serviette hygiénique**
sauce **la sauce**
saucepan **la casserole**
saucer **la soucoupe**
sauna **le sauna**
sausage **la saucisse, le saucisson**
to save (*rescue*) **sauver**
  (*money*) **économiser**
to say **dire**
  how do you say it? **comment est-ce qu'on dit ça?**
  people say that . . . **on dit que . . .**
  that's to say **c'est-à-dire**
scales **la balance**
scarf **l'écharpe** (*f*)
  (*square*) **le foulard**
scene (*theatre*) **la scène**
  (*view*) **la vue**
scenery (*countryside*) **le paysage**
scent **le parfum**
school **l'école** (*f*)
science **la science**
  (*subject*) **les sciences** (*fpl*)
scientist **le/la scientifique**
scissors **les ciseaux** (*mpl*)
score: what's the score? **où en est le jeu/match?**
  final score **le résultat**
Scotland **l'Écosse** (*f*)
Scottish **écossais(e)**
scrambled eggs **les oeufs brouillés** (*mpl*)
scratch **l'éraflure** (*f*)

(*on skin*) **l'égratignure** (*f*)
screen (*TV, cinema etc.*) **l'écran** (*m*)
  (*partition*) **le paravent**
screw **la vis**
screwdriver **le tournevis**
sculpture **la sculpture**
sea **la mer**
seafood **les fruits de mer** (*mpl*)
sea-sick: to be sea-sick **avoir le mal de mer** (avoir, *see page 195*)
season (*of year*) **la saison**
season ticket **l'abonnement**
seat **le siège**
  (*place*) **la place**
seatbelt **la ceinture de sécurité**
second **second(e), deuxième**
second (*time*) **la seconde**
secret **le secret**
secret **secret, secrète**
secretary **le/la secrétaire**
section **la section**
to see **voir**
  I see **je vois**
  I can't see it **je ne le vois pas**
to seem **sembler**
  it seems . . . **il semble . . .**
self-service **le libre-service**
to sell **vendre**
to send **envoyer**
senior citizen **le/la retraité(e)**
sensible **raisonnable**
sentence **la phrase**
  (*prison*) **la sentence**
separate, separated **séparé(e)**
serious **grave**
to serve **servir**
service charge **le service**

set (*group*) **le jeu**
   (*series*) **la série**
   (*hair*) **la mise en plis**
setting lotion **la lotion pour
   mise en plis**
several **plusieurs**
to sew **coudre**
sewing **la couture**
sex (*gender*) **le sexe**
   (*intercourse*) **les rapports
   sexuels** (*mpl*)
shade (*colour*) **le ton**
shadow **l'ombre** (*f*)
shampoo **le shampooing**
shampoo and set **le
   shampooing et mise en plis**
shampoo and blow-dry
   **le shampooing et brushing**
sharp (*edge*) **tranchant(e)**
   (*pain*) **vif, vive**
to shave (oneself) **(se) raser**
shaver **le rasoir (électrique)**
shaving cream **la crème à
   raser**
she **elle**
sheep **le mouton**
sheet **le drap**
shelf **le rayon**
shell (*egg, nut*) **la coquille**
   (*seashell*) **le coquillage**
shellfish **le crustacé**
shelter **l'abri** (*m*)
shiny **brillant(e)**
ship **le navire**
shirt **la chemise**
shock **le choc**
shoe **la chaussure**
shoelace **le lacet**
shoe polish **le cirage**
shoe shop **le magasin de
   chaussures**

shop **le magasin**
shop assistant **le vendeur,
   la vendeuse**
shopping: to go shopping
   **faire des courses (faire,** *see
   page 195*)
shopping centre **le centre
   commercial**
short **court(e)**
shorts **le short**
to shout **crier**
show **le spectacle**
to show **montrer**
shower **la douche**
to shrink **rétrécir**
shut **fermé(e)**
shutter **le volet**
   (*camera*) **l'obturateur** (*m*)
sick (*ill*) **malade**
   to be sick **vomir**
   to feel sick **avoir mal au
   cœur (avoir,** *see page 195*)
side **le côté**
sieve **la passoire**
sight (*vision*) **la vue**
sightseeing **le tourisme**
sign **le panneau**
to sign **signer**
signal **le signal**
signature **la signature**
silent **silencieux/euse**
silk **la soie**
silver **l'argent** (*m*)
similar **semblable**
simple **simple**
since **depuis**
to sing **chanter**
single (*room, bed*) **pour une
   personne**
   (*ticket*) **aller simple**
   (*unmarried*) **célibataire**

**281**

single (*record*) **le 45 (quarante-cinq) tours**
sink **l'évier** (*m*)
sir **monsieur**
sister **la sœur**
sister-in-law **la belle-sœur**
to sit (down) **s'asseoir**
sitting (down) **assis(e)**
size **la dimension**
  (*clothing*) **la taille**
  (*shoes*) **la pointure**
skate **le patin**
to skate **patiner**
ski **le ski**
to ski **skier**
ski boot **la chaussure de ski**
skiing **le ski**
ski-lift **le téléski**
skimmed milk **le lait écrémé**
skin **la peau**
skindiving **la plongée sous-marine**
ski pole **le bâton de ski**
skirt **la jupe**
ski-run/slope **la piste**
ski suit **la combinaison de ski**
sky **le ciel**
to sleep **dormir**
sleeper/sleeping-car **le wagon-lit**
sleeping bag **le sac de couchage**
sleeve **la manche**
slice **la tranche**
slide (*film*) **la diapositive**
slim **mince**
slip (*petticoat*) **la combinaison**
slippery **glissant(e)**
slow **lent(e)**
slowly **lentement**
small **petit(e)**

smell **l'odeur** (*f*)
smell **sentir**
  it smells bad/good **ça sent mauvais/bon**
  it smells of . . . **ça a une odeur de . . .**
smile **le sourire**
smoke **la fumée**
to smoke **fumer**
smoked **fumé(e)**
smooth **lisse**
to sneeze **éternuer**
snorkel **le tuba**
snow **la neige**
snow: it's snowing **il neige**
so **si**
  (*thus*) **ainsi, comme ça**
so much **tant**
soap **le savon**
socialism **le socialisme**
socialist **socialiste**
social worker **l'assistant(e) social(e)** (*m/f*)
sociology **la sociologie**
sock **la chaussette**
socket (*electrical*) **la prise de courant**
soda (water) **l'eau de Seltz** (*f*)
soft **doux, douce**
soft drink **la boisson non alcoolisée**
soldier **le soldat**
solid **solide**
some **quelques**
someone **quelqu'un**
something **quelque chose**
sometimes **quelquefois**
somewhere **quelque part**
son **le fils**
song **la chanson**
son-in-law **le beau-fils**

soon **bientôt**
    as soon as possible **aussitôt que possible**
sore throat **le mal de gorge**
sorry (*pardon me*) **pardon**
    I'm sorry (je suis) **désolé(e), je m'excuse**
sort **la sorte, le genre**
sound **le son**
soup **la soupe**
sour **acide**
south **le sud**
    southern **du sud**
souvenir **le souvenir**
space **l'espace** (*f*)
    (*place*) **la place**
spade **la pelle**
spanner **la clé anglaise**
spare **de rechange**
    (*left over*) **en trop**
spare time **le temps libre, le loisir**
spare wheel **la roue de rechange**
sparkling (*wine*) **mousseux/euse**
to speak **parler**
special **spécial(e)**
specialist **le/la spécialiste** (*m/f*)
speciality **la spécialité**
spectacles **les lunettes** (*fpl*)
speed **la vitesse**
speed limit **la limitation de vitesse**
to spend (*money*) **dépenser**
    (*time*) **passer**
spice **l'épice** (*f*)
spicy **épicé(e)**
spinach **les épinards** (*mpl*)
spirits **les spiritueux** (*mpl*)
splinter **l'écharde** (*f*)

to spoil **abîmer**
sponge (*bath*) **l'éponge** (*f*)
    (*cake*) **le gâteau de Savoie**
spoon **la cuiller**
sport **le sport**
spot **la tache**
    (*place*) **l'endroit** (*m*)
sprain **l'entorse** (*f*)
sprained **foulé(e)**
spray (*can*) **la bombe**
spring (*season*) **le printemps**
square **la place**
square (*shape*) **le carré**
stadium **le stade**
stain **la tache**
stainless steel **l'acier inoxydable** (*m*)
stairs **l'escalier** (*m*)
stalls (*theatre*) **l'orchestre** (*m*)
stamp (*postage*) **le timbre**
stand (*stadium*) **la tribune**
standing (up) **debout**
staple **l'agrafe** (*f*)
stapler **l'agrafeuse** (*f*)
star **l'étoile** (*f*)
start (*beginning*) **le début**
to start **commencer**
starter (*food*) **le hors d'œuvre**
state **l'état** (*m*)
station **la gare; (*underground*) la station**
station master **le chef de gare**
stationer's **la librairie**
statue **la statue**
stay **le séjour**
to stay **loger**
steak **le bifteck**
to steal **voler**
steam **la vapeur**
steel **l'acier** (*m*)
steep **raide**

step le pas
  (stair) la marche
stepbrother le demi-frère
stepdaughter la belle-fille
stepfather le beau-père
stepmother la belle-mère
stepsister la demi-sœur
stepson le beau-fils
stereo la stéréo
sterling: pound sterling la livre
  sterling
steward (air) le steward
stewardess (air) l'hôtesse (f)
stick le bâton
to stick coller
sticking plaster le sparadrap (m)
sticky (e.g. with jam)
  poisseux/euse
sticky tape le ruban adhésif
stiff raide
still toujours
still (non-fizzy) non
  gazeux/euse
sting la piqûre
to sting piquer
stock exchange la bourse
stockings les bas (mpl)
stolen: my . . . has been stolen
  on m'a volé mon/ma . . .
  (see page 191)
stomach l'estomac (m)
  upset stomach l'estomac
  dérangé
stomach ache le mal
  d'estomac
stone la pierre
stop (bus) l'arrêt (m)
to stop arrêter
  stop! arrêtez!
stopcock le robinet d'arrêt

storey l'étage (m)
story l'histoire (f)
stove (cooker) la cuisinière
straight droit(e)
straight on tout droit
strange bizarre
strap la courroie
straw (inc. drinking) la paille
strawberry la fraise
stream le ruisseau
street la rue
street light le réverbère
stretcher le brancard
strike la grève
string la ficelle
stripe la raie
striped rayé(e)
strong fort(e)
student l'étudiant(e) (m/f)
studio le studio
to study étudier
stupid stupide
style le style
styling mousse la mousse
  croissante
subtitled sous-titré(e)
suburb la banlieue
to succeed, be successful
  réussir
success le succès
such tel, telle
sudden soudain(e)
suddenly soudain
sugar le sucre
sugar lump le morceau de
  sucre
suit le costume
suitcase la valise
summer l'été (m)
sun le soleil
sunburn le coup de soleil

sunglasses **les lunettes** (*fpl*) **de soleil**
sunshade **le parasol**
sunstroke **l'insolation** (*f*)
suntan **le bronzage**
suntan cream **la crème solaire**
supermarket **le supermarché**
supper **le souper**
supplement **le supplément**
suppose: I suppose so/not **je suppose que oui/non**
suppository **le suppositoire**
sure **sûr(e)**
surface **la surface**
surname **le nom de famille**
surprise **la surprise**
surprised **surpris(e)**
surrounded (by) **entouré(e) (de)**
sweat **la sueur**
sweater **le pull**
sweatshirt **le sweat-shirt**
to sweep **balayer**
sweet **doux, douce**
sweetener **la sucrette**
sweets **les bonbons** (*mpl*)
swelling **l'enflure** (*f*)
to swim **nager**
swimming **la natation**
swimming pool **la piscine**
swimming trunks, swimsuit **le maillot de bain**
Swiss **suisse**
switch **le bouton**
to switch off **éteindre** (*engine*) **arrêter**
to switch on **allumer** (*engine*) **mettre en marche**
Switzerland **la Suisse**
swollen **enflé(e)**
symptom **le symptôme**

synagogue **la synagogue**
synthetic **synthétique**
system **le système**

# T

table **la table**
tablet **la pastille**
table tennis **le ping-pong**
tailor **le tailleur**
to take **prendre**
to take off (*plane*) **décoller**
to take out (*remove*) **arracher**
taken (*seat*) **occupé(e)**
talcum powder **le talc**
to talk **parler**
tall **haut(e)**
tame **apprivoisé(e)**
tampon **le tampon**
tap **le robinet**
tape **le ruban** (*recording*) **la bande magnétique**
tape measure **le mètre à ruban**
tape recorder **le magnétophone**
taste **le goût**
tasty **savoureux/euse**
tax **l'impôt** (*m*)
taxi **le taxi**
taxi rank **la station de taxis**
tea **le thé**
teabag **le sachet de thé**
to teach **enseigner**
teacher **le professeur** (*primary school*) **l'instituteur** (*m*), **l'institutrice** (*f*)
team **l'équipe** (*f*)
teapot **la théière**
to tear **déchirer**
teaspoon **la cuiller à café**
teat (*for baby's bottle*) **la tétine**

tea-towel **le torchon (à vaisselle)**
technical **technique**
technology **la technologie**
teenager **l'adolescent(e)** *(m/f)*
telegram **le télégramme**
telephone **le téléphone**
to telephone **téléphoner**
telephone directory **l'annuaire** *(m)*
television **la télévision**
to tell **dire**
temperature **la température**
  to have a temperature **avoir de la fièvre** (**avoir**, *see page 195*)
temporary **provisoire**
tender **tendre**
tennis **le tennis**
tennis court **le court de tennis**
tennis shoes/trainers **les tennis** *(fpl)*
tent **la tente**
tent peg **le piquet de tente**
tent pole **le montant de tente**
terminal, terminus **le terminus**
terrace **la terrasse**
terrible **affreux/euse**
terrorist **le/la terroriste**
thank you (very much) **merci (beaucoup/bien)**
that **ce, cette** (*see page 191*)
that one **celui-là, celle-là**
the **le, la;** *(pl)* **les**
theatre **le théâtre**
their **leur(s)** (*see page 191*)
theirs: it's theirs **c'est à eux**
them **les; leur; eux**
then **alors**
  (*afterwards*) **après**
there **là**

there is/are **il y a**
therefore **donc**
thermometer **le thermomètre**
these **ces** (*see page 191*)
they **ils, elles**
thick **épais, épaisse**
thief **le voleur**
thin **mince**
thing **la chose**
to think **penser**
  I think so/not **je pense que oui/non**
third **troisième**
thirsty: to be thirsty **avoir soif** (**avoir**, *see page 195*)
this **ce, cette** (*see page 191*)
this one **celui-ci, celle-ci**
those **ces** (*see page 191*)
thread **le fil**
throat **la gorge**
throat lozenges/pastilles **les pastilles pour la gorge**
through **à travers**
to throw **lancer**
to throw away **jeter**
thumb **le pouce**
thunder **le tonnerre**
ticket **le billet**
  (*bus, metro*) **le ticket**
ticket office **le guichet**
tide **la marée**
tidy **bien rangé(e)**
tie **la cravate**
to tie **nouer**
tight (*clothes etc.*) **étroit(e)**
tights **le collant**
till (*until*) **jusqu'à**
time (*once etc.*) **la fois**
time **l'heure** *(f)* (*see page 201*) there's no time **il n'y a pas de temps**

timetable l'horaire (m)
tin la boîte
tin foil le papier aluminium
tinned en boîte
tin opener l'ouvre-boîtes (m)
tip (money) le pourboire
tired fatigué(e)
tissue le kleenex
to à
toast le toast, le pain grillé
tobacco le tabac
tobacconist's le (bureau de) tabac
today aujourd'hui
together ensemble
toilet(s) les toilettes (fpl)
toilet paper le papier hygiénique
toiletries les articles (mpl) de toilette
toilet water l'eau (f) de toilette
toll le péage
tomato la tomate
tomorrow demain
tongue la langue
tonic water le Schweppes
tonight ce soir
too (also) aussi
too (excessively) trop
tool l'outil (m)
tooth la dent
toothache le mal de dents
toothbrush la brosse à dents
toothpaste le dentifrice, la pâte dentifrice
top le haut
  on top (of) sur
  at the top (of) en haut (de)
top floor le dernier étage
torch la lampe de poche
torn déchiré(e)

total le total
to touch toucher
tough (meat) dur(e)
tour (excursion) l'excursion (f)
  (visit) la visite
tourism le tourisme
tourist le/la touriste
tourist office le syndicat d'initiative, l'office (m) du tourisme
to tow remorquer
tow rope le câble de remorque
towards vers
towel la serviette
tower la tour
town la ville
town centre le centre-ville
town hall l'hôtel de ville (m)
toy le jouet
track (path) le sentier
tracksuit le survêtement
trade union le syndicat
traditional traditionnel(le)
traffic la circulation
traffic jam l'embouteillage (m)
traffic lights les feux (de signalisation) (mpl)
trailer la remorque
train le train
  by train en train
training shoes/trainers les tennis (fpl)
tram le tram(way)
tranquilliser le calmant
to translate traduire
translation la traduction
to travel voyager
travel agency l'agence (f) de voyages
traveller's cheque le chèque de voyage

tray le plateau
treatment le traitement
tree l'arbre (m)
trip le voyage
trolley le chariot
   (supermarket) le caddy
trousers le pantalon
trout la truite
true vrai(e)
   that's true c'est vrai
to try (on) essayer
T-shirt le T-shirt
tube le tube
tuna le thon
tunnel le tunnel
to turn tourner
turning (side road) la rue
   latérale
to turn off fermer
   (light) éteindre
   (engine) arrêter
to turn on allumer
   (tap) ouvrir
   (engine) mettre en marche
TV la télé
twice deux fois
twin beds deux lits; lits
   jumeaux
twins les jumeaux (mpl),
   les jumelles (fpl)
twisted tordu(e)
type (sort) la sorte
to type taper à la machine
typewriter la machine à écrire
typical typique

## U

ugly laid(e)
ulcer l'ulcère (m)
umbrella le parapluie
uncle l'oncle (m)

uncomfortable
   inconfortable
under sous
underground le métro
underneath dessous
underpants le slip
to understand comprendre
   I don't understand je
   ne comprends pas
underwear les sous-
   vêtements (mpl)
underwater sous-marin(e)
unemployed en/au
   chômage
unfortunately
   malheureusement
unhappy malheureux/euse
   (sad) triste
uniform l'uniforme (m)
university l'université (f)
unleaded petrol l'essence (f)
   sans plomb
unless à moins que
unpleasant désagréable
to unscrew dévisser
until jusqu'à
unusual insolite
unwell malade
up en haut
upper supérieur(e)
upstairs en haut
urgent urgent(e)
urine l'urine (f)
us nous
use l'emploi (m)
to use utiliser
useful utile
useless inutile
usual: as usual comme
   d'habitude
usually normalement,
   d'habitude

## V

vacant (*room etc.*) **libre**
vacuum cleaner **l'aspirateur** (*m*)
vacuum flask **le thermos**
valid **valable**
valley **la vallée**
valuable **de valeur**
valuables **les objets de valeur**
van **la camionnette**
vanilla **la vanille**
vase **le vase**
VAT **la TVA**
veal **le veau**
vegetable **le légume**
vegetarian **végétarien(ne)**
vehicle **le véhicule**
vermouth **le vermouth**
very **très**
very much **beaucoup**
vest **le maillot de corps**
vet **le vétérinaire**
via **par**
video cassette **la vidéocassette**
video recorder **le magnétoscope**
view **la vue**
villa (*country*) **la maison de campagne** (*by sea*) **la villa**
village **le village**
vinegar **le vinaigre**
vineyard **le vignoble**
virgin **la vierge**
Virgin Mary **la Sainte Vierge**
visit **la visite**
to visit **visiter**
visitor (*tourist*) **le visiteur, la visiteuse**
vitamin **la vitamine**
vodka **la vodka**

voice **la voix**
volleyball **le volley(-ball)**
voltage **la tension**
to vote **voter**

## W

wage **le salaire**
waist **la taille**
waistcoat **le gilet**
to wait (for) **attendre**
waiter **le garçon**
waiting room **la salle d'attente**
waitress **la serveuse**
   waitress! **mademoiselle!**
Wales **le Pays de Galles**
walk **la promenade**
   to go for a walk **faire une promenade** (faire, *see page 195*)
to walk **marcher**
walking stick **la canne**
wall **le mur**
wallet **le portefeuille**
walnut **la noix**
to want **vouloir** (*see page 195*)
   would like: I would like **je voudrais**
war **la guerre**
warm **chaud(e)**
to wash **laver**
washable **lavable**
wash-basin **le lavabo**
washing **la lessive**
washing machine **la machine à laver**
washing powder **la lessive**
washing-up: to do the washing-up **faire la vaisselle** (faire, *see page 195*)
washing-up liquid **le lave-vaisselle**

wasp la guêpe
wastepaper basket la corbeille à papier
watch (*wristwatch*) la montre
to watch (*TV etc.*) regarder
watchstrap le bracelet de montre
water l'eau (*f*)
water heater le chauffe-eau
water melon la pastèque
waterfall la chute d'eau
waterproof imperméable
water-skiing le ski nautique
wave (*sea*) la vague
wax la cire
way (*route*) le chemin
  that way par là
  this way par ici
  (*method*) la manière
way in l'entrée (*f*)
way out la sortie
we nous
weather le temps
  what's the weather like? **quel temps fait-il?**
wedding le mariage
week la semaine
weekday le jour de semaine
weekend le weekend
weekly par semaine
  (*each week*) chaque semaine
to weigh peser
weight le poids
welcome bienvenu(e)
well (*water*) le puits
well bien
  as well aussi
well done (*steak*) bien cuit(e)
Welsh gallois(e)
west l'ouest (*m*)
western occidental(e)
wet mouillé(e)

wetsuit la combinaison de plongée
what quoi
what? quoi?
  what? qu'est-ce que?
  what is . . .? qu'est-ce que c'est . . .?
wheel la roue
wheelchair le fauteuil roulant
when quand
when? quand?
  (*what time?*) à quelle heure?
where où
where? où?
  where is/are . . .? où se trouve/trouvent . . .?
which quel, quelle
which? lequel?, laquelle?; (*pl*) lesquel(le)s?
while pendant que
whisky le whisky
  whisky and soda le whisky soda
white blanc, blanche
  (*with milk*) au lait
who qui
who? qui?
  who is it? qui est-ce?
whole entier, entière
wholemeal bread le pain complet
whose? à qui?
why? pourquoi?
  why not? pourquoi pas?
wide large
widow la veuve
widower le veuf
wife la femme
wild sauvage
win la victoire

to win **gagner**
who won? **qui a gagné?**
wind **le vent**
windmill **le moulin à vent**
window **la fenêtre**
(*car/train*) **la vitre**
(*shop*) **la vitrine**
windsurfing **la planche à voile**
windy: it's windy **il y a du vent**
wine **le vin**
wine merchant **le marchand de vin**
wine waiter **le sommelier**
wing **l'aile** (*f*)
winter **l'hiver** (*m*)
winter sports **les sports** (*mpl*) **d'hiver**
with **avec**
without **sans**
woman **la femme**
wonderful **merveilleux/euse**
wood **le bois**
wool **la laine**
word **le mot**
work **le travail**
to work (*job*) **travailler**
(*function*) **marcher**
world **le monde**
world (*of the world*) **mondial(e)**
First/Second World War **la Première/Seconde Guerre Mondiale**
worried **inquiet, inquiète**
worry: don't worry **ne vous inquiétez pas**
worse **pire**
worth: it's worth . . . **ça vaut . . .**
it's not worth it **ce n'est pas la peine**
would like (*see* to want)
wound (*injury*) **la blessure**
to wrap (up) **envelopper**

to write **écrire**
writer **l'écrivain** (*m*), **la femme-écrivain**
writing pad **le bloc-notes**
writing paper **le papier à écrire**
wrong (*incorrect*) **inexact(e)**
you're wrong **vous vous êtes trompé(e)(s); vous avez tort**
there's something wrong **il y a quelque chose qui ne va pas**

# X

X-ray **la radiographie**

# Y

yacht **le yacht**
to yawn **bâiller**
year **l'an** (*m*), **l'année** (*f*)
yellow **jaune**
yes **oui**
yesterday **hier**
yet **encore**
not yet **pas encore**
yoghurt **le yaourt**
you **vous** (*formal*); **tu** (*informal*) (*see page 192*)
young **jeune**
your (*formal*) **votre**; (*pl*) **vos** (*informal*) **ton, ta**; (*pl*) **tes**
yours: it's yours **c'est à vous; c'est à toi**
youth **la jeunesse**
youth hostel **l'auberge** (*m*) **de jeunesse**

# Z

zip **la fermeture éclair**
zoo **le zoo**
zoology **la zoologie**

# EMERGENCIES

(*See also* Problems and complaints, *page 179*; Health, *page 165*)

## You may want to say

### Phoning the emergency services

(Emergency telephone numbers, *page 297*)

The police, please
**La police, s'il vous plaît**
*la polees seelvooplay*

The fire brigade, please
**Les pompiers, s'il vous plaît**
*lay pawmpyay seelvooplay*

I need an ambulance
**J'aurais besoin d'une
ambulance**
*johray buhzwañ dewn
ombewloñs*

There's been a robbery
**Il y a eu un vol**
*eelya ew uñ vol*

There's been a burglary
**Il y a eu un cambriolage**
*eelya ew uñ kombree-olaj*

There's been an accident
**Il y a eu un accident**
*eelya ew un akseedoñ*

There's a fire
**Il y a un incendie**
*eelya un añsoñdee*

I've been attacked/mugged
**J'ai été attaqué(e)**
*jay aytay atakay*

I've been raped
**J'ai été violée**
*jay aytay vee-olay*

There's someone injured/ill
**Il y a une personne blessée/
malade**
*eelya ewn person blesay/
malad*

It's my husband/son
**C'est mon mari/fils**
*say mawñ maree/fees*

It's my wife/daughter
**C'est ma femme/fille**
*say ma fam/feey*

It's my friend
**C'est mon ami(e)**
*say mawn amee*

Come immediately
**Venez tout de suite**
*vuhnay toot sweet*

I am at . . .
**Je suis à . . .**
*juh sweez a . . .*

My address is . . .
**Mon adresse est . . .**
*mawn adres e . . .*

My name is . . .
**Je m'appelle . . .**
*juh mapel . . .*

My telephone number is . . .
**Mon numéro de téléphone est . . .**
*mawñ newmayroh duh taylayfon e . . .*

Where is the police station?
**Où est le poste de police?**
*oo e luh post duh polees*

Where is the hospital?
**Où est l'hôpital?**
*oo e lopeetal*

Is there anybody who speaks English?
**Est-ce qu'il y a quelqu'un qui parle l'anglais?**
*eskeelya kelkuñ kee parl loñglay*

I want to speak to a woman
**Je voudrais parler à une femme**
*juh voodray parlay a ewn fam*

Please call the British Embassy
**Appelez l'ambassade de Grande-Bretagne, s'il vous plaît**
*apuhlay lombasad duh groñd bruhtanyuh seelvooplay*

I want a lawyer
**Je voudrais un avocat**
*juh voodray un avoka*

## You may hear

### When you phone the emergency services

**Allô, Police-Secours, ne quittez pas**
*alo polees suhkoor, nuh keetay pa*
Hello, Police, please hold on

**Qu'est-ce qui s'est passé?**
*keskee se pasay*
What has happened?

**Où est-ce que vous êtes?**
*oo eskuh vooz et*
Where are you?

**Votre adresse, s'il vous plaît?**
*votr adres seelvooplay*
Your address, please?

**Votre nom, s'il vous plaît?**
*votr nawñ seelvooplay*
Your name, please?

**Une voiture de police est en route**
*ewn vwatewr duh polees et oñ root*
A police car is on its way

**Une voiture de pompiers est en route**
*ewn vwatewr duh pawmpyay et oñ root*
A fire engine is on its way

**Une ambulance est en route**
*ewn ombewloñs et oñ root*
An ambulance is on its way

**Je vous envoie toute de suite une ambulance**
*juh vooz oñvwa toot sweet ewn ombewloñs*
I'm sending you an ambulance right away

## The police

**Comment vous appelez-vous?**
*komoñ vooz apuhlay voo*
What is your name?

**Quelle est votre adresse?**
*kel e votr adres*
What is your address?

**Où ça s'est passé?**
*oo sa se pasay*
Where did it happen?

**Quand ça s'est passé?**
*koñ sa se pasay*
When did it happen?

**Pourriez-vous décrire . . .?**
*pooree-ay voo daykreer . . .*
Can you describe . . .?

**Venez avec moi/nous au poste**
*vuhnay avek mwa/noo oh post*
Come with me/us to the police station

**Vous êtes en état d'arrestation**
*vooz et on ayta darestasyawñ*
You are under arrest

## The doctor

**Il faut que vous alliez à l'hôpital**
*eel foh kuh vooz alee-ay a lopeetal*
You will have to go to hospital

**Il faut qu'il/qu'elle aille à l'hôpital**
*eel faut keel/kel iy a lopeetal*
He/she will have to go to hospital

**Où avez-vous mal?**
*oo avay voo mal*
Where is the pain?

**Depuis combien de temps avez-vous ça?**
*duhpwee kawmbyañ duh toñ avay voo sa*
How long have you been like this?

**Depuis combien de temps il/elle a ça?**
*duhpwee kawmbyañ duh toñ eel/el a sa*
How long has he/she been like this?

| | |
|---|---|
| Help! | **Au secours!** |
| | *oh suhkoor* |
| Help me | **Aidez-moi!** |
| | *ayday mwa* |
| Police! | **Police!** |
| | *polees* |
| Stop! | **Arrêtez!** |
| | *aretay* |
| Stop thief! | **Au voleur!** |
| | *oh voluhr* |
| Fire! | **Au feu!** |
| | *oh fuh* |
| Look out!/Danger! | **Attention!** |
| | *atoñsyawñ* |
| Gas! | **C'est le gaz!** |
| | *say luh gaz* |
| Get out of the way! | **Allez-vous-en!** |
| | *alay vooz oñ* |

| | |
|---|---|
| Call the police | **Appelez la police** |
| | *apuhlay la polees* |
| Call the fire brigade | **Appelez les pompiers** |
| | *apuhlay lay pawmpyay* |
| Call an ambulance | **Appelez une ambulance** |
| | *apuhlay ewn ombewloñs* |
| Get a doctor | **Appelez un médecin** |
| | *apuhlay uñ maydsañ* |
| Get help | **À l'aide** |
| | *a led* |
| Quick | **Vite** |
| | *veet* |
| It's very urgent (an emergency) | **C'est très urgent!** |
| | *say trez ewrjoñ* |

## Emergency telephone numbers

|             | POLICE | FIRE | AMBULANCE |
|-------------|--------|------|-----------|
| France      | 17     | 18   | 18        |
| Belgium     | 101    | 100  | 100       |
| Luxembourg  | 012    | 012  | 012       |
| Switzerland | 117    | 118  | 144       |

# NOTES